Traveling Home

Traveling Home

Sacred Harp Singing and American Pluralism

KIRI MILLER

UNIVERSITY OF ILLINOIS PRESS
Urbana and Chicago

Library of Congress Cataloging-in-Publication Data

Miller, Kiri.
Traveling home : sacred harp singing and American pluralism / Kiri Miller.
p.   cm. — (Music in American life)
Includes bibliographical references and index.
ISBN-10 0-252-03214-4 (cloth : alk. paper)
ISBN-13 978-0-252-03214-1 (cloth : alk. paper)
1. Sacred harp.   2. Shape-note singing—United States—History and criticism.
3. Pluralism.   I. Title.
ML3111.M54   2008
782.270975—dc22   2007030756

For D.J.W.H., A.R.G., and J.M.B.

Contents

List of Illustrations

Figures

Tables

Recommended Sound Examples

The following sound examples come from a small selection of publicly available recordings. They include tracks from two recent conventions at which the author was present, one historical compilation, and two commercial recordings. The code at the end of each listing refers to the original recording, disc number (if applicable), and track number. Consult the Source Recordings key for information on obtaining these recordings.

1. "Holy Manna" (59) / A1-14
2. "Clamanda" (42) / B1-17
3. "Parting Hand" (62) / A2-32
4. "Mear" (49b) / C2-2
5. "Save, Lord, Or We Perish" (224) / A1-13
6. "Sweet Morning" (421) / C1-7
7. Memorial Lesson by Marcia Johnson (1999) / A2-16
8. "I'm On My Journey Home" (345b) / D2-3
9. "The Golden Harp" (274t) / D2-13
10. "Evening Shade" (209) / E-4
11. "Cowper" (168) / E-3
12. "Cowper" (168) / C1-2
13. "Idumea" (47b) / E-20
14. "North Port" (324) / E-9
15. "Liberty" (137) / A2-21
16. "I'm Going Home" (282) / F-9

Source Recordings

A *In Sweetest Union Join.* Double-disc set recorded at the 1999 United Sacred Harp Convention, held at Liberty Baptist Church in Henagar, Alabama (Community Music School of Santa Cruz 2000). Distributed by CD Baby (http://www.cdbaby.com/cd/ushma) and the Sacred Harp Musical Heritage Association (http://www.fasola.org/shmha). Available as streaming audio through CD Baby.

B/C *150th Anniversary Chattahoochee Sacred Harp Singing Convention.* Two separate double-disc sets recorded at the 2002 Chattahoochee Convention in Cross Plains, Georgia (Denney 2002–3). B is Saturday; C is Sunday. Distributed by Morning Trumpet Recordings (http://www.morningtrumpet .com).

D *Joe Beasley Memorial Sacred Harp Album.* Double-disc set of songs recorded by Joseph Beasley at Alabama singings in 1954 and the 1970s (Seiler 1999). Distributed by the Joe Beasley Memorial Foundation (http://joe beasleymemorialfoundation.org). Available as streaming audio through Pilgrim Productions (http://www.pilgrimproduction.org/sacredharp/beasley/ beasleyharp.html).

E *Rivers of Delight: American Folk Hymns from the Sacred Harp Tradition.* Professional recording by the Word of Mouth Chorus (1979). Widely available.

F   *Cold Mountain* [soundtrack]. Includes two Sacred Harp songs recorded at Liberty Baptist Church, performed by a diverse group of singers (Burnett 2003). Widely available.

Many excellent historical recordings and tunebooks can be obtained through Morning Trumpet Recordings (http://www.morningtrumpet .com) and Rising Dove Fine Arts (http://www.risingdove.com).

The 1991 revision of *The Sacred Harp* tunebook can be obtained by contacting the Sacred Harp Publishing Company. The executive secretary, Richard Mauldin, can be reached at rkmauldin@att.net. See http://www .originalsacredharp.com for more information.

Acknowledgments

I must begin by thanking the singers—and I will never feel that I have finished. The Chicago Sacred Harp singers, writ large, supported my singing and my research from the beginning. Special thanks are due to Ted Mercer, Ted and Marcia Johnson, Dean Slaton (in loving memory), Suzanne Flandreau, and Lisa Grayson for their help with interviews, reading drafts, fact-checking, and general feedback. I had been citing Steve Warner's work on the sociology of religion for some time before I realized that he was the same man who brought joy to the bass section at every Chicago convention; since I made that connection he has proved doubly meaningful in my work. John Plunkett not only housed and transported me to singings virtually every time I visited Georgia but got me involved in ambitious historical projects of his own devising. He has shared all of his findings from interviews, archival research, and travels to far-flung Southern cemeteries. Richard DeLong, David Lee, and Kelly House were gracious enough to read and comment on sections about themselves or their families, always a peculiar experience. I can't thank them enough for their support and encouragement. Carolyn Deacy provided me with housing, delightful companionship, and a window into California Sacred Harp singing on many occasions. Gary and Sarah Smith always welcomed me (and dozens of other singers) into their Alabama home. D.J. Hatfield's friendship, scholarly work, and voice have informed every page of this book. In my own generation of singers, Megan Jennings, Mark Miller, Aaron Girard, and Duncan Vinson often challenged my understanding of the "newcomer" experience in productive ways. Aaron was a constant presence for much of my work and was generous with his ample gifts as a singer, musicologist, writer, and editor. All the participants on the fasola.org listservs deserve thanks for their thoughtful, knowledgeable postings over the years; in these pages I have only been able to address a tiny fraction of what I learned from those online discussions.

I owe my introduction to critical thinking, writing, and Sacred Harp singing itself to four extraordinary teachers and singers at the Putney School: George Emlen, Alec Ewald, Joe Holland, and Hugh Silbaugh. It is no exaggeration to say that this project began when I was a teenager under their tutelage. In later years, my mentors, colleagues, and students made the writing process a pleasure. Kay Kaufman Shelemay, Richard Wolf, Sean Gallagher, Hoon Song, Martin Stokes, Phil Bohlman, Carol Oja, Ginny Danielson, Leo Treitler, Ruth Solie, Lewis Lockwood, Tom Kelly, Regula Qureshi, and Henry Klumpenhouwer have supported my work with erudition, warmth, and all manner of advice. My friends and colleagues Molly Kovel, Lilith Wood, Christina Linklater, Anneka Lenssen, Victoria Widican, Te-Yi Lee, Mary Greitzer, Sindhu Revuluri, Petra Gelbart, Natalie Kirschstein, Sarah Morelli, Anicia Timberlake, and David Kaminsky helped me imagine making a happy life in academia. Laurie Matheson, Judith McCulloh, and the staff of the University of Illinois Press have made the publication process smooth, swift, and even occasionally fun. The Press's two readers offered not only invaluable feedback but also much-appreciated encouragement.

I gratefully acknowledge the material support I received from a Mellon Fellowship in the Humanities; term-time and summer research grants from Harvard University; the Alvin H. Johnson AMS 50 Fellowship from the American Musicological Society; and a Killam Memorial Postdoctoral Fellowship at the University of Alberta. On another material front, the Sacred Harp Publishing Company has graciously permitted me to reproduce a wide range of materials from the 1991 revision of *The Sacred Harp*.

Finally, thanks to the many branches of my family for their support. My partner, James Baumgartner, has earned my undying gratitude by learning to sing with me.

Ye fleeting charms of earth, farewell,
Your springs of joy are dry;
My soul now seeks another home,
A brighter world on high.

I'm a long time trav'ling here below,
I'm a long time trav'ling away from home,
I'm a long time trav'ling here below,
To lay this body down.

—"White" (288); text from Dobell's
  New Selection, 1810

Traveling Home

Introduction

IN SEARCH OF TRADITION

On a summer Saturday morning in the South, at the end of a gravel road, cars filled in the fringes of a clearing where a plain white building stood. Off to the side, coolers and covered dishes were scattered on a long cement table shaded by a roof. There was a cemetery in back, and just behind that there was a highway—down a drop-off and through a screen of brush, trees, and kudzu, its presence betrayed by a near-imperceptible hum. A different sound, a steady pulse of voices, came from the building. A latecomer pulled in, hopped out of his car—from which the soundtrack to *O Brother, Where Art Thou?* briefly blasted—and headed for the building, a bag of cough drops and an oblong dark-red book in hand. He slipped in the door; it stood open for a moment as he filled out his registration form, and a few lines of song roared into the sweltering air:

Then He'll call us home to heaven,
At His table we'll sit down;
Christ will gird Himself, and serve us
With sweet manna all around.
("Holy Manna" [59]; see Figure 1,
Sound Example 1)[1]

I had also arrived late; a sudden summer storm had forced us to the shoulder of the interstate for a while. I knew from the fragment of song that we had only missed the very beginning of the singings—"Holy Manna" is a popular choice for the first song of the day. Now there would be the opening prayer, which we knew we shouldn't interrupt by coming inside. So we took a few moments to gather our things, smell the wet ground, distribute some paper fans among ourselves. I shook out the skirt of my summer dress, grateful that I didn't have to wear long sleeves and long pants to look respectable. Then we went in, made ourselves nametags, chose seats in the appropriate vocal sections, and sang from our copies of *The Sacred Harp*.

This scene is probably a familiar one to my readers. For me and for them, it is shaped by layers of associations. In my own memories of Sacred Harp conventions, several different arrivals at Holly Springs Primitive Baptist Church have coalesced into this account of the tantalizing moment just before I step inside a wood-paneled room that vibrates with voices and thumping feet. But most Americans have encountered other versions of this arrival at an end-of-the-line clearing where there's a little Southern church full of singers—versions from movies, documentaries, public television specials, folklore and ethnomusicology writings, a century of local-color journalism, and all the other reverent, satirical, nostalgic, or condescending representations of community practices in the rural South. The revival, the camp meeting, the family reunion with dinner-on-the-grounds—they turn up often, along with the tale of the traveler's discovery of this little pocket of peculiar customs and time-worn ritual.[2] Such scenes are quintessentially local, traditional, and authentic. In my account, the only clues to the contrary—or at least to complications—are the registration form, the nametags, and the car stereo playing a beautifully produced Hollywood homage to scenes just like this one.

The Sacred Harp convention held at Holly Springs every June is one of hundreds of gatherings of singers that take place all over the United States each year. Many of the voices that filled the little church belonged not to west Georgia locals but to people from Chicago, New England, Minneapolis, Texas, and California. They sat on rows of pews arranged to form a "hollow square," with one voice part to a side and everyone facing the center (see Figure 2). Singers took turns standing in the middle of the square to choose and lead a song from *The Sacred Harp*. They sang all day Saturday and Sunday, with breaks for a sociable lunch and for memorial speeches about recently deceased fellow singers. Then they drove to homes or airports. Some would see each other the following weekend at another singing in another state; others might go to only one or two Sacred Harp singings a year. A first-time visitor who'd made a long road-trip to Georgia to check out this traditional Southern practice might learn that a group back home in Ohio had been holding monthly Sacred Harp singings for years.

HOLY MANNA. 8s & 7s.
"Worship the Lord in the beauty of holiness." -- Ps. 29:2.

William Moore, 1825.

C Major George Atkin, 1819.

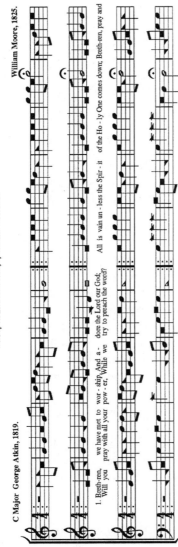

1. Breth-ren, we have met to wor-ship, And a-dore the Lord our God; All is vain un-less the Spir-it of the Ho-ly One comes down; Breth-ren, pray and
   Will you pray with all your pow-er, While we try to preach the word?

ho-ly man-na Will be show-ered all a-round.

2. Brethren, see poor sinners round you,
   Trembling on the brink of woe;
   Death is coming, hell is moving,
   Can you bear to let them go?
   See our fathers, see our mothers,
   And our children sinking down;
   Brethren, pray and holy manna
   Will be showered all around.

3. Sisters, will you join and help us?
   Moses' sisters aided him;
   Will you help the trembling mourners,
   Who are struggling hard with sin?
   Tell them all about the Saviour,
   Tell them that He will be found;
   Sisters, pray, and holy manna
   Will be showered all around.

4. Is there here a trembling jailer,
   Seeking grace, and filled with fears?
   Is there here a weeping Mary,
   Pouring forth a flood of tears?
   Brethren, join your cries to help them;
   Sisters, let your prayers abound;
   Pray, O pray that holy manna
   May be scattered all around.

5. Let us love our God supremely,
   Let us love each other, too;
   Let us love and pray for sinners,
   Till our God makes all things new.
   Then He'll call us home to heaven,
   At His table we'll sit down;
   Christ will gird Himself, and serve us
   With sweet manna all around.

Figure 1: The tune "Holy Manna" (59), which is often used to open a singing (Sound Example 1). All songs from *The Sacred Harp* are reproduced here with the kind permission of the Sacred Harp Publishing Company.

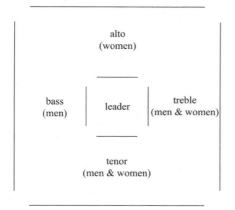

Figure 2: The "hollow square" seating arrangement. Sections are divided by aisles to allow access to the center. Men and women double the tenor and treble parts at the octave; the tenor part is the melody line, and leaders face the tenor "front bench" at the beginning and end of songs.

Today the singers who gather at annual Sacred Harp conventions include young children born into rural Southern "singing families"; Southern urbanites in search of regional cultural heritage; American folk music fans from college-age to graying; Christian and Jewish singers who have grown dissatisfied with their institutional religious experience; early-music lovers who think the open harmonies and straight-tone singing have a medieval sound; and young punk musicians who appreciate the volume, "rawness," and do-it-yourself anticommercial ethos of Sacred Harp. Generational, religious, political, and geographical differences would ordinarily prevent these people from crossing paths at all, let alone forming a tight-knit community. Their ideas of just what "the tradition" is are as diverse as the singers themselves.

Some singers, especially in the rural South, sing because of long-standing family involvement and religious conviction. Local Sacred Harp practice was passed down in rural Southern communities for about a hundred years with only intermittent interest from urban folk revivalists. These lifelong participants are often called "traditional singers"—although some would say that "traditional singing" is more a state of mind and spirit than a birthright. Southern singers *without* family connections to Sacred Harp sometimes come in search of an antidote for the poisonous stereotypes of the South that they've been swallowing for years. As one man told me, "I think one of the reasons Sacred Harp appealed to me as a college student was that it gave me a reason to be proud of being from Alabama." Other new singers are looking for "truly American music," national roots to which they can lay claim. They might approach Sacred Harp as one among many forms of participatory music making that regained popularity during the folk revival of the 1950s–1970s.

In all these categories of participation there are singers who see Sacred Harp as their primary source of spiritual or religious experience, as Christians or otherwise. This is especially true of those who were brought up with no religion, who have "lapsed" from a childhood faith, or who maintain a religious affiliation but now feel unwelcome in their places of worship—due to sexual orientation, for example, or to shifting political convictions.

All these people sing from *The Sacred Harp,* an American collection of hymns and anthems first published in 1844 by the Georgians B. F. White and E. J. King. Many singers place themselves within a single national Sacred Harp community, with roots in the American South and flourishing branches in the Midwest and on both coasts. Participants regularly travel hundreds of miles to attend certain annual singings, returning year after year. But why do they keep coming back? What binds Sacred Harp singers across the geographic, religious, political, and generational divides that they constantly invoke? This book is about the physical and metaphoric travels of Sacred Harp singers as they meet and sing around the country, creating and sustaining an ethos of mutual tolerance by lifting their voices together.

Shape-Notes and Singing Schools

Sacred Harp falls under the broad rubric of "shape-note" music, which takes its name from a late-eighteenth-century innovation in musical notation. Shape-note systems notate each pitch in a scale with a shaped note head that corresponds to a solfege syllable. In *The Sacred Harp,* for example, all the major-key tonic notes have triangular heads and are called "Fa." These systems were designed to promote music literacy, improve sight-singing skills, and sell tunebooks.[3] Singers could use the shaped note heads and their corresponding solfege syllables to read through the music before contending with the words of the song.

Scholars often credit the system used in *The Sacred Harp* to William Little and William Smith, but in fact these men adopted the notation from fellow Philadelphian John Connelly.[4] Little and Smith's tunebook *The Easy Instructor* (1801) employed four shaped note heads to represent the four-syllable British solfege system, which designated the major scale with the syllables Fa–Sol–La–Fa–Sol–La–Mi–Fa.[5] *The Sacred Harp* of 1844 was only one of many nineteenth-century song compilations to use this system, but

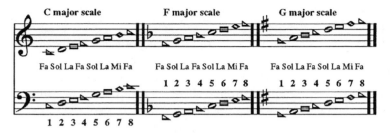

Figure 3: Explanation of shape-note scales from the "Rudiments of Music" printed in the front of *The Sacred Harp.*

over the course of a century it emerged as the main victor in a fierce competition among the adherents of different shape-note books (Bealle 1997: 5). The notation has played an integral part in Sacred Harp transmission and performance practice since the 1840s. At a Sacred Harp singing, participants sing through each tune on "the notes"—the solfege syllables represented by the shapes—before proceeding with the verses chosen by the leader. (See Figure 3.)

Shape-note singing has a rich and varied history, much of which has been documented by scholars of early American history and hymnody.[6] The bare-bones version that experienced singers provide to newcomers usually focuses on New England origins, persecution by the nineteenth-century "better music movement," and preservation and historical continuity in the South. The following excerpts from the brief history that Minnesota singer Keith Willard provides at the Sacred Harp website www.fasola.org can be considered representative of contemporary singers' accounts:

> In New England, the singing school institution flowered briefly in the period prior to the Revolutionary war but then faded. A post war influx of European style trained musicians, systematically campaigned for the removal of this "crude and lewd" music and its schools. Under the influence of Lowell Mason and like ilk, the teaching of singing moved from the informal process of community singing schools to the rigid (and regulated) control of the public schools. The "Better Music Movement" was largely successful in the cities of the North. . . .
>
> Books such as *Kentucky Harmony, Missouri Harmony, Southern Harmony,* and *Sacred Harp* were published in four-shape notation and used widely by a people isolated from the tyranny of citified "experts." It was in the south where the marriage of the New England singing school music

forms to the oral Celtic folk tune heritage was completed, and the folk-hymn was born. It was here that the singing school found a permanent home in the rural areas of the Appalachians and the Piedmont. (Willard 2004)

More detailed versions expand on two threads of this narrative: the spread of singing schools and the role of revival meetings tied to the Second Great Awakening. Shape-note singings have now diverged considerably from the revival tradition in form and content, but singing schools continue to take place.[7] Sacred Harp conventions still use terminology derived from the singing school tradition: the assembled group of singers is called a "class," and leading a song is "giving a lesson."

The singing school movement began in the eighteenth century as a corrective for low levels of music literacy and the perceived chaos of lined-out psalm singing. Eventually the movement "succeeded in creating a large body of singers capable of handling a repertoire of increasing complexity and variety" (Bruce 2000: 136). In the early nineteenth century, outlying American settlements provided a market for the services of itinerant singing masters; their multi-week singing schools met a need for music education and provided a chaperoned social space for young people to mingle. As the singing masters made inroads further south and west, however, the style and the shape-note notation of the music they taught fell out of favor in northeastern cities. Reformers vilified them as unqualified tricksters who were cheating honest Americans out of a civilizing musical education. A Cincinnati music periodical reported in 1848 that "Hundreds of country idlers, too lazy or too stupid for farmers or mechanics, 'go to singing school for a spell,' get diplomas from others scarcely better qualified than themselves, and then with their brethren, the far famed 'Yankee Peddlars,' itinerate to all parts of the land, to corrupt the taste and pervert the judgment of the unfortunate people who, for want of better, have to put up with them."[8] John Bealle has described how the crusading New England music reformer Lowell Mason (1792–1872) and his colleagues placed editorials in such publications; they heaped ridicule on shape-notation and promoted a musical idiom and pedagogy based on contemporary Western European models in its stead (Bealle 1997).

In rural frontier areas, however, shape-note singing still flourished as wholesome family entertainment. In the same regions, camp-meeting revivals transmitted religious songs among huge crowds, diverse in both race and theology. Shape-note tunebooks absorbed popular musical forms of the day, becoming "virtual catalogs of musical and religious dissent";

compilers and arrangers paired dance tunes with sacred texts by Isaac Watts and other popular Evangelical poets (Bealle 1997: 127). These texts were themselves "popular" in every sense of the word. Watts was "the most widely published and read writer in eighteenth-century America," as Marini has observed, and nineteenth-century revivalists adopted his work. Watts's verses created a Christian antitype for Old Testament psalms—*The Psalms of David Imitated in the Language of the New Testament and Applied to the Christian State and Worship,* as Watts's 1719 psalter was titled.

In the wake of the music reform campaigns in the northeast, and with the help of gathered and dispersed revivals in frontier regions, by the mid-nineteenth century the American South was the primary home of shape-note singing traditions. The tradition of unaccompanied hymn singing was maintained in that region partly because it was home to so many independent Baptist sects, some of which consider the use of musical instruments in church to be sacrilegious; elsewhere, four-part congregational singing declined in favor of prestigious organ music and formal choirs.[9] In addition, some communities maintained the four-shape system and its associated musical repertoire as a gesture of loyalty to antebellum rural Southern culture. Like other innovative technologies, shape-note notation carried "the burden, prestige, and controversy of being made to speak for specific ideological projects" (Ginsberg 2002: 20). Before the Civil War *The Sacred Harp* was still a fairly new compendium, adopted by only a few singing conventions. But as the book's popularity surged in the postwar decades, its four-shape notation came to signal an affinity with antebellum traditions (Campbell 1997).

"Sacred Harp" and "shape-note" are often used interchangeably now. This practice obscures the existence of several ongoing, distinct shape-note singing traditions linked with other nineteenth-century tunebooks, such as the Mennonite *Harmonia Sacra* (1832),[10] the *Southern Harmony* (1835), the *Social Harp* (1855), the *Christian Harmony* (1866), and the *New Harp of Columbia* (1867). These books include quite different repertoire than the *Sacred Harp;* some employ a seven-shape notation system that corresponds to moveable-tonic Do–Re–Mi solfege. There are also many flourishing Sacred Harp communities today who sing from "the Cooper book." In 1902 W. M. Cooper of Dothan, Alabama presided over a major revision of *The Sacred Harp,* bringing many "gospel" songs and hymns with more regularized harmonic arrangements into the book. A substantial portion of the Cooper repertoire presents textual and harmonic features typical of turn-of-the-century "new-book" or gospel singing, a style popularized by the urban revivalists Dwight L. Moody and Ira D. Sankey in the 1870s.

In any given community the adoption of one tunebook and rejection of others was oriented around local politics, practical ease of access, and ideological positions on seven-shape gospel music. The cheap and frequently revised paperback seven-shape books that traveled South from the urban northeastern gospel movement were emblematic of "simplicity, speed, and efficiency," the ideals of a postbellum progressive New South, but both the books and the ideology met with resistance in some quarters—particularly when the New South's economic developments did not benefit all communities equally (Campbell 1997: 173). While Cooper's 1902 revision of *The Sacred Harp* retained the four-shape system, its gospel elements made it unpalatable to many singers.

In 1911 Joe S. James produced a rival to Cooper's edition. He eliminated most gospel songs, restored material from B. F. White's earlier editions, and called his book the *Original Sacred Harp*. James advertised the fact that the book's pagination was consistent with the 1869 White edition, an editorial decision that emphasized points of common repertoire and facilitated side-by-side use of the two books. But he also appealed to "the industrial New South's obsession with numbers, output, and quantification" by including features like statistics on the numbers of printed words, Scripture citations, and repeat signs in the book (Campbell 1997: 182). James's book found followers, and in 1936 Paine Denson led the publication of a new revision of the James edition. Subsequent "Denson revisions" took place in 1960, 1967, 1971, 1987, and 1991; the editorial committees added older tunes from other shape-note sources as well as newly composed tunes considered to resonate with the musical styles prevalent in the earlier editions.

The 1991 "Denson book" revision of *The Sacred Harp*—produced by a committee led by the eminent Georgia singing school teacher Hugh McGraw—currently enjoys the most widespread use of all the shape-note tunebooks. For practical purposes my observations should be considered limited to singings using the 1991 revision, although a number of my informants and the participants on the fasola.org Internet listservs take part in other shape-note traditions on a regular basis. Most Sacred Harp conventions operate in accordance with written bylaws that specify which revision of *The Sacred Harp* is to be used.

The Legacy of "White Spirituals"

The early-twentieth-century designation "white spirituals" continues to cling to Sacred Harp singing. In 1997 shape-note singing could still be glossed as "the quintessential expression of white, Anglo-Celtic ethnicity" in a multiculturalist American music textbook (Lornell and Rasmussen 1997: 209), a description that elides a long history of racially-charged controversy by implying that "Anglo-Celtic" whiteness is just one ethnicity among many. Sacred Harp first came to be associated with whiteness under very different political circumstances.

In the decades around the turn of the twentieth century, anxieties about urban immigrants and the social mobility of African Americans fueled eugenicist ideologies all over the United States. At the same time, rapid changes to the Southern economy inspired antimodernist nostalgia, giving rise to the Southern Agrarian movement by the 1930s. In this context the whiteness of rural Southern Sacred Harp singers was construed as one aspect of their valuable preservation of distinctive local culture in the face of assimilationist rhetoric (cf. Lauter 2001: 133).

George Pullen Jackson (1874–1953) was a key figure in the development of this discourse. His book *White Spirituals in the Southern Uplands* famously described shape-note singers as a "lost tonal tribe," and he considered their singing traditions central to the "lyric-religious folk-ways" of the rural South (Jackson 1933: 4, viii).[11] Jackson's work argued that both black and white American spiritual song traditions were derived from Anglo-Celtic hymnody and folksong repertoires. While he acknowledged that the black spirituals of his own time displayed some African elements in the realm of rhythm, harmony, and performance practice, he considered these to be adaptations to a European-derived repertoire acquired by black singers at Southern Uplands camp meetings.

Jackson's devotion to the idea that the flow of musical influence ran primarily from white to black singers—and his emphasis on the authentic, historical value of white rural culture—made his work appealing to the racist ideologues of his era (Bealle 1997: 119). His ideas proved useful to xenophobic contemporaries who lauded the racial purity of "mountain whites"—"the Scotch-Irish type which . . . has been touched very little by the great stream of immigration which has flooded other parts of the country and has almost obliterated the racial characteristics of the founders of the nation" (Caldwell 1930, reprinted in McNeil 1995: 221). But Jackson's personal history suggests that his thesis about "white spirituals" had different ideological underpinnings.

In the 1920s Jackson was an influential figure in Nashville public life and an ardent supporter of progressive institutions like Fisk University, Nashville's African American college. He was a constant advocate for the Fisk

Jubilee Singers over the course of many years as the music reviewer for the Nashville *Banner*. Upon his retirement from this position in 1931 he received letters of thanks from both John W. Work Jr., director of the Fisk Singers, and Ray F. Brown, the University's director. (Work's warm, hand-written letter related that "whenever you attend a concert in which I am concerned I always feel that I have a 'friend at court.'") Late in his life Jackson carefully pasted these letters into retrospective scrapbooks, along with many of his own articles praising performances by the Fisk Singers.[12] On the last page of this scrapbook volume he juxtaposed two images of black religious practice: the early-nineteenth-century Pavel Petrovich Svinin watercolor titled "Negro Methodists in Old Philadelphia" and a photograph of himself engaged in extending the "hand of fellowship" among worshippers at an African American church service.[13]

These biographical details (and Jackson's own writings) suggest that his shortchanging of African American originality and influence in spiritual traditions was rooted not in racial antipathy but in a defense of the impoverished rural white Southerners who were being cited as disgraceful examples of the need for progressive reform in the South. Jackson stressed the value of rural culture in the context of a derisive discourse that dismissed these people as "white trash" or, at best, as backward remnants of a past that must inevitably fade. As one reviewer wrote of *White Spirituals in the Southern Uplands*, "[O]ne is wrought upon to consider how quickly the 'yokels' of only yesterday are being transformed into the conservators of the native arts that we did not know we had. The country folks have innocently kept alive the sacred fire that the prophets of the modern temper had all but extinguished with their tears."[14]

In a 1932 article, Jackson laid blame at the feet of two groups of white Southerners for their failure to recognize the cultural value of "white spirituals": "the professional Southerners of big-plantation presumptions who would do anything to lower the stock of the poor white trash" and "the Southern urban church folk, who have always been eager to forget and disown the camp-meeting songs, the illegitimate children of their own early hymnody" (Jackson 1932: 246). Jackson championed white rural culture for its deep historical connections to English Protestantism, and he insisted that African American culture come along for the ride. Both black and white rural Southerners became the keepers of an indigenous American folk culture shaped by its natural environment.[15]

Jackson's conviction that these rural tradition-bearers were fundamentally shaped by American history and the American landscape led him to project them into the past and discount their creative agency regardless of their race. For him, all contemporary composition in the genre was anachronistic and derivative. As he wrote of black composers in *White and Negro Spirituals,* "it should be said to the credit of the makers of such songs that their product seems to be about as 'original' as is that of the more recent 'fuguists' whose productions have found their way into the white Sacred Harp" (Jackson 1943: 274). Jackson's shape-note-singing octet, the Nashville "Old Harp Singers," costumed themselves in Colonial-era accessories. Official portraits in his scrapbooks show the group singing by candlelight while sporting bonnets, white wigs, and muttonchops.

The legacy of Jackson's work lies not only in its association of Sacred Harp singing with white rural Southerners—and of these citizens with early American history—but in the establishment of the practice as indigenous American folksong. Under the auspices of progressive multiculturalism, these two associations have been deployed in tandem to clear Sacred Harp singing from charges of racial exclusivity. As the description from *Musics of Multicultural America* indicates, if Sacred Harp is "the quintessential expression" of an "ethnic" cultural practice then it is no more surprising for a long-established rural Southern convention to be all-white than for a New York *sonidero baile* to be all-Mexican (Lornell and Rasmussen 1997: 209, see above; Ragland 2003).

But the fact that recently-established urban and Northern conventions are not more racially diverse gives some singers pause. As the Southern historian and Sacred Harp singer David Carlton has noted, "To the intense regret of many Sacred Harpers, the most widespread stream of the tradition . . . remains virtually all white. . . . [T]he few African Americans appearing at most white 1991 Edition singings are typically middle-class northerners" (Carlton 2003: 60). This situation stems from historical competition among different shape-note tunebooks, racial segregation of Southern churches and social institutions, and the different nature of the relationship between shape-note singing and specific local church affiliations among black and white Southerners.

Community-based African American Sacred Harp singing has existed since the nineteenth century. The vast majority of black singing communities adopted the Cooper revision of *The Sacred Harp* in the early twentieth century, as did white singers in the same regions: southern Georgia and Alabama, northern Florida and Texas. The "Wiregrass" singers in southeast Alabama remain the best-known community of black singers, owing to the composition, publishing, and recording work of Judge Jackson (compiler of *The Colored Sacred Harp*, 1934; no relation to G. P. Jackson). After Jackson's death, his friend Dewey Williams facilitated the Wiregrass singers' participation alongside white Sacred Harp singers at the 1970 Smithsonian Festival of American Folklife and at the Montreal "Man and His World" exposition the following year. A few Wiregrass singers made regular appearances at the (largely white) National Sacred Harp Convention in Alabama during my fieldwork years, with strong encouragement from the convention's organizers. However, the number of black singers in the Wiregrass region and elsewhere has diminished greatly over the past several generations.[16]

In the 1970s, the folklorist Joe Dan Boyd sought out but was unable to uncover links among different regional communities of black Sacred Harp singers. He concluded that the importance of local church bonds resulted in a singing tradition where "blacks appear to have less enthusiasm than do whites for a widely scattered 'brotherhood of Harpers' throughout the country bound together symbolically by a common denominator: the book itself" (Boyd 1971: 77). One should also bear in mind that long-distance travel was more limited for black singers—owing to their systematically restricted economic and social circumstances and the risk of encountering racial violence on long journeys—and that huge nondenominational gatherings of black singers on the scale of contemporary white conventions might have attracted hostile attention. For all these reasons, African American Sacred Harp conventions have never formed long-distance travel networks like those that are my subject here.

Nevertheless, race and ethnicity remain important issues for today's national singing community. As I will discuss in Chapter 6, the guilt some singers feel about Sacred Harp's racial homogeneity encourages them to find and emphasize other proofs of diversity. The difference between Northern and Southern singers is often treated like an ethnic distinction—one that can deceptively subsume other distinctions, such as traditional versus newcomer and urban versus rural. The affiliations among singers and singing families are modeled like ethnic affiliations. And perhaps the most powerful legacy of the ethnicization of traditional singers is the double bind in which they may find themselves now, when their rural Southern background can stigmatize them as uneducated, backward, or racist "white trash" while also serving as the mark of their musical authenticity.[17] The creative co-option of these stereotypes by both Southern and Northern singers has important musical and social results in the singing community today.

A Middle Ages for America: Sacred Harp's Double History

From the late nineteenth century on, the practitioners of shape-note singing traditions were repeatedly "discovered" by journalists, historians, folksong enthusiasts, and musicologists who sent word of "the fasola folk," "white spirituals," and "our living musical ancestors" out to the urbane reading public.[18] Such discoveries reproduced central elements of European historical narratives within highly condensed evolutionary accounts of American history (Batteau 1990, Miller 2003b). Contextualized in this way, the brisk pace of that history became an asset rather than a liability—it mirrored the speed of American industrialization. American progress was so rapid that American "ancestors" were still alive and well when the nation as a whole reached civilized maturity. Instead of centuries-old documents, America had human beings from another time available for scrutiny, interrogation, and eventual assimilation into modern life—a progressive humanitarian goal to be achieved through the efforts of genteel female schoolteachers and Protestant missionaries (Batteau 1990, Whisnant 1983). These homegrown primitives were conceived as both familiar and alien, with the ambivalence characteristic of all stereotypes. The Southern uplands region and its citizens were not only quintessentially American but also "a strange land and a peculiar people" (Harney 1873), "an anachronism" requiring objective scientific investigation by moderns (Frost 1899, reprinted in McNeil 1995: 92).[19]

Rural Southerners were conceived as specifically *our* living ancestors, where "we" denoted white middle-class American Protestants. This quality divided them from other kinds of contemporary primitives—including distant exotic peoples and Native Americans—who were made to represent humanity's more general and ancient origins (Miller 2003a). In their presumed racial purity and proximity to modern culture, the Southern mountaineers could be invoked as a parallel to the medieval ancestors of Europeans. Like medieval society, rural Southern society was glossed as "old-fashioned, primitive, irrational, superstitious, cruel" (Treitler 2003: 104). The invention of the rural South recapitulated the nineteenth-century invention of the Middle Ages as a means for self-definition through rich cultural heritage, self-congratulation through distance from the primitive past, and self-escape into an ancient, romantic wilderness (Stock 1974: 543).[20]

Like much rural Southern music, Sacred Harp singing has long been marked as explicitly and indigenously American—not only for its Southernness but for its earlier connections to colonial New England. Flyers promoting singing conventions or folk festival workshops often describe

Sacred Harp as "America's oldest choral art" or "a quintessential expression of American democracy." Music historians and contemporary singers alike frequently link Sacred Harp to the composer William Billings and other "New England tunesmiths." The "independence" attributed to Colonial-era musical style has become closely associated with a later generation's resistance to the "better music movement." For example, in 1940 Charles Seeger identified Billings as "our first musical rebel"; on the same page he described shape-notes as "an effort to free the ordinary man from bondage to the high priests of the musical profession and their difficult notation" (Seeger 1940: 492). This association is so strong that many singers are surprised to learn that Billings himself did not publish music in shape-notes. (Little and Smith's *Easy Instructor* was published a year after his death.) The relationship between Billings, Sacred Harp singing, and independent-minded dissent holds a prominent place in the "Rudiments of Music" printed at the front of *The Sacred Harp*: "*Sacred Harp* harmony does not follow the rules of *conventional harmony* [bold in original], which were well established by the late 18th century. Billings fiercely declared his independence ('I don't think myself confined to any rules of composition laid down by any who went before me') and he practiced what he preached" (Garst 1991: 21). The Billings quotation is from the passage in *The New-England Psalm-Singer* (1770) that continues with the famous assertion that "every *Composer* should be his own *Carver*," a turn of phrase that has been cited countless times as evidence of his American individualism.

Stephen Marini notes that Billings "created a vocational model for other tunesmiths," many of whom chose to compose, publish, and teach from their own settings of the massively popular texts of Isaac Watts (Marini 2003: 79). Richard Crawford has traced the shifting reputation of Billings as another sort of model: in the twentieth century the composer and his cohort began to be considered "the first creators of an unmistakably American music" (Crawford 1990: 225). Early-nineteenth-century critics located American qualities in what they viewed as technical crudity and impiety. But twentieth-century scholars began to celebrate the same repertoire as projecting qualities of independence, individualism, egalitarianism, and primitive power. In 1940, Seeger referred to "a rigorous, spare, disciplined beauty in the choral writing that is all the more to be prized for having been conceived in the 'backwoods' for which many professional musicians have such scorn, and in the face of the determined opposition of sophisticated zealots in no small number, from Lowell Mason down to those of this very day" (Seeger 1940: 488). At the turn of the millennium, Neely Bruce suggested that Mason had "replaced something vital and indigenous with something derivative and imported" (Bruce 2000: 139).

Both singers and scholars have invoked independence, egalitarianism, and resistance to mainstream convention as key characteristics of Sacred Harp practitioners and the styles represented in their tunebook. Like independent-minded frontiersmen, the story goes, this democratic and physically engaging singing moved from stodgy New England to a rougher but more liberated landscape. The history of shape-note singing reproduces a recurring narrative theme of American history, the westward push in search of freedom. It also articulates a central drama of American historiography: the productive tension of egalitarianism and rugged individualism.[21] Both singing practices and songs are made to play out this drama, often in the same breath. Consider Ron Pen's assessment: "This new singing school music clearly reflected the important question that was at the heart of America's experiment in participatory democracy—how was this country going to reconcile the tension between individual freedom and the constraints of social order. Each vocal line was fiercely independent in following its own path" (Pen 1997: 214).

The continuous transmission of Sacred Harp singing in the South has often been linked to the presumed natural musicality and stubborn backwardness of rural Southerners. They are imagined as old-fashioned conservators of any and all traditions, far removed from the vigorous, innovative independence of a figure like Billings. Crawford implies as much in assessing B. F. White, one of the compilers of the 1844 *Sacred Harp:* "[T]he lesson taught by White's life was that to achieve eminence in the culture where *The Sacred Harp* flourished was to be remembered as a typical figure, not an innovative one" (Crawford 2001: 166). But it was the establishment of Sacred Harp conventions, not the essentialized conservative qualities of Southern singers, that carried the tradition into the present.

The term "convention" refers both to an association of singers—with membership sometimes recorded in writing—and to the annual multiday singing events hosted by such associations. At nineteenth-century singing conventions, which were typically governed by written constitutions, delegates from different regional singing associations gathered to sing, socialize, share meals, campaign for political office, court future spouses, and keep parliamentary-style order during the singing sessions. Constitution writers consciously adopted the language of American political institutions. An 1866 constitution begins, "We, the vocalists of the Chattahoochee Musical Convention feeling it to be the duty of the present generation to make an effort, in common with the interest of the subject, to renovate, improve & systematize our Southern Music, do therefore, form an association for that purpose, that by our united aid and influence, we may assist in advancing this cause, do adopt the following Constitution for our government" (Miller 2002: 154).

The stated mission here has both progressive and conservative aspects. It is rooted in the ideals and potential of "the present generation," those who faced the duty of restoring regional culture after the depredations of the Civil War. The preamble implicitly celebrates antebellum Southern cultural heritage, but it also emphasizes a forward-looking agenda—not simply to restore old practices but "to renovate, improve, & systematize." Yet within the lifespan of some of the first Chattahoochee Convention singers, Sacred Harp singing became associated with cultural conservatism, rural isolation, "natural" musicianship, and "our musical ancestors" (see Chapter 5). Sacred Harp acquired a double history, reliant on contrasting visions of Revolution-era New England independence and nineteenth-century Southern conservatism.

In the twentieth century the advent of portable recording technology—coupled with a new interest in specifically and authentically American cultural traditions—brought descriptions and recordings of shape-note singing to an ever-widening audience. Recordings made by academic folk-music collectors and by singers themselves in the 1920s and 1930s became influential during the folk revival of the 1950s and 1960s. The revival substantially expanded the market for Sacred Harp recordings, including decades-old tracks that resurfaced in Americana compilations like the Smithsonian Folkways *Anthology of American Folk Music* (Smith 1997 [1952]). Some new recordings were made at Southern singing conventions, the classic example being Alan Lomax's 1959 Alabama recording *All Day Singing from "The Sacred Harp"* (Lomax 1960)—which was actually a recording of songs requested by Lomax during a break in the convention proceedings (Bealle 1997: 253). Recordings produced by the Sacred Harp Publishing Company were played on the radio in many Southern communities, often on call-in shows that allowed listeners to request particular songs. Some radio shows had live singers who would perform requested songs on the spot.

Other recordings were produced by folk revival or early music ensembles without ties to Southern singing communities. It wasn't difficult to learn and circulate songs from the shape-note repertoire, since they were available in printed notation. These singers were attracted to the American antiquity of the music and to its open, "medieval-sounding" harmonies. Some members of these ensembles became interested in traditional Southern practice and gradually deepened their relationships to particular singing communities. They helped organize new conventions and became regular travelers in the national convention network.

Gradually, Sacred Harp singing became part of the American folksong canon: a ubiquitous presence at folk festivals large and small, a frequent subject of short features on TV news programs and National Public Radio, and a natural part of the lineup in documentaries like the tremendously popular *Amazing Grace with Bill Moyers* (1990). More and more people began seeking out local singing groups or founding their own. This task was facilitated by the development of the Internet and eventually by www .fasola.org, a clearinghouse for Sacred Harp information of all kinds.

In the years since the folk revival, several factors have contributed to the formation of a self-identifying national community of Sacred Harp singers: the growing popularity of shape-note singing in the Midwest, New England, and in urban areas on both coasts; reduced numbers of lifelong singers in the South, as fewer young singers have stepped into the places of the elderly and deceased; and dramatic changes in transportation and communication technology. My work focuses on the state of Sacred Harp practice in the wake of these changes, but the historical events and recurrent themes I have sketched here will reappear and gain detail and color as they inform singers' narratives and my own analysis.

Singers and scholars perpetually consult and reshuffle the available repertoire of facts about tunebook compilers, shape-note composers, revisions, musical and textual influences, and convention history. My own approach to Sacred Harp history explores how people use such data to meet their own needs as they take stands on the overlapping musical, historical, and ideological controversies that engage the singing community. Sacred Harp culture is saturated with layers of meaning drawn from personal experience and received history, meaning that is ever-present, ever-emergent, and continually transformed by and transforming of individual experience within the tradition. Each singer's experience is necessarily distinct, but over years of such experiences certain commonalities gradually appear, like paths worn across an open field.[22] These paths form a record of ambivalence and choice: with all their intersections, soft borders, and parallel routes to different destinations, they map the history at the core of my work.

The Politics of Nostalgia: A Guiding Principle and a Look Ahead

The physical, intellectual, and spiritual travels that Sacred Harp singers undertake in search of tradition are often fueled by nostalgia. I have come to conceive of that nostalgia as political and even activist in character. But how can nostalgia be political? Several singers asked me this question after I used the phrase in a posting to the Sacred Harp listservs. One woman remarked on the negative connotations of "politics"—which she glossed as "conniving, brown-nosing, cliquish and exclusive behavior and maneuvering to get what you want at the expense of someone else"—and contrasted them with the positive, "sad but sweet" connotations of nostalgia. My response relied partly on pointing out the less-charged definition of "politics" as a term that describes how people negotiate life in a social community. But in fact my "politics of nostalgia" also relates to that loaded, sharper-edged, painful kind of politics, the polarizing politics that has been the subject of so much anxiety and anger in the early years of the American twenty-first century. Nostalgia in the Sacred Harp community has to do with establishing a shared terrain that cuts across that kind of politics, as well as with eminently political conflicts over who has the right to feel nostalgic at all.

Making a nostalgic claim about Sacred Harp singing constitutes a statement of affiliation, affinity, and at least partial authority. In a tradition where authenticity of feeling is a paramount emblem of valid participation, nostalgia is a feeling that stakes claims and creates relationships among singers. Nostalgia is built into the rhetoric of vanishing traditions and cultural crisis; it promises "compensation for the forgetfulness, homelessness and alienation of [modernity's] guilt-ridden conscience" (Steinwand 1997: 10).[23] As such, nostalgic practices and discourses offer the Sacred Harp community a realm of powerful sentiment that lifelong and new singers can share.

But while the politics of nostalgia deeply informs singers' ideologies and practices, there is more to this community than a collective rejection of or by modern society. As Christopher Waterman has written, any kind of modernity has to "focus retrospectively, fix ideologically, and contour aesthetically a master tradition in terms of which its own pragmatic and up-to-date identity makes sense and appears inevitable" (Waterman 1990: 377). I practice and write about Sacred Harp singing because so many Americans are bringing such diverse beliefs and powers to bear in this process of making sense of tradition and modernity.

*   *   *

The following chapters are first and foremost an ethnography of a musical community, but they also speak to themes that are of burning importance in both American cultural studies and on-the-ground American politics: tolerance, voluntary association, diaspora, pluralism, authenticity, stereotype, and nostalgia. Chapter 1 describes my ethnographic "venture to the field" and the dispersed, diverse community of committed singers that I encountered there—all of them travelers in their own right. Chapter 2 explores the nature of "traditional singing" through description of a typical Sacred Harp convention, including the travels of its participants from far-flung geographical and cultural points of origin to "the center of the square," a physical and metaphorical location at the core of Sacred Harp practice and transmission. In Chapter 3, I approach the musical and social markers of traditional singing from another angle: how is competence acquired and recognized in different contexts? Here I discuss the Sacred Harp repertoire, elements of performance practice, and matrices of transmission, including the productive tension between oral and written traditions.

Chapters 4 and 5 analyze more deliberate representations of Sacred Harp, explicit efforts to account for the tradition's importance in personal or national narratives. Chapter 4 assesses the recurring themes found in Sacred Harp texts and in singers' interpretations of them, especially texts about travel, family, death, and homecoming. I demonstrate how songs acquire layers of meaning that are specific to individual singers but are also deployed to account for shared values. Chapter 5 turns to media representations of Sacred Harp produced within and outside the singing community, beginning with the early-twentieth-century local-color journalism that essentialized rural Southerners in general and Sacred Harp singers in particular by projecting them into a romanticized past. I discuss the affinities of this material with post–folk-revival representations of Sacred Harp, including newspaper journalism and recordings by early-music and folk-revival ensembles. After identifying some longstanding themes of outsider representations, I show how Sacred Harp singers have reproduced or subverted them in their own use of media technology.

Finally, in Chapter 6, I address Sacred Harp as traveling culture, containing aspects of both diaspora and pilgrimage, characterized by core values of sincerity, authenticity, and tolerance. I discuss singers' use of humor and irony in the service of their ideals, analyze their debates about the nature of authentic Sacred Harp experience, and show how they stake ownership claims by addressing the tradition variously as ethnic music, sacred music, historical music, and American music. This chapter illuminates the nature of "the politics of nostalgia" and the role Sacred Harp has played in broader American cultural narratives. I conclude by suggesting how the specifically musical and American nature of this tradition shapes its capacity to inform ethical, religious, and political modes of engagement with American society.

1

A Venture to the Field

The texts of Sacred Harp tunes resonate with singers' personal experiences in curious ways. For me, the chorus of "Clamanda" has become inextricably associated with my thoughts on ethnographic method:

O have you ventured to the field,
Well-armed with helmet, sword and shield?
And shall the world, with dread alarms,
Compel you now to ground your arms?[1]
(42, Sound Example 2)

These words have often reminded me of the cultural history of fieldwork, with its connections to missionary expeditions and aggressive colonialist endeavors. With varying degrees of discomfort, scholars have acknowledged that ethnographic fieldwork can resemble a capture-and-conquer mission. An explorer well-armed with the "helmet, sword, and shield" of methodology and recording equipment sets out into unknown territory in search of raw cultural goods that can be converted into intellectual capital. But the world of human relationships in "the field" can compel the ethnographer to ground her arms; practice confounds methodology and will not hold still to be recorded.

I first attended a Sacred Harp convention in college, although as a child of the folk-revival generation I was already familiar with some of the early American shape-note hymns the tunebook contains. It was at my second convention, in the fall of 1997, that I realized I was becoming involved in a musical tradition that might demand a great deal of my intellectual and emotional energy in the years to come. The singing was the Illinois State Convention, an impressive name for an event that draws only forty or so singers each year and takes place in a rural church surrounded by corn-fields. Just before the lunch recess on the last day of a convention, Sacred Harp singers usually hold a "memorial lesson": two or more respected par-ticipants read a list of the names of those singers who have died in the past year, make some remarks of their own, and lead the assembled "class" in singing songs in memory of the dead and of those too ill or elderly to attend the convention. Although I knew none of the names on the list at the Illi-nois State, I found myself in tears as we sang.

Afterward, as I left the church with wet eyes and emerged into the blind-ing midwestern noontime sun, I found a fellow University of Chicago student transfixed with amazement before a large tree that stood alone in the churchyard. Dozens of cicada shells were stuck to the trunk. "There's good luck here—our singing is blessed," he said, and told me that the cica-das were a Taiwanese mark of good fortune. A man who had been raised as a Mennonite and was currently finishing a doctorate in anthropology was finding Taiwanese omens in an Illinois cornfield and applying them to hours of Protestant hymn-singing—singing that had profoundly moved me, though I was not a Christian. I was to find that this kind of multilayered consciousness was characteristic of Sacred Harp singers as they negotiated an approach to the tradition. With or without doctorates in anthropol-ogy, the people who were to be my "informants" were also travelers, social analysts, and documenters of tradition; many were consciously engaged in some form of fieldwork of their own. Lifelong Southern singers and new enthusiasts alike regularly left home for three or four days at a time to go to distant conventions, just as I did, and they often brought some recording equipment alongside their pie-safes for "dinner-on-the-grounds."

It is impossible to draw precise boundaries around Sacred Harp practice on a national scale. Increased ease of transportation and communication over the last fifty years has resulted in a singing community in constant flux; a small convention in rural Georgia might draw singers from Califor-nia and be described in detail on one of the fasola.org listservs the next day. Countless musical traditions are currently in similar situations, suddenly rendered more accessible to tourists, academics, and the commercial music scene. The children who are expected to carry on a tradition within a local community may turn to a different kind of life. Some traditions disappear as their last practitioners die; others change beyond recognition.

These potentially dire consequences of shifting social relations lend themselves to "discourses of the vanishing" (Ivy 1995). Such discourses draw on broader modern anxieties about "the acceleration of history," in Nora's terms, "an increasingly rapid slippage of the present into a historical past that has gone for good, a general perception that anything and everything may disappear" (Nora 1989: 7). The "vanishing tradition" concept has powerfully influenced the experience of new Sacred Harp singers, invoking nostalgia for what modernity has destroyed and making Sacred Harp participation into something of a politicized lifestyle choice. Singing can fall into the same category as other radical practices adopted by Americans on both the far left and right—for example, home-schooling one's children, tightly restricting consumption of mass media products, inventing traditions for the explicit purpose of building social bonds, and establishing back-to-the-land communes or religious communities.

Different constituencies in the national singing community respond to these concerns about disappearance or dilution in different ways, from undertaking community documentation projects to engaging seriously with the question "Should Northerners learn to sing Sacred Harp?"[2] This question was also the title of a 1990s *Chicago Sacred Harp Newsletter* article by Ted Mercer, who answered in the affirmative but warned, "Without wanting to get into questions like, 'How diluted by other musical influences can Sacred Harp be and still retain that ancient power?' I believe that the old-time fasola sound, compared by an Ohio paper last year to a 'brightly patterned but coarsely woven tapestry,' has to be regarded as seriously endangered."[3]

New technologies of communication, including the Internet listserv through which Mercer's article was redistributed in 2003, have undoubtedly altered Sacred Harp transmission and diminished face-to-face social activity in America in general. But not all changes driven by technological shifts are as hostile to musical and social traditions as the typical rhetoric of crisis would suggest. Indeed, Sacred Harp practice is itself the product of the distinctly modern technological phenomenon of mass-produced tunebooks intended for a literate population (Miller 2004a). In many cases, the widened world created by new technologies engenders both the threat of extinction and the means of continuation—but continuation by a different community.

The national Sacred Harp community today is a community of travelers. Singers liken themselves to religious pilgrims, to the itinerant singing masters of the nineteenth century, and more generally to the "strangers here below" or "poor wayfaring stranger" figures who often appear in Sacred Harp hymn texts. My research methods and theoretical framework have been organized around the core metaphor and practice of travel. Much of my fieldwork took place at singings where a majority of participants were not born into a Sacred Harp singing tradition.

This approach tends to obscure certain aspects of the traditional Southern singing experience, such as the importance of singing within a family context or in a highly localized community. However, it places other aspects in relief: the emotional and intellectual appeal of the tradition to new adult singers, their confrontations with religious and political difference, and the unwritten priorities that govern procedure at singings. Like fieldworkers, singers who actively travel are constantly negotiating insider-outsider status in new contexts. They have chosen Sacred Harp as a tradition in which to acquire competence and perform, much as religious converts model an "achieved" religiosity when they actively choose among the plethora of religious options in America (Warner 1993: 1076).

I became a Sacred Harp singer and organizer as a college student in Chicago, a singing region with particular affiliations to Southern singing communities. Inevitably, I still exhibit some of the biases of the Chicago contingent. In the course of my research, however, I have focused on interactions that criss-cross the national scene rather than spending a traditional "year in the field" with a single local singing community. I attended over ninety annual conventions in fifteen states between 1997 and 2006 (see Table 1). In most cases I returned to an annual event at least once. In 1999 I established connections with singers all over the country by asking for written responses to open-ended survey questions about their Sacred Harp experience.[4] On the Sacred Harp listserv discussions@fasola.org, a singer once admonished a student who had sent a set of questions to the list: "[Y]ou should not be writing a paper about Sacred Harp if you have just been introduced to the world of Sacred Harp, & certainly not under deadline-pressure. You should attend conventions & related occasions for about 20 years, & then remember, if at that time you still wish to write papers on the subject, that you are still writing on a subject that you know all too little about, except as a guest to it."[5]

This writer's tone is atypical of singers I have encountered in my own Sacred Harp experience. Still, many agree on the importance of the basic concern expressed here. I am not a lifelong singer, and whether or not someone like me might ever be considered a "traditional" singer is a matter of ongoing debate. Yet, as another relatively new singer put it in his 1999

Table 1. **Annual Sacred Harp Singings Attended, 1997–2006**

Midwest Convention (Ill.): 1997–2005
Fox Valley Folk Festival Singing (Ill.): 1997–1999
Illinois State Convention: 1997–99
Southern Wisconsin Singing: 1997–99
Chicago Anniversary Singing: 1998–2003, 2005
Lincoln's Birthday Singing (Ill.): 1998–2000
National Convention (Ala.): 1998–99, 2001
God's Little Vine Singing (Ala.): 1998–99
Michiana Singing (Ind.): 1998–99, 2001, 2003–4
New England Convention (Vt., Conn., Mass.): 1998, 2000, 2002
University of Chicago Anniversary Singing: 1998–2001
Holly Springs Convention (Ga.): 1999–2003
Kalamazoo Singing (Mich.): 1999, 2001, 2003–4
Chattahoochee Convention (Ga.): 1999, 2001–4, 2006
Young People's Singing (Tenn.): 1999
United Convention (Ala., Ga., Tenn.): 1999, 2001, 2004–5
All-California Convention: 2000, 2003, 2006
Joe Beasley Memorial Singing (Ala.): 2000
Keeton Cemetery Singing (Ala.): 2000
Western Massachusetts Convention: 2001–5
Georgia State Convention: 2001–3, 2005
Pioneer Valley Singing (Mass.): 2001, 2003–4
Bethel Singing (Ga.): 2001
West Georgia College Singing: 2002
Hoboken Elementary School Singing [Cooper book] (Ga.): 2002, 2004
Minnesota State Convention: 2003
Shenandoah Valley Singing (Va.): 2004
Salem United Methodist Church Singing (Ala.): 2004–5
DeLong-Roberts Memorial Singing (Ga.): 2004–5
East Texas Convention [Cooper book]: 2004
Golden Gate Singing (Calif.): 2005

Note: My participation at local weekly or monthly singings in Illinois, Massachusetts, California, Michigan, Virginia, and Alberta (Canada) is not listed here.

survey response, "I do seem willy-nilly to be sticking my oar into the future of the tradition in some perhaps small (but readily identifiable) ways." Sacred Harp is particularly accommodating of participant-observation because it welcomes new singers of any age, background, or level of musical training. I would never want to abuse the privilege of that welcome. However, few singers would deny that Sacred Harp has proved remarkably resilient across its long and varied history. That resilience is one subject of this study, and also one ethical justification for it.[6]

"A Long Time Trav'ling": The Sacred Harp Diaspora

My work addresses the phenomenon of the Sacred Harp convention that draws many travelers from far-off places rather than the local singing in an isolated area where most participants are related by blood or marriage. Some aspects of local practice are sure to change as large conventions proliferate, and some new singers worry that their participation (or scholarship like mine) might eventually destroy Southern traditional singing. But my travels have also led me to resist the suggestion that new Sacred Harp conventions have to be viewed as well-meant dilutions, corruptions, or flawed reenactments of Southern traditional practice. Instead, I approach conventions around the country with an eye to different forms of localism and authenticity. I have come to think of this dispersed landscape of singing communities as a "Sacred Harp diaspora."

This model of social relations might seem a curious choice. I have not borrowed it from singers; I have heard a few use the term, but it is not a common way of accounting for the national singing community. "Diaspora" usually implies a community with blood ties to a foreign nation, often a community dispersed by violence (the African diaspora, the Jewish diaspora) or by the social vectors of globalization. The seeds of a people are scattered and sown (Greek: *speirein*) in a foreign land. My use of the term relies not on blood ties but on this metaphorical claim of organic dispersal and reproduction.

Scholars of diaspora have identified fundamental common traits that enable comparative analysis of different dispersed communities. For William Safran, these include geographic dispersal from an idealized homeland; a sense of alienation or resistance to assimilation in the host society; a commitment to supporting the homeland both materially and ideologically; a desire for eventual return there; and "diaspora consciousness," a self-aware solidarity defined by an ongoing relationship with the homeland (Safran 1991: 83–84). James Clifford's suggested emendations to Safran's criteria draw attention to decentered diasporas oriented around "a reinvented 'tradition,' a 'book,' a portable eschatology" rather than a national territory (Clifford 1997: 269). In these terms, the Sacred Harp community has substantial diasporic credentials. The diaspora concept resonates with singers' anxieties about corruption and assimilation, the rural South's long history of representation as a foreign land within America's borders, and the "white ethnic" model that singers have used to account for Sacred Harp's present-day racial homogeneity. "Diaspora consciousness" effectively models the experience and stated commitments of many singers, particularly in terms of their relationship to Southern singing.

Emphasizing the distinctive qualities that the Sacred Harp community shares with ethnic diasporas usefully distinguishes this group from other dispersed communities united around a common leisure interest, such as Grateful Dead fans, role-playing gamers, or the Society for Creative Anachronism. Unlike these groups, the Sacred Harp diaspora is oriented around descent-based kinship discourses and a strong sense of obligation to a historical and geographical homeland in the rural South.[7]

Many singers who did not grow up in the rural South differentiate their own home singing region from the homeland for "the tradition" as they experience it, which they link to a particular Southern convention, region, or singing family (e.g., the Holly Springs Convention; Sand Mountain, in Alabama; the Lee family, in southern Georgia). New conventions spring up on foreign soil—in urban areas or the North—where they are not well-integrated into local social practices, and organizers must actively decide whether and how to maintain connections to the "home" tradition. Like the founders of ethnic cultural organizations, the officers of these new Sacred Harp conventions do things like inviting traditional singers to visit from the homeland, publicizing the tradition as culturally valuable to nonpractitioners, and recruiting new participants to join diaspora singing culture by emphasizing its affiliations with ongoing Southern practice rather than with generic "folk music" or "early music."[8]

I characterize members of these Southern-tradition-affiliated singing communities as diaspora singers. Some of them fit the descent-based ethnic diaspora model very closely—perhaps they grew up in the rural South, were raised elsewhere by Southern parents, or regularly travel south to visit family. "Expatriate" Southern singers have had a transformative impact on singing communities in other parts of the country. For example, Joseph Beasley (1929–95), the first of ten children born into an Alabama singing family, forged close connections with many new singers during decades spent living in New York City. Those New York and New Jersey singers now make regular visits to Beasley family memorial singings in Alabama, and they produced a CD of recordings made by Beasley to help fund a nonprofit organization in his memory (Seiler 1999; see http://www.joebeasleymemorialfoundation.org). Through such relationships, many singers strongly identify with the South even without a descent-based connection to the region. Some hope to "return to the homeland" by retiring to a Southern Sacred Harp area one day.

Diaspora singers experience the tensions and ambivalent feelings typical of ethnic diaspora communities, including persistent nostalgia, divided loyalties, and anxieties about assimilation. Some diaspora singers have fundamentally different political or religious beliefs than most "homeland" singers. They might also have a guilty sense that their nostalgia is unearned, or worry that they are themselves potential diluters of the tradition. A New England singer with years of traveling experience and strong personal ties in the South surprised me with the force of her fears on this point:

> *Singer:* See, I've got a real prejudice for unfettered Southern singings. My goal in life is if I go South to be either the only foreigner there or one of so few foreigners that it doesn't muck up the sound. . . .
>
> *KM:* What do you mean when you talk about "foreigners mucking up the sound"?
>
> *Singer:* Exactly that. It's not a question of sticking out in terms of decibel. Have you ever been in a foreign country and way across the room you heard somebody speaking English? Well, I stand out both ways. . . .
>
> *KM:* So you don't think you should be having any influence on the way people are singing?
>
> *Singer:* I dread the kind of influence that Northern singers and music readers are having and continue to have on Sacred Harp singing.[9]

Later I discussed these issues with another singer from a similar background, someone who worked hard to establish Southern convention norms at singings in her region. Her approach did not draw the "foreigner" line in the same way. I asked why she felt it was important for new singers to travel South. She replied,

> *Singer:* I would say it connects to the source. [*laughs*] You know, it really connects to the source of the music, the founding, the tradition. I don't really like to use the word tradition, because it implies that it's a stuck thing, and it's not. It's an oral tradition, it's changed, it's changed two times since I've been singing.
>
> *KM:* What do you mean exactly by that?
>
> *Singer:* Well, it changed, I think it changed when the Chicago people and then all the other midwestern people started going south. It just changed it, it can't help [changing], you know, it

kind of changed things, it just changed the sound. And then the
Lees. That slowed the songs.[10]
KM: So you think that that influenced the whole national scene,
both of those things?
Singer: Yeah, I think Northerners and then the Lees.
KM: But that's not a bad thing, it's just a—
Singer: No, because—it makes it an oral tradition, it makes it, it
gives it—oral tradition, or oral, yeah—it changes, it's flexible.
So that's why "the tradition," I don't like to say tradition, that
implies to me that it's static, it doesn't change. And you have to
allow flexibility for different areas.[11]

While this singer clearly locates "the source" in the South, she also cites
the interaction of singers from different regions as characteristic of Sacred
Harp singing. These interactions and the ensuing changes in musical
style "make [Sacred Harp] an oral tradition," certainly a positive thing in
post–folk-revival "traditional music" circles. There is a source but there
is also a diaspora of distinctive regional communities, and the reciprocal
flows between them shape the future of the tradition. This singer believes
that lifelong Southern singers consciously permitted such relationships to
develop rather than see the tradition vanish: "That is something that's just
so amazing, them realizing that—and that's part of them letting us into the
tradition, it's like the whole thing about the singing, it's so open, it's open.
So that makes sense. And the singing would have died out if they had not
been open to the Northerners. And that's a big deal, to let your—but they
were smart enough to know that if they didn't do that, and they love the
music that much, and they're not that attached really to the way that it
sounds. They just want people to sing and enjoy it."

The singers who talk about a Southern "source" often cannot claim a
blood-based right to the heritage of this imagined homeland. They jus-
tify their sense of connection and traditional legitimacy in other ways, by
actively working to prove their loyalty and maintain their ties to lifelong
Southern singers. Some also extrapolate Sacred Harp community values
out to the realm of *American* values, creating an access point for new singers to feel invested in the practice; for example, at a Chicago convention
one singer called Sacred Harp "the best democracy in America." But a kind
of civic duty to maintain reciprocal relationships is an integral part of such
claims. "Every singer from far away that you see here is an obligation star-
ing you back in the face," a Minnesota convention organizer told the class

at the end of two days of singing. He urged people to go and learn from Southern singers "before they're gone."

Sacred Harp's diasporic resonances do not stop with individual identifications. Patterns of community practice also resemble those observed in ethnic diasporas.[12] Cultural products and financial resources circulate through long-distance networks, some of which are shaped by airline service routes. Recordings, recipes, newly composed tunes (photocopied and distributed at singings), and photographs flow from region to region, along with less tangible goods like vocal ornaments, gossip, and parodies of song texts. People who only know each other from singings arrange to travel together or call on one another for housing and transportation assistance. Financial capital makes its way around the country to help refurbish a church, fund air travel for college students, create a memorial fund for a prominent singer, maintain a cemetery, or produce commemorative recordings and books. And diaspora begets diaspora: after Chicago Sacred Harp singing was well-established, a cluster of Chicago singers who had moved to the West Coast jump-started the All-California Convention by inviting singers from around the country to attend the wedding of two former Chicago singers in 1989.

This last case raises some important points about the contours and margins of the Sacred Harp diaspora. There were other groups singing Sacred Harp in California before the establishment of the state convention, some active since the 1960s. But they had picked up shape-note singing as one of many American folk music genres and did not necessarily adhere to Southern-traditional norms. Some of them used a tuning fork or pitch pipe to set the pitch for songs, for example—a practice that both eliminated a Southern skill set attached to "keying" songs at a comfortable level by ear and occluded the traces of a religious restriction on musical instruments in sacred contexts. The former Chicago singers deliberately set about changing this state of affairs, running their own annual convention along Southern lines and inviting a prominent Southern singer to give singing schools beforehand.[13]

As this bit of regional history suggests, some Sacred Harp singers do not claim an affiliation to Southern practice. They might prefer to cite New England as the practice's historic homeland, or rely on a utopian vision of a folk music that "belongs to everyone." Other singers might indeed claim a Southern affiliation but not have their claim recognized. Still others seem to use the terms of diasporic discourse while disavowing diaspora consciousness; as one survey respondent wrote, "I'm a Yankee who did not grow up with this music, and 'what I am' (i.e., Yankee) & sense of myself will not change—I have no intention of emigrating or pretense of trying to 'pass' as a Southern traditional singer" (Massachusetts singer, nineteen years of experience). But one of the most important attributes of my imagined diaspora is that so many lifelong Southern singers *do* implicitly include all other Sacred Harp singers within its borders. With encouragement from sympathetic diaspora singers, they assert the right to dictate what practices can be termed traditional and to assume that newer singers will be receptive to such instruction.

These matters were neatly summarized in an exchange I jotted down at a local Chicago singing in the spring of 1999:

> "Fourteen years is long enough for a tradition."
> "Maybe in Palo Alto!"

With offhand remarks like these, along with activist gestures like inviting a lifelong singer to teach a singing school, diaspora singers attribute traditional authority to "homeland" people and practices.

There is no final answer to the question of how long it takes to create a local tradition whose authenticity cannot be challenged. Singers negotiate the issue at every diaspora convention as they claim, project, or reject traditional authority. As lifelong Alabama singer Daphene Causey joked at a Seattle convention in 2004, "I saw on the registration card how it asks if you would like help with leading. Well, if anyone here has been singing for more than seventy-five years, I'd like them to come up and give me some help!"[14] It was a comment unlikely to be heard at a long-established Southern singing—but not because there are no conflicts of authority or hierarchical status relationships there. Rather, in that context, Causey would not be the only person holding the winning hand of age, singing experience, and Southern origin, and the registration card would probably not offer "help with leading." Such offers communicate the diaspora convention's missionary spirit: they are meant to persuade newcomers to stand in the middle of the square, a powerful and sometimes transformative experience that can cement new singers' commitment to future participation.

The imagined diaspora provides a membership category that transcends the binary distinctions of South versus North, insider versus outsider, traditional versus newcomer, rural versus urban, and Christian versus folk enthusiast, without eliminating the very real importance of these divisions in individual conceptions of the national community. These persistent dichotomies are stumbling blocks for those who attempt to speak for the singing community; they make it difficult to account for the many singers whose experience cross-cuts these categories. For example, an assumed sharp distinction between Northern singers (read: baby boomer, liberal folk revivalists) and Southern singers (read: somewhat older, fundamentalist "traditional singers") led Stephen Marini to write that "Southern singers grew up before the modernization of the rural South, and in response to its devastating effects they have shifted their sacred worldview on to Sacred Harp, the last institutional vestige of the life they have experienced together. Northern singers, by contrast, have grown up after modernization disenchanted the worldview of primary religious institutions" (Marini 2003: 87). This analysis may apply quite well to the experience of a particular generation of rural Southern singers and certain groups of Northern revivalists, but it is a poor fit for the national community in general. Many of the most influential Southern singers who travel to teach singing schools around the country today were born in the 1950s and 1960s; they have a perfectly good claim to the "postmodern sensibility" that Marini reserves for Northern singers (2003: 90). Many Northern singers have evangelical Christian convictions and are neither liberal nor "postmodernist."

Southern singers are not exclusively Christian or politically conservative—nor are these categories equivalent. And regardless of the strength of their religious convictions, Christian singers who attend a lot of Sacred Harp conventions are not the most church-oriented members of their home communities: they have chosen to prioritize Sacred Harp above Sunday services. The Georgia State Convention—which meets on the fourth Sunday and the Saturday before in March—happened to fall on Easter weekend in 2005. The convention was held in a rural west Georgia church; the vast majority of singers were practicing Christians. Yet the convention had as many singers on Easter Sunday morning as it had on Saturday. The church's regular congregation, which rotates among several churches, attended Easter services elsewhere.[15]

But Marini's observations were not unfounded—rather, they relied on binary divisions articulated in the singing community. That community is constructed "in and through relations of difference," as Radway writes of American identity politics generally (2002 [1999]: 54). In imagining a Sacred Harp diaspora, I aim to acknowledge the differences singers use to place themselves in the national community but also to avoid reinforcing stereotypical dichotomies. Instead, my approach foregrounds the importance of ascribed and experienced relationships among community members and their agency in crafting these affiliations.[16]

Above all, the diaspora model makes space for two large groups of singers who cut across these dichotomies in complicated ways: singers who *aspire* to "traditional singer" status, and singers who were *born into* a community with regular Sacred Harp singing but didn't get involved themselves until adulthood. Different kinds of authority accrue to a Northern singer who has been organizing Southern-style conventions in Chicago for twenty years as opposed to a singer whose family name and regional accent mark him as a "traditional singer" despite his own lack of involvement with Sacred Harp until reaching middle age. As in an ethnic diaspora community, disparate forms of evidence inform the evaluation of an individual's status. But these two singers are both marked by their deliberate, voluntary involvement with the tradition; they account for their participation differently than do lifelong singers.

"What Poor Despised Company": Pilgrimage, Diversity, and Resistance

The tune "Irwinton" (229) describes a band of travelers on the road, in difficult straits but united in song:

> What poor, despised company
> Of travelers are these,
> That walk in yonder narrow way,
> Along the rugged maze.
> Ah, they are of a royal line,
> All children of a King;
> Heirs of immortal crowns divine,
> And loud for joy they sing.[17]

Sacred Harp singers adopt such texts as metaphors for their own experience, envisioning the singing community as a band of pilgrims. The voluntary aspect of diaspora commitments, combined with the requisite activity of travel to distant conventions and the authenticity credited to particular locations, makes pilgrimage an attractive model. Pilgrimage constitutes particular sites as spiritually efficacious. It also partly accounts for the status that singers gain through their travels, derived both from their perceived commitment and from the humility implicit in making such a journey. Singers who make "pilgrimages" are announcing that they are receptive to instruction from others and vulnerable to transformation. Pilgrimage and diasporic resettlement are similar in their demands for voluntary commitment and their consequent liminoid qualities.[18]

As one might expect, I have only heard the term "pilgrimage" applied to the journeys of diaspora singers to Southern conventions. No one has ever referred to the local singers at such conventions as saints—that would be taking things a bit far, especially given that most lifelong singers are from Protestant sects that oppose the notion of sainthood. But some "pilgrims" do attribute something like holiness to these singers, in that anything they do is considered traditional, socially appropriate, and generous. Lifelong singers are not necessarily comfortable with veneration from diaspora singers, and that veneration has at times engendered resentment—especially when certain singing families receive more attention, more singing school commissions, and more listserv praise than others. But the tradition of reciprocity in the singing community provides a way to diffuse the intensity of status relationships built up by pilgrimage: the tradition-bearers who inspire such journeys also make visits to the home conventions of the "pilgrims," gradually building up a network of travel routes more characteristic of a diaspora than of a "pilgrimage field" (Turner and Turner 1978: 22).

It is important to remember that the diversity of this singing community is atypical of a band of pilgrims or an ethnic diaspora community. Singers' differences extend far beyond the stereotypical division of Northern secular liberal and Southern Christian conservative. Their religious and political affiliations vary so widely that they seem bound to create conflict. Many self-identified liberals in the singing community belong to Christian congregations that actively oppose conservative evangelical theology. Liberal Jews, agnostics, and atheists are also well represented. Most lifelong singers are churchgoing Baptists, but even this category includes a wide range of affiliations—from predestinarian, nonproselytizing, Primitive sects to those with a strong commitment to missionary work and political activism. Some of these groups are ordinarily staunch opponents, the active-duty troops in the "culture wars." As a rule, they do not willingly interact on warm terms. Yet much of the singing community's strength seems to lie in the participants' sense of voluntary association. Sacred Harp singing today bears the marks of its history as part of an American religious culture that has been "disestablished, culturally pluralistic, structurally adaptable, and often empowering" from its earliest days (Warner 2005: 63).

The metaphors of diaspora and pilgrimage that I employ suggest that Sacred Harp singers form a consent-based community, but I might just as easily locate its foundations in dissent.[19] Participants not only express a sense of alienation from mainstream American life but also identify the entire musical tradition as marginalized across its history, starting from the days of the "better music movement." Some singers identify a class-based conflict in the tradition's present-day cultural context, believing the American mainstream places Sacred Harp and many of its lifelong practitioners under the derogatory heading of "poor white trash." For others, Sacred Harp is bound up with the Christian conservative struggle against a perceived secularizing mainstream. When I am presented with these discourses of marginalization, it is hard not to construct a narrative that identifies and celebrates resistance from the margins—a common approach in current ethnography and American music history (Tick 2003: 728).

Elements of such a narrative do exist in the national Sacred Harp community. Lifelong singers subvert common stereotypes of rural Southerners with irony and wit. Conservative Christians and gay liberals come to identify with each other's social positions as they join together to sing, eat, and mourn for the dead. Newcomers move from alienation to a profound sense of homecoming. But such celebratory narratives of resistance tend to essentialize both mainstream society and marginal communities, obscuring complex divisions of power and ideology. A purely egalitarian vision of Sacred Harp singing—in which each participant travels freely to her favorite conventions and has an equal chance to lead a song—ignores not only the status relationships that are plainly evident at any singing but also the different regional cultures, material assets, and ideological affiliations that influence singers' experiences and itineraries.

Public discourse at singings does tend to occlude matters of politics, religion, and economic status in exactly this way, focusing on egalitarianism and common purpose. Politics and religion are potentially divisive, and class is rarely considered a polite topic anywhere. Singers discuss the presence of travelers—or "visitors"—a great deal, but rarely acknowledge that a certain person might not be traveling to a distant convention because he can't afford it, or that another might suddenly have the time to do lots of traveling because she is out of work. While vague references to "different faiths" and "different backgrounds" abound, rhetorical celebrations of Sacred Harp singers' diversity only get down to details on the matter of geographic origin, which serves as a stand-in for all the other forms of diversity at a convention. Singers attribute authority and value to various regions depending on their own experience, of course. Still, the most fundamental regional division is between the South and not-the-South. In a context where singers' origins and affiliations are hard to determine by sight, regional accents and their counterparts in musical performance practice become signposts pointing to other realms of difference.

Audible Otherness: The South Imagined and Performed

The extremes of the Sacred Harp ideological spectrum—the Northern folk-music revivalist and the Southern traditional singer—seem to exemplify perfectly the culture wars that are a recurring feature of American political discourse today. What are a Southern conservative Christian and a liberal queer agnostic intellectual doing singing hymns together, one weekend in a university hall in Chicago and the next in a one-room church in rural Alabama? Surely one of them is being disingenuous, or at least naïve. A few Sacred Harp singers of my acquaintance think this is the case in one way or another. But most see something more meaningful in this strange conjunction.

I have come to believe that the social transformation that takes place at Sacred Harp singings, whereby groups that tend to be mutually intolerant sit down together to sing, eat, trade gossip, and experience transcendent fellowship, is made possible in part by stereotypes of rural white Southern-ers. As a first piece of evidence for this perhaps counterintuitive theory, consider the bemused exclamation of a newcomer who drifted into Chica-go's 2000 Midwest Convention: "They're singing with a Southern accent!"

By now many scholars have observed that certain subsets of the nebulous American category called "white people" are stereotyped and fetishized in much the same way as racially marked groups.[20] They can be differentiated from other "white people" by means of visible signs, but signs consisting primarily in costume and dialect rather than embodied characteristics like skin color. One can recognize whites from the rural South by their over-alls, corncob pipes, banjos, missing teeth, and moonshine, among other accessories; think of *Deliverance,* or the recurring minor character "Cletus the Slack-Jawed Yokel" on "The Simpsons." These caricatures continue to turn up regularly in the American mass media, both domestically and for export. (See Figure 4.) Of course, Southerners use these redneck, trailer-trash, "sleeping with your cousin" caricatures all the time for their own purposes. Stereotyped groups strategically deploy and perform stereotypes in complicated and productive ways. Southerners often displace hillbilly stereotypes onto other Southerners. Just as often, they transform them into a point of pride.[21]

People who grew up in the North typically cannot differentiate and decode the regional, urban/rural, and class connotations of different South-ern accents. They tend to read all Southern accents as vaguely rural—as the Georgia rap artist Big Boi succinctly put it, "You might call us country, but

"I hope we can still be cousins."

Figure 4: Received ideas of the rural South: two found objects from 2004. Left: *New Yorker* cartoon (October 25, 2004; © The New Yorker Collection 2004, Matthew Diffee from cartoonbank.com. All Rights Reserved). Right: San Francisco newspaper advertisement for Treat Street Cocktails (courtesy of Terry Nauslar; designed by him in conjunction with customers).

we's only Southern."[22] But most Southerners are adept at making fine distinctions based on accent or mannerisms; often they are skilled at imitating Southern accents other than their own. At a singing in the summer of 2004 a young west Georgia woman got up to lead and chose the song "Alabama" (196), "because I married a redneck. No, just kidding, but I married an Alabama boy." While finding the right page in the book she told how her little girl "the other day asked me 'Is redneck a bad word?' Well, *that's* an interesting question." Indeed it is, and it demonstrates how interpreting signs of difference can be far from straightforward.

To focus exclusively on visible marks as the site of stereotype is to miss an important variation on the essentializing gaze—what one might call the "essentializing ear."[23] Just as an academic reading a paper aloud can somehow communicate the capital O in "Other" to her listeners, a white man speaking with a Southern accent can create immediately recognizable—but not visible—difference where the category "white man" previously stood.

In a discussion of cultural food prohibitions, I once heard a University of Chicago anthropology professor ask his class, "How many of you are squirrel-eaters?" Greeted with silence, he provided the punch line—that he himself was a squirrel-eater. "We were hillbillies, hicks." The class laughed; the incomprehensible question had been rendered transparent through the invocation of stereotype. The fact that a squirrel-eating hillbilly could grow up into an esteemed anthropology professor with no apparent marks of his background illustrates some of the peculiarities of his status.[24] The otherness of the squirrel-eater seems to be something he can overcome: he can "pass," becoming indistinguishable from regular "white people," as long as he doesn't go squirrel-hunting on the college quadrangles and doesn't mind the occasional laugh at the expense of hillbillies. One of the crucial components of passing is the elimination or at least the modification of one's Southern accent. An Alabama singer who had moved to Nashville told me, "I had to get rid of it because I'm working with people from all over now, and you know with a Southern accent people think you don't have any education, and a lot of the black people think you're a bigot." This capacity for disguise—rarely available to the visibly marked—is as multivalent and ambiguous as stereotype itself: sometimes it seems to be a privilege, sometimes a coercive force that cannot be denied.

In Sacred Harp circles the Southern accent has become a strategic resource, a mark of authenticity and authority. All "traditional singers" have Southern accents, and such singers are revered as keepers of sacred musical and spiritual wisdom. Thus one encounters Northern singers who affect a Southern accent as part of "traditional Sacred Harp style," not only when singing but also when calling out page numbers or intoning "Good" at the close of a hymn. This acquired Southern accent is a source of guilt, embarrassment, or irritation for some singers. One survey respondent, a young man who had been singing in Chicago for a few years, related that "I used to (maybe I still do) sing with a bit of a Southern accent, which is partly from learning to sing from people singing that way, I guess, but I think it has also been a way of distancing myself from what I'm singing, so that it isn't really me that's singing the song (though I still vicariously get a certain relief from doing it)." This singer suggests that the distancing effect of his acquired accent connotes dishonesty, or even a betrayal of singers with "standard Christian beliefs" (to whom he referred elsewhere). Even though he picked up the accent through the usually lauded medium of oral tradition, he views it as a kind of disguise, a symbol of insincere role-playing.

Another singer, a middle-aged woman who grew up in the South but has no discernible Southern accent and began singing as an adult in a Northern city, spoke more harshly about adopted accents. Over the course of a long conversation she referred to the practice as condescending, insulting, and "like a parody." Even as I unintentionally steered her toward something closer to the previous singer's interpretation—role-playing, trying to appear authentic, perhaps even expressing respect by adopting a normally stigmatized marker—she remained focused on the "offensive" nature of the "imitation."

> *Singer:* And then there's the whole thing of people in the North trying to imitate the Southerners by singing in a Southern accent, and that's more offensive to me than someone in the North going down and singing loud in the South.
>
> *KM:* Why does it bother you?
>
> *Singer:* It just seems so fake-y, you know?
>
> *KM:* I don't notice it as much when people are singing the words, but when people call the numbers in a Southern accent that's kind of weird. But then on the other hand you know, Southern accents are so stigmatized in America that it might feel kind of interesting to have somebody come and affect a Southern accent. So many Southerners go to great pains to hide their Southern accents.
>
> *Singer:* Well, the whole Southern accent thing—someone said to me once that people sound dumb with a Southern accent, and that's—because I grew up in _____ where people speak with Southern accents, so for me, I just find that kind of shocking, because my family has Southern accents, mild Southern accents. [Calling out] the numbers—well, here, when people do that here, I am offended. When a singer who's not been to the South, has only heard people visiting here, imitates them, not so much in the singing, in the talking, I am offended. Because I feel like they're making fun of them.
>
> *KM:* You feel like they're making fun? You don't feel like they're kind of posing as authentic or whatever?
>
> *Singer:* No. They've never been to the South. They're just copying people who've come here, who they might consider dumb.
>
> *KM:* So they're sort of role playing.
>
> *Singer:* Yeah, or mocking. So that really irritates me.[25]

This singer consistently resisted my suggestions that Northern singers might consciously or unconsciously adopt a Southern accent to sound more authentic, important, or prestigious—unless a singer had actually been South, or perhaps moved North after a childhood in the South. These affiliations might earn a singer the right to Southernisms, or at least to the benefit of the doubt; as the singer acknowledged, "Well, I mean, I go to the South and I come back with a Southern accent, I come back with a drawl. . . . [M]y family history is not as strong as what I come back from the South with." She emphasized that even for someone as conscious of negative Southern stereotypes as herself, they were internalized at a deep level:

> *Singer:* And I've been driving with someone, in the deep South,
>   in the middle of some of those churches, with a gay person, he
>   goes, "I could be killed for being who I am," feeling like they
>   could. And then I've driven up the wrong driveway sometimes.
>   I don't know where I was going. . . . I drove up the wrong place,
>   and there was this shack, with a couch out front and these dogs,
>   and I was like "Hooah! Get me out of here!" I just immediately
>   assumed that these people are going to come out with guns.
> *KM:* That they're hostile, like in *Deliverance.*
> *Singer:* Yes, yes!

I had similar discussions with many diaspora singers, discussions that were wryly confessional and tinged with liberal guilt. The issue of when a singer has the right to self-represent as Southern has some of the same hallmarks as the media flap over whether the white rap artist Eminem should "drop the N-bomb" in his lyrics. As in that case, affirmative answers rely on evaluations of an outsider's connections to a community that has unquestionable rights to self-representation, self-parody, and co-option of stereotypes.

During my years in Chicago I found that Southern pronunciation conventions for certain words in songs were imparted to new singers with all the fixity of eternal laws: "The correct pronunciation is 'gâping' graves, not 'gāping' graves," one experienced Northern singer told several new University of Chicago singers in April 2000, so they would do credit to their teachers when the Southerners arrived for the Midwest Convention. "And it's 'in-fǐ-nīte day' and the river is 'Jərdan' not Jordan," another added. "How come?" a student asked. "Because that's the way the Southerners do it." The student rejoined, "And people only sing this music in the South?"

This question went unanswered as the next person rose to lead a tune. But the answer would have been, "People sing this music the right way in the South." For most of the singers I have spoken with since 1997, this is a basic article of faith. For some it is so crucial that the lifelong Southern singers who come to big annual events like Chicago's Midwest Convention are not considered sufficiently authentic. They are delightful friends, but as traditional singers they are growing tainted by association. One diaspora singer, shaking her head, described how a particular lifelong singer used to automatically sing the minor scale with a raised sixth (for some, a hallmark of traditional singing) but now had begun to correct herself. Only the most isolated communities of singers can meet the rigorous standards of purity maintained by some diaspora singers, who feel their own presence at a traditional Southern convention is a mark of corruption.

This attitude depends upon an imagined rural South that is fundamentally isolated and conservative. The stories I have recounted—as well as pop culture examples from "The Waltons" to "The Beverly Hillbillies" to *O Brother, Where Art Thou?*—show that these traits can be read both positively and negatively (cf. Newcombe 1979–80). Diaspora singers read them positively, for the most part. But in some ways their anxieties about the dilution and corruption of Southern singing unconsciously reproduce the arguments of racial nativists of the 1930s, who also celebrated the homogeneity of rural Southern communities. Sacred Harp discussions of the gradual erosion of distinctive local or family performance practices can bear a perilous resemblance to an earlier era's fears about racial miscegenation, as well as to current White Power discourses of "the minoritization of whiteness," where "whiteness is seen to be under threat, to have been superseded demographically on a global scale" (Ware and Back 2002: 131). But singers would disavow the rhetorical company they are keeping, of course, because their celebration of the homogeneous character of particular Southern singings is premised on the value of diversity. They don't want to restock America with racially pure Celtic mountaineers; they want to preserve the pockets of cultural difference they glimpse at the margins of their own experienced American mainstream.

In a curious reversal, at diaspora conventions it is lifelong Southern singers—whom new singers often imagine as culturally and politically conservative—who most consistently recognize and embrace the diversity of the national singing community.[26] New singers sometimes cover over their discomfort with the racial homogeneity of most conventions by imagining traditional singers as something like an ethnic group; nondiversity becomes authentic purity, something to be respected by outsiders. But lifelong singers regularly point out the ways in which the broader community actually *is* more diverse than a glance at a room full of white, mostly middle-aged Americans would suggest. Their arguments, too, are sometimes predicated on assumptions about genetic purity. One lifelong singer suggested to me that Chicago singers should not be trying to sound like Alabama singers because they *can't;* the Alabama singers have different vocal cords, owing to their Celtic rather than Scandinavian ancestry. He felt that Chicago singers should be satisfied with sounding like themselves, and he identified this diversity of sound as one of his main pleasures in traveling to distant conventions.

While the Chicago singers are not, in fact, predominantly of Scandinavian ancestry, this singer's observation about imitation and authenticity is still important. It implies that no matter how much diaspora singers worry that assimilation will destroy the distinctive sound quality of particular Southern singing communities, they will not save that sound by imitating it and might do better to acknowledge and develop their own distinctiveness. Rather than precisely reproducing certain regional styles in a nostalgic, orthopraxic obsession with oral tradition, they could strive to reproduce the convention structures and social values that engendered cohesive community styles in the South.[27] This is the stance that a diaspora singer glossed as "they're not that attached really to the way that it *sounds.*"[28] It is not a dismissal of traditional performance practice but a prioritization of other values, the nature of which will unfold over the coming chapters.

In a musical tradition where "traveling" is deeply embedded in practice, rhetoric, and metaphoric imaginary alike, the strange and the familiar become a repertoire upon which each singer draws as she imagines her own identity and her place within the tradition. These individual choices create areas of intensely local sensibility across a diverse and mobile community. Shared travels, mourning, and nostalgia are as important as shared singing as the Sacred Harp community gathers new adherents and recreates its core values. Over time, these practices have enabled singers of sometimes radically opposed religious and political beliefs to develop a pluralist ethos of tolerance and empathy, living against the grain of present-day American political life.

2

Travels to the Center of the Square

Sacred Harp singers like to quote Hugh McGraw, who headed the 1991 revision of *The Sacred Harp,* as saying, "I wouldn't cross the street to listen to Sacred Harp singing, but I'd travel five hundred miles to sing it myself." This statement encapsulates important principles: that Sacred Harp is participatory, that its aesthetic priorities are different from those of most choral performances, and that committed participants travel long distances to sing together. "Five hundred miles" is not hyperbole—many singers travel to conventions that far away several times a year.

In the late nineteenth century, when the longer trips were closer to fifty miles than five hundred, the nature of roads and vehicles made the journeys arduous. Round-trip travel to a major convention could take a week or more, requiring overnight stays with friends and extended family on the journey and at the convention. As lifelong Georgia singer Lonnie Rogers explained, "Now you can go to a singing in north Georgia, south Alabama, and do it in one day. You take when the Chattahoochee [Convention] started; you traveled by ox cart, that would be two days if you lived forty, fifty miles away. That plus the four days of singing then two days back home. Well, you had to live, eat for those eight days. They relied on friendship a lot. . . . When I was a kid, at Hopewell we just had local folks, now we have people from Minnesota at a small singing."[1]

Hugh McGraw reiterated this point with special reference to the work performed by women on such journeys: "I hope you'll say somewhere up in there how much the ladies were appreciated for what all they had to do. They had a hard time. And you can imagine going in an ox wagon for four days and have a drove of kids following, you had to camp every night and you had to cook—a woman, she never did get to go to bed till time was to get up, she had to do all that cooking."[2] Today, too, going to a convention is not only about singing together but about cooking on a massive scale, finding all the spare bedclothes in the house, and undertaking long trips. Reciprocal travels have created, sustained, and gradually extended relationships across the Sacred Harp diaspora.

There are no more ox wagons, but singers still pack up their battered tunebooks, their preferred brand of throat lozenges, publicity flyers for their own local singings, and enormous hampers of food to contribute to "dinner-on-the-grounds." Women still tend to do more of the cooking; many female singers have commented on the bonds that develop from getting up at four in the morning to make final food preparations with mothers, daughters, sisters, or friends who are staying the night. With the car loaded, singers make the rounds to pick up friends and family at the crack of dawn. They may drive for hours or days, gossiping about the singing community and listening to Sacred Harp recordings on the way. Or they fly, to be met by local volunteers at an airport that may still be hours from the singing site by car. When they get to the singing, they sing hymns about traveling—as a "poor wayfaring stranger" or "poor despised company," "a long time trav'ling here below," going to "the better land where troubles are unknown," "over Jordan," "to the new Jerusalem," or simply "on my journey home."[3] The appointed chaplain never fails to give thanks for the presence of travelers and to pray for their safe journey home. The memorial committee discusses the earthly travels of recently deceased singers, the pain the "sick and shut-in" feel at not being able to travel, and the final journey of death.

At Sacred Harp conventions, directed motion in time and space—not only physical space but also musical, emotional, and theological space—shapes the singing day and the singer's memory of a lifetime of singing days. This chapter cycles in and out of the "hollow square," the physical and metaphorical space at the center of Sacred Harp practice, in order to illuminate the relationship between the codified elements of traditional Sacred Harp practice and the lived experience and perpetuation of that practice.[4] The hollow square is a frame for the accumulation of layers of experience; it converts space into place and distraction or detachment into a body vibrating with voices coming from all sides.

If Sacred Harp travels are like pilgrimage, then the hollow square is the sanctuary where the icon stands—voices, faces, tunebooks, and moving hands are symbols, relics, and proofs of commitment. Stepping into the square to lead, the singer is completely surrounded by these symbols, in space and in imagined historical time. She is stepping into the place of every other leader who has ever stood in the square.[5] Leading, or just standing in the square with a leader, can overwhelm the senses. An enveloping wave of sound bounces off the walls and ceiling to fill in the gaps and aisles in the hollow square. The excitement and fatigue of travel, the nervous anticipation of waiting to be called to lead, and the move from sitting tightly packed with one's friends in the tenor section to standing alone in a space where everyone is watching and the voice parts can be heard equally—all these conditions heighten the leader's experience and promote identification with other leaders. Both new and lifelong singers are often breathless and shaky when they return to their seats.[6] (See Figures 5 and 6.)

And if these pilgrimages and miraculous transformative experiences gradually engender diaspora consciousness, then the hollow square is that diaspora's portable homeland, a place that gathers family together. As singer Eric Morgan said in a Western Massachusetts memorial lesson, "We really are a family. Not just the idea of a family, but a family in practice."[7] In the rhetoric of memorial lessons, prayers, and reports to the fasola.org listservs, home in the hollow square is only one small step removed from home in heaven, where the singing never lets up, voices never get tired, and singers who have crossed over Jordan are waiting for their family and friends to come "sing around the throne."[8] Even for singers who would not usually express belief in an afterlife, the compelling repetitions that characterize the hollow square can engender such belief—a "living hope," in the language of the hymn texts—if only for a few moments.[9] Any given class of singers can evoke past assemblages and inspire hope for a kind of future-perfect class: a crowd or cloud of witnesses, a parallel class of past and future singers that seems to hover above the square.[10]

In order to show how the hollow square can compose such crowds, I must leave its seductive confines and step back into the realm of the "tradition" debate. The kind of hollow square experience I have described here is a foundational element of a "traditional" singing or convention, but it is made possible by other practices and experiences: repeatedly traveled routes, framing devices, deliberate codification, affiliations, and claims of authority. Before I take another turn in the square, I will address the nature of a "traditional convention," the structure of the singing day at such an event, and singers' struggles to create a working definition of what constitutes a "traditional singer."

Figure 5: The empty square awaits singers. All-California Convention, San Carlos, January 14, 2006. (Photograph by the author.)

Figure 6: The All-California hollow square in full swing. (Photograph by the author.)

Convention and Tradition

To most contemporary Sacred Harp singers the rapid leader-by-leader, song-by-song progression that characterizes both conventions and local singings serves as the primary source for acquiring competence in the tradition. Like ethnographers, newcomers are expected to learn through participant-observation: all singings are considered "entry-level," and formal instruction as to the nature of shape-note notation and convention procedure is often limited to printed flyers made available at the registration table. The situation was different in the late nineteenth and early twentieth centuries. Children learned to read music and lead in singing school. The membership of a convention comprised a body of competent delegates from different singing communities, and only the most skilled were invited to lead—often "giving a lesson" for a half-hour or more. Some Southern conventions drew thousands of singers and listeners, most of whom would have to crowd around outside the church or courthouse where the singing took place.

Today there are many fewer singing schools, the largest conventions only draw about three hundred singers, and there is no need for delegates. Anyone who walks in is welcome to sign up to lead a song, and the convention sessions themselves serve as a singing school for a wide range of newcomers. A "convention" is an annual multi-day singing event, as opposed to a one-day "annual singing" or a weekly or monthly local singing (sometimes called a "practice singing").[11] Most annual conventions and singings are listed in the directory portion of the annual *Minutes of Sacred Harp Singings*, a paperback volume compiled, edited, and typeset by singers. A convention's secretary is expected to submit minutes that report who led which tunes, the names of committee members, and the names on memorial lists. A fee of $40 for each day of minutes supports the publication of the minutebook; in return, the editors will ship back ten copies of the next annual volume for distribution among local singers. Singers use the minutebook to choose which conventions to attend, confirm dates and locations for a particular year, and catch up on the proceedings when they have missed a favorite convention.

There is no system of accreditation for Sacred Harp conventions. Anyone may start one anywhere without consulting any kind of governing body, and if a new convention sends minutes to the minutebook they will be printed. However, the 1991 revision of *The Sacred Harp* includes codified guidelines for running a convention as part of the "Rudiments of Music" (a pedagogical section present in many shape-note tunebooks). In thirteen pages, the Rudiments address the basic principles of music notation—including the staff, rhythmic values, time signatures, key signatures, and dynamics—along with information specific to Sacred Harp singing. John Garst, a singer and scholar, revised the 1991 Rudiments and added a final chapter entitled "Organization and Conduct of Singings and Conventions." It concisely outlines the structure of proceedings at a typical "Southern traditional" Sacred Harp singing.

1. An annual singing lasts one day and a convention two days or more. In another sense, a convention is an organization that sponsors singings. A special singing occurs only once, has a frequency other than annual, or occurs irregularly. Most all-day singings last from 9 or 10 a.m. to 3 or 4 p.m. Conventions, churches, or other groups sponsor singing schools, where one can learn to read music and sing from the Sacred Harp.
2. Although the proceedings at singings tend to be informal, there is a formal structure of officers and committees, and the minutes of singings are usually published.

3. The singers sit in rows of pews or chairs that face to the center of a hollow square. To the immediate left and right of the tenors are the basses and trebles, respectively. The altos face the tenors.

4. A session begins with a call to order by the chairman, who leads a selection, calls upon the chaplain (or another) for an opening prayer, makes welcoming remarks, and presides over the election of new officers. Typically, officers include chairman, vice chairman, secretary, treasurer, and chaplain. Arranging and memorial committees, and sometimes others such as finance, hospitality, and resolutions committees, are appointed by the chairman.

5. The chairman calls the group to order after each recess and generally presides. . . . The secretary keeps the minutes, which include a brief description of the proceedings, a list of leaders and the page numbers of the pieces led, and reports of committees. The treasurer collects donations, the main purpose of which, usually, is to cover the expense of having the minutes printed. . . . The chaplain may be called on to lead in prayer at opening, dinner, and closing. The arranging committee identifies leaders and calls on them to lead, often giving notice to the next leader as well. The memorial committee identifies those who have died since the last meeting (and sometimes others) and formulates a memorial lesson and report. . . .

6. When called, the leader steps into the hollow square, faces the tenor section, and announces the page number of his or her selection. . . . After everyone has a chance to find the page, the leader or other designated person sounds the pitches of the tonic and others, possibly the dyad or triad built on the tonic or the opening pitches of all the parts. . . . The notes (syllables Fa, Sol, La, and Mi) are sung first, then the words of one or more verses. . . . After finishing ("teaching a lesson"), the leader retires to his or her regular seat, making way for a new leader.

7. A recess of five minutes or more is taken every hour or so. . . .

8. At the memorial lesson, usually just before lunch, the chairman of the memorial committee may make remarks, read the names of the deceased, and lead songs in their memory. These duties may be shared with others.

9. Where circumstances permit, dinner on the grounds is from 12 noon to 1 p.m. There is a blessing by the chaplain or another, after which all help themselves from a long table. Usually, the food is

provided by local people, often by members of the host church or community.

10. HOLY MANNA (59) and PARTING HAND (62) are often, but by no means always, used as opening and closing songs. (Garst 1991: 25)

While these guidelines have a prescriptive aim as far as new conventions are concerned, Garst presented them in a descriptive style. He left room for the diversity of local Southern practice while taking a more authoritative stance with respect to new conventions. When such a convention adopts the protocol described in the Rudiments, its officers are aligning themselves with Southern practice and sometimes implicitly distancing themselves from folk-revival practice (Herman 1997: 47). Basic elements of performance practice—vocal timbre, rhythmic style, treatment of repeats and verses, seating arrangement, means of finding a starting pitch, distribution of singers among the parts, and leading method—have all become sites of contestation in areas where diaspora singers have begun to influence established folk-revival shape-note groups.

Regardless of their own feelings about "traditional" singing, most singers use the term to denote Sacred Harp singings, singers, and customs that are considered to belong to an unbroken line of Southern practice. Within this broad framework, however, what constitutes "the tradition" is debatable. Such discussions rarely take place at conventions, even during breaks or dinner-on-the-grounds. Under these circumstances most singers consciously avoid behavior that might jeopardize the atmosphere of fellowship. They take up sensitive topics in more private settings, on long car trips or at the homes of hosts. Long-distance travel creates cooling-off periods and appropriate venues for hashing out points of controversy and criticism. Now that so many singers have cell phones, post-mortem conversations begin to take place between cars as soon as they are pulling away from a convention.

The two Internet lists devoted to shape-note singing—singings@fasola .org and its more recently introduced cousin, discussions@fasola.org— have shaped the nature of diaspora discourse by providing a relatively public forum for the kind of discussion that is tacitly discouraged at singings. Listservs engender some of the intimacy of private conversation without the social restraints of face-to-face interaction. These days, though, the volunteer moderators will occasionally deny passage to a message that could cause heated conflict. The administrators of a previous incarnation of the list shut it down after it descended into what one singer called "virulent hostility"; participants on the new lists are expected to be on their best behavior.

On both lists writers usually sign their messages with their real names and hometowns. Unlike many members of online communities, Sacred Harp singers tend to post messages with the tacit assumption that listserv participants could or should eventually meet in person, at a singing.

Discussions@fasola.org split from singings@fasola.org in 1999. In introducing the new list, to be moderated by John Bealle, singings@fasola.org moderator Keith Willard of Minnesota wrote,

> When the singings list became moderated, one of my major goals was to create a place not only free from the rancor that was occasionally previously present but also one that focused on the activity of singing. Thus the focus on singers, singing announcements, singing experiences, and discussions of such. During the tenure of the old fasola list I became convinced that certain kinds of topics, particularly those associated with a "musicology/ ethnomusicology" flavor could drown out other posters and postings. In contrast, I wanted a list which is hospitable to those principally interested in traditional singings and singers.

The advent of the new list acknowledged the interests of the more "musicological" contingent of singers but offered others the chance to opt out of witnessing the conflicts engendered by active debate over Sacred Harp history and tradition.

In February of 1999, prior to the inception of the discussions list, Martha Henderson of Minnesota initiated a series of postings on the nature of "the tradition." She asked, "How far from the center of the tradition, as it has been practiced in the south for the last 150 years, can a local group get, before the singing ceases to be Sacred Harp and becomes something else?"[12] There were many replies to Henderson's posting, many of which defended the importance of "tradition." Singer and hymnody scholar Warren Steel answered by citing Hugh McGraw:

> In his career of teaching Sacred Harp to singers of widely varied backgrounds, Hugh McGraw has identified four essential and defining practices that he will normally insist on, in addition to the Sacred Harp songbook:
>
> 1. a hollow square arrangement of voice-parts
> 2. the rotation of leaders
> 3. the use of "fasola" syllables
> 4. opening and closing prayers.[13]

Prayer stands out here as the only item not connected with musical performance. Even when practicing Christians are a minority in a singing community, diaspora convention organizers include opening and closing prayers at their all-day singings. Agnostic or atheist singers characterize their tolerance of prayer as a matter of courtesy and respect for tradition—tacitly acknowledging that this tradition is religious, not simply folksong, and that it is not wholly theirs.

When I asked singers to describe the characteristics of traditional Sacred Harp practice, they overwhelmingly pointed to the South, and within the South to people born into "singing families." But when I asked whether they considered *themselves* to be traditional singers, they approached "tradition" differently. Of the 109 singers who responded to my survey questions in 1999, only 16 percent identified themselves as lifelong Sacred Harp singers, but 39 percent responded positively to the question "Do you consider yourself a traditional singer?" Another 25 percent responded with some variation on "I try to be." 32 percent responded negatively. Some of them applied strict standards related to regional origin, family connection, musical training, or religious affiliation:

> No. I am an amateur (see the dictionary!) but I did not grow up in the tradition, so I do not consider myself a traditional singer. (New York singer, twenty-four years of experience)

> Nope. Pretty nontraditional. Our regular singings are secular. Our big summer and winter sings are organized by one of our Jewish members. (Canadian singer, three years of experience)

> Not really, I'm too "north," I'll go with tradition when it's important to other people, but deviations don't upset me. (New Jersey singer, eight years of experience)

> Would be presumptuous because I did not begin singing from the time I was two years old. . . . Could consider myself traditional if I consider the people that I learn most from, but that is an odd way of defining. Tradition is a very loose and dangerous concept. (Illinois singer, seven years of experience)

But apart from the lifelong singers, most respondents who claimed "traditional" status or aspirations to that status used exactly the definition that this last singer deemed "odd." They cited personal experience with Southern singers or regular trips to Southern singings. Some drew a straightforward connection between Southern practice and traditional status; as one Minnesota singer wrote, "We follow southern traditions (rotation of leaders, standing in the middle, dinner-on-the-grounds, not much time spent on election of officers . . .) so we are traditional singers." Among Northern singers, claiming or denying affiliation with the South emerged as a common means of addressing the question of traditionality.

For Southern singers, however, the question was more complex. Many Northern singers tacitly treat the South as a place where old customs hold sway and all Sacred Harp singers/singings are traditional.[14] But in fact large numbers of Southern singers first encounter Sacred Harp as adults. Singers fitting this description, who accounted for roughly a quarter of my survey respondents, typically did not claim traditional status on the basis of their Southernness. Instead they crafted definitions of "traditional" that might include themselves without usurping the authority of lifelong singers:

> Yes—assuming "traditional" means an appreciation and respect for the tradition of singing the shapes, maintaining the format with inclusion of prayer and respect for the text/poetry and that some of these texts bear a direct relation to the singers' spiritual life and religious belief system. (Georgia singer, seven years of experience)

> I'm probably about 50 percent traditional. All of my early experience with SH singing was with traditional Southern singers. However, I grew up singing regular church music in choirs and congregations. (Tennessee singer, thirty years of experience)

> Yes, and no. If I am stylistically it must just be by some form of osmosis, because I have no idea what I am doing as a "vocal stylist." I just sing and don't think much about what it sounds like, and I don't think it sounds very good!! But I believe what really counts is NOT what it sounds like. It is to me a form of worship, praise and entreaty to God. I suppose spiritual values make me a "traditional singer." (Texas singer, one year of experience)

> Yes. In every way I can, I try to imitate the traditional Southern singers, i.e., Charlene Wallace, Hugh McGraw, Richard DeLong, etc. The "rituals" of running a convention, the Memorial Lesson, the accent and intonation of the music—I try to "seek the old paths & walk therein."(Georgia singer, six years of experience)

The Scriptural passage (Jeremiah 6:16) cited by the last singer is included in the dedication of the 1991 revision of *The Sacred Harp;* it turns up as often as Hugh McGraw's "five hundred miles" in Sacred Harp discourse.

These reflections on the nature of tradition suggest that there is a process through which a "visitor" might come to self-identify as traditional. That process is driven by newcomers' engagement with the diverse concepts of tradition that they encounter in the singing community.

Encounters in the Hollow Square

For many newcomers, Sacred Harp begins with sound. Some first heard it on recordings or public radio features; others walked by a singing in a church basement or at a folk festival and wandered into the room. When singers describe their first impression of Sacred Harp, they use words like "weird," "compelling," "authentic," and "primitive." The high volume, bright timbre and driving rhythm typical of the singing style produce a visceral response in many listeners. As a diaspora singer told me, "The very first time that I ever went South I got a headache that beat in time to the pulse of the music. I mean, I'm talking about a full-fledged temples to the back of my skull headache, you know, like those idiot teenagers who have their bass speakers in the back, and the trunk is vibrating? If I ever had to define pulse—"[15]

Visitors to conventions are welcome to sit and listen; there is no formally recognized audience, but there are usually some sparsely populated rows of chairs at the back of the tenor section. In the South, family members of devoted singers often attend a family memorial singing every year, bringing food for dinner-on-the-grounds and sitting in the back rows all day to listen and watch. But most newcomers feel they are expected to sing, and they will either leave the room and never return or (at the urging of experienced singers) pick up a loaner tunebook and try to at least follow along with the words. Soon they take up the new challenge of reading the fasola syllables. Once they can "sing the notes," they gradually develop a personal repertoire of favorite songs to lead, practice at home, or to note as favorites when others call them.

Any participant may lead a tune at a convention, as long as he makes his wish known to the "arranging committee" (which determines the order of leaders). For the many new participants who have never before read music or performed in public, standing up to lead in the midst of hundreds of singers is a momentous and nerve-wracking experience that requires practice in advance. Some singers wait years to lead, but most do eventually make their way into the center of the square.

Ideally, leaders know both the solfege syllables and the words of their chosen song by heart, but the vast majority still hold their books open to the appropriate page and look down from time to time. Leaders face the tenor section, which consists of men and women singing in parallel octaves. Basses (men) are to the leader's right, trebles (men and women in octaves) to the left, and altos (women) directly behind. A leader is expected to sing the tenor part, since it is the melody line. This requirement can limit the leading repertoire of those who ordinarily sing other parts, not only because learning another line is confusing but also because tenor parts often have a range of an octave and a half.

Leading can be elaborate and dance-like: leaders spin around to cue the staggered entrances in the imitative "fuging" tunes, and some use hand gestures to indicate high notes, held notes, and distinctive figures in particular parts. To lead is to put one's body on display; in a kind of inverted panopticon, one is being stared at from all sides, including from behind.[16] The extraordinary physical grace and musicality of many leaders are transformative; the elderly, overweight, or just ordinary-looking suddenly display physical mastery, self-possession, and charisma.

The most basic leading requirement is "beating time" to show the tempo and meter. A simple down-up arm motion indicates duple meters. For triple meters the downward motion is divided into two parts, making a beat pattern different from the triangular version employed by conductors. Young children are encouraged to learn how to beat time as soon as they begin to come into the square. (See Figure 7.) Newcomers with little experience reading music often memorize or write down which beat pattern goes with which song rather than consulting the time signature. In their nervousness, amid the overwhelming sound at the center of the square, inexperienced leaders mix up their beat patterns or otherwise become out-of-step with the downbeat. Fears about such mistakes prevent many singers from adding to their repertoire, and some singers lead only one or two tunes over decades of Sacred Harp singing.

Many singers beat time in their seats. Beating time helps singers maintain a steady, emphatic rhythm and keep track of rests when entrances are staggered among the voice parts. A disoriented leader can find the downbeat or correct his beat pattern by mirroring the singers' hands. This constant motion can also provide a physical outlet for emotion; when the class's energy is high, a look around the room shows some singers making expansive gestures, others clenching fists, many with eyes and books closed and both hands in the air.

Beating time sharpens the distinction between the time of singing and the time between songs. The repetitive, essentially circular hand motion reinforces the structure of tunes with repeated choruses or imitative "fuging" sections. Leaders usually select specific verses to sing, so as not to take up too much time in the square, and it is conventional to observe written repeats only when singing "the notes" and the last selected verse. Repeating a fuging chorus on the solfege syllables provides an additional practice run

Figure 7: Laura Webb Frey and her daughter Jenna beat time while leading at the 2005 Georgia State Convention, held at Emmaus Primitive Baptist Church in Carrollton, Georgia. Jenna is a sixth-generation Georgia Sacred Harp singer. (Photograph by the author.)

for difficult entrances and prepares the ground for the repeat on the final verse, when most singers can look away from their books and engage with one another. During these repeats many leaders walk or pivot around in a circle in the center of the square, making eye contact with members of each section as they cue successive entrances in fuging tunes. If the class is deeply engaged the leader might cue a third or fourth repeat. Ordinary experience of time is displaced by these indefinite circular repeats; as Qureshi writes, "[R]epetition serves to enrich and expand the meaning of a 'meaningful moment' by creating for it an exclusive perceptual space, an autonomous existence" (Qureshi 1994: 520). Singers characterize these moments as some of the most affecting of the singing day.

"Singing the notes," beating time, and observing repeat conventions are the technical skills that form the basis of individual competence and provide an intellectual point of entry for newcomers. The all-day singing and the multi-day "convention" are built from the basic unit of a leader and his or her choice of tune. Roughly seventy to one hundred leaders may be called to the center of the square in a single day of singing, and no one (with the exception of very small children or very inexperienced leaders) may call a tune that has already been led that day. Repetition is an internal feature of every song—via "singing the notes," multiple verses, and repeated choruses—but the sequence of songs is unique and nonrepetitive within the singing day. Sometimes a singer almost always leads the same song; others will not knowingly lead it if called before him, since a given song can only be led once a day. When a singer is missing, owing to death, illness, or some other circumstance, a friend or relative might lead that person's song and remark: "This was Virgil's song" or "Karen asked me to lead this for her since she can't be here today."

Recently, some leaders have enlisted a friend to hold up a cell phone so the absent singer can listen from his nursing home or sickbed. But even before cell phones made regular appearances in the hollow square, leaders often asserted that missing singers could hear the singing. Singers also allude to hearing the specific voice of a dead or absent singer in the mass of voices of those present. After hearing these kinds of stories I discovered I could create the experience of hearing a missing voice for myself. If I listened intently to the rich layering of overtones emerging from hundreds of distinctive individual timbres, my ear could construct a beloved absent voice from the available sonic materials. Voices pile up, drift, return to the surface, and become incorporated into the musical-cultural terrain. Layered memories of renditions of a song accumulate; a song can be a kind of hypertext referent that links conventions, informal singing occasions, and recordings in a singer's personal history. Swinging hands, tapping feet, voices growing hoarse in time with one another, the tight throat that feels like grief embodied when silence falls for the memorial lesson—the felt body, the heard voice, and musical and calendrical rhythms all govern each singer's experience of time at a Sacred Harp convention.

Realizing the Rudiments: A Sacred Harp Convention Day

The repetitive flow of leaders moving in, around, and out of the square is framed and broken up by a few distinctive events that lend structure to the singing day. Realizing this standard convention procedure requires careful preparation from organizers; the simple guidelines in the Rudiments balloon out into a detailed timetable, often meticulously scripted in advance. The events discussed here distinguish a convention or all-day singing from a weekly or monthly local singing, where small groups of singers meet in living rooms or church basements for two or three hours at a time on a regular schedule. The various committees that look after logistics at a Sacred Harp convention are unnecessary when only ten or twenty singers are present. These practical matters aside, elements like prayer, the memorial lesson, and the ritual of farewell called the "parting hand" serve to formalize and intensify the effects of an annual singing event.

OPENING

The singing day usually starts between 9 and 10:30 A.M., depending on how many participants are expected to be driving long distances or crossing time zones. Many singers try to arrive early to get good seats in the square, socialize, or set up recording equipment. The chairman of the previous year's convention moves to the center of the square and calls out the page number for an opening song, often the same from year to year. The chairman or another person competent at "keying" gives the starting pitch, which cues the singers to stop socializing and take their seats in the hollow square. The singers rise to their feet on the final verse of the opening song and remain standing for the opening prayer, delivered by a previously appointed chaplain.

PRAYER

Prayers vary in length, content, and style depending on region and the individual chaplain. They include the opening prayer, a grace before the shared midday meal, a prayer to close the memorial lesson (usually), and a closing prayer immediately following the "parting hand."

In general, prayers at diaspora conventions are less explicitly Christian than those at long-established Southern conventions; they are less likely to end with "in Christ's name," for example. These stylistic choices sometimes reflect the influence of the liberal churches and divinity schools with which many diaspora singers are associated (especially in urban areas).[17] But prayers do not necessarily correlate with the beliefs of a majority of the class or of local organizers. A convention's local singers often have diverse religious affiliations, and a visiting singer may be asked to serve as a convention's chaplain as a gesture of respect irrespective of her particular beliefs. The more ecumenical nature of prayers at diaspora conventions may derive from the chaplain's sensitivity to greater religious diversity in the class rather than from weak or nonsectarian Christian convictions on her own part.

Two fairly typical opening prayers by experienced chaplains follow, the first by Chicago singer Jim Swanson and the second by Georgia singer Louis Hughes Sr.:

> Jim Swanson: Let us pray. Lord, we thank you for this opportunity to join from near and far and unite in song and friendship and praise. Bless us who are here, be with those who may still be on the way here. Grant them a safe journey that they may soon add their voices to ours. Help dispel the gloom of

this gray day, transform it into the experience of joy that this music is about to give us. Be with those who wish they were here but are unable. We think of them now and we thank you for each and every one of them as well. We thank you for this place, for this circle of friends, for this wonderful music. Infuse us with your love and your joy. Amen. (Chicago Anniversary Singing, 2001)[18]

Louis Hughes Sr.: Gracious Lord, we want to thank you for this day, for the privilege of being able to come together once again to sing with our friends and loved ones. We ask a special blessing on each one that has come this way. Bless and be with those who wish they could be here but could not. Go with us through the further part of this service; lead, guide and direct us. Forgive us of our sins, for Christ's sake, Amen. (Holly Springs Convention, Georgia, 2001)[19]

After the opening prayer, the singers take their seats again and the chairman makes welcoming remarks and logistical announcements. A few more leaders—often the previous year's officers—may be called by the arranging committee before the elections.

ELECTIONS

Within the first hour of singing, the arranging committee calls the chairman again and he or she presides over the election of new officers, taking nominations and motions from the floor in formal parliamentary style. The officers have typically been selected in advance; the new chairman is usually the previous year's vice-chair and, as the "rising chair," has already been responsible for the singing's advance organization. Thus elections are almost never contested; most are completed with dispatch and some humor, as singers employ parliamentary language with ironic, over-the-top verve. The new chairman and vice-chair appoint the committees, including the arranging committee, the memorial committee (which collects the names of the sick and the dead and prepares the memorial lesson), the finance committee (which takes up a collection to cover any expenses), and the resolutions committee (which presents resolutions for approval by the class at the close of the singing). A chaplain is appointed to say grace before lunch, deliver the closing prayer at the end of the day, and sometimes to close the memorial lesson. A secretary is charged with copying down the names of the officers, the sequence of leaders, and their chosen songs, which are subsequently submitted to the annual minutebook. A summary of the memorial lesson and resolutions may also be included in the minutes.

LEADERS

The arranging committee determines the order of leaders (usually with the aid of registration forms) and calls out their names. At some small singings there is time for each leader to choose two songs when she is called, providing an opportunity for her to demonstrate the range of her taste and skill. At others, the arranging committee struggles to call every singer who wants to lead over the course of a two-day convention. As Hugh McGraw noted in an interview,

> In the olden time they didn't have as many leaders. They'd lead for forty, forty-five minutes, and they would talk about everything under the sun. And now, we're just in a hurry because we want to lead everybody that's there, men and women. Back then, they didn't. They just led the men, and they'd talk about the crops and they'd talk about the weather, and they'd talk about various things. . . . It was because more people got to coming that were qualified to lead, and they thought that if they would recognize people and let 'em lead, see, when you recognize a leader, a leader demonstrates their ability at what they can do. They wanted to recognize as many people as they possibly could.[20]

With today's system of equal-opportunity leading, the arranging committee keeps things moving by giving notice to a leader one song in advance, so that he has time to choose a song: "Kiri Miller of Somerville, Massachusetts, will be followed by Richard DeLong."

The order in which leaders should be called is not prescribed in the Rudiments, and it may be random if the arranging committee is inexperienced and lacks advisors. Random arranging can seriously detract from the quality of a large convention, in terms of both musical experience and goodwill among singers, so convention officers usually appoint the committee with care. Arranging is widely regarded as the most demanding committee job. It requires experience and tact, and the committee usually has to sit at the fringes of the hollow square and cannot concentrate on singing.

At its most effective, arranging is governed by complex status assessments and knowledge of leaders' preferences. Since some singers, but not all, may get to lead more than once, politeness dictates calling those who have traveled the farthest to lead the most times. The committee must also take into account the energy level of the class: when voices are tired they try to call competent, sensitive, and engaging leaders, avoiding those who tend to request five verses of a slow tune, prefer difficult, showy anthems, or have too small a repertoire to choose something that will be easy on the class. The committee's desire to match high-status leaders with an energetic class can yield long low-energy periods; for example, arrangers tend to reserve the best leaders (or those who have traveled furthest) for the hour after lunch, when singers are warmed up, refreshed, and energized by a dizzying variety of sugary desserts. Maintaining variation in leading style and repertoire helps keep the class attentive; their voices, bodies, and minds are exhausted by the end of the day.

The arranging committee calls a break of five to ten minutes roughly every hour so singers can get a drink, converse, or change seats. The chair or another appointed person "calls back the class" by beginning a song; experienced singers join in from memory as they hurry back to their seats and tunebooks.

MEMORIAL LESSON

The arranging committee usually calls on the memorial committee before lunch on the last day of a convention, or sometimes after lunch at a one-day singing (to allow more time to collect names of the dead and the sick). The memorial committee consists of at least two people, one to speak and lead a song for those who have died in the past year and the other to speak and lead for the "sick and shut-in." Others may be asked to speak about one or two individuals who have died, e.g., an influential singing-school teacher, a dedicated traveler, or a member of a major Southern singing family. There is no prescribed style or content for the memorial lesson, aside from reading the lists of the dead and the sick. Some speakers may quote from Scripture, while others make no mention of religion at all. The room is silent and still, in marked contradistinction to the constant singing, talking, and physical movement of the rest of the day; the perpetual motion of hands beating time is suspended.

Amid the cyclic repetitions of annual conventions, movement in and out of the square, and imitative choruses, memorial narratives and the reading of the names of the dead interpose a moment of finality. At the same time, these narratives draw attention to the inadequacy of speech as compared to singing; they reinforce singers' perception of music as a "particularly affective and direct way of knowing" (Turino 1999: 221). The songs led after each section of the memorial lesson carry a greater burden of emotional intensity after these moments of speech, and the committee often asks the class to omit "singing the notes" in order to focus on the words. This musical choice "reconfigures the emotional texture" of the convention (Wolf 2001: 414), enforcing an immediacy of experience that suggests a song of grief bears no rehearsing.

The altered sense of time and place that a singing constructs, character-ized by an inward focus on the center of the square, becomes more con-centrated and formalized during the memorial lesson: time set apart stands within time set apart. But while the hollow square turns singers' backs on the outside world, the memorial lesson looks beyond the square's borders to address death, illness, grief, and remembrance. This fundamentally reflexive event is emotionally accessible to newer singers because it may be interpreted as addressing not only particular human deaths but also the progress of modernity, with all the fragmentation and loss that progress is considered to entail. Memorial narratives are invitations to participate in nostalgia, anticipations of loss that frame the discourse of the vanishing tradition in specific human terms.

Public performances of grief intensify the emotional state of the per-former by creating a feedback loop. The verbal and nonverbal markers of emotion displayed in memorial lessons—including tears and cracking voices—function as "emotives," William Reddy's term for expressions that change the feeling-states of those who utter them (Reddy 1997: 327).[21] Memorial lessons also encourage listeners to try on an emotion for size, attempting a rehearsal of the feeling in question (Reddy 2001: 107). New singers experiment with the idea that "There'll come a time when you'll know" what Sacred Harp means, as Richard DeLong once promised in a memorial speech. These speeches by the grief-stricken place newcomers in an intimate circle: they are witnessing risky social behavior, and that witnessing may inspire empathy even in those who don't know any of the names on the memorial lists. When memorial speakers invite the class to prepare themselves for the day when their own loved ones are missing from the square, they encourage *preemptive* nostalgia as a prelude to grief. To earn the right to this nostalgia, newcomers must invest themselves in the task of perpetuating the singing tradition.

A few more leaders may be called after the memorial lesson to make time for food to be set out for dinner—otherwise, some singers have to miss the memorial. The trade-off is that leaders called after the memorial lesson may face a decimated alto section, since women still do most of the food preparation and layout.

DINNER-ON-THE-GROUNDS

The chairman calls a one-hour break for dinner. Many country churches in the South have long outdoor tables made of reinforced concrete, some-times sheltered by a roof, where the food is laid out buffet-style. The singers pour out of the singing room and crowd around the tables, admiring the offerings and waiting for the chaplain to say grace before filling their plates; one diaspora singer recounted, "The only time I've been chastised for my behavior at any sing was [for] eagerly grabbing at a biscuit pre-prayer." Outdoors, singers eat on their feet or sit on the ground in small groups. Indoors, they eat at tables or (rarely) sit back down in the singing space.

The spread of food is vast and varied, a visible and edible representation of the diversity of the participants. Southern staples like barbecue, fried chicken, biscuits, and red velvet cake appear alongside elaborate pasta sal-ads, sushi, pilafs, and midwestern "hot dish." Individual singers or fami-lies have trademark dishes, some of which are promised in advance as part of advertising for a singing (on flyers or the fasola.org lists). Sacred Harp newsletters feature photographs and lavish descriptions of the laden tables, and organizers exhort local singers to be sure the food at their home con-vention will be good enough and plentiful enough to draw visitors back the following year.

Such dinners are a fabled component of rural Southern hospitality. As lifelong Georgia singer Lonnie Rogers explained in an interview,

> No sir, never gone home hungry. While I was in the hospital one of my roommates asked me—ward-mate, we were in a ward—he said, "I want you to tell me, Lonnie, why it's so much different up here in Atlanta and in Heard County where you live." He said, "I got a aunt here in Atlanta and got a aunt down in Heard County." He says, "I go over there to visit my aunt in Atlanta," he was a federal guard out at the federal prison was what his job was, he says, "there'll be a little bit of stuff in the bowl with a little bit in it, there'll be a little bit in another bowl with a little bit in it," he says, "she'll have plenty to eat, but it won't be any excess. But see, I go down to Heard County down there, I know that's poor as Job's turkey. They rentin' land." Says, "You'll have a good big bowl of peas, great big pone of bread, two or three other kind of vegetables, you'll have something sweet, big plates of it, it ain't just like—" He says, "I want you tell me what it is." I said, "I can tell you exactly what it is." I said, "Poor folks, why they want you to make yourself at home when you're around them, and they raise that stuff. And they don't mind putting it out there. Now see, the other people in town are buying it, and they know exactly what it costs, and just naturally they're a little more economical about their cooking. But you eat down there in the country where I live—" and I imag-ine it was that way pretty well everywhere back then especially, there'd be a plenty of food on the table. My daddy, if he was around here at dinnertime, you ate here. Yessirree, I don't care if you lived in Bowdon or Carrollton or where you lived, yes sir, he had insisted on you eating here.[22]

Figure 8: Commemorative markers for B. F. White (Hamilton, Georgia) and the Denson brothers (Double Springs, Alabama). The Denson marker celebrates the centennial of *The Sacred Harp* and the family's part in its history. (Photographs courtesy of John Plunkett. Denson marker photograph reproduced by Plunkett from the personal files of George Pullen Jackson; thanks to Jackson's granddaughters Pam Helms and Ellen Jackson for access to these materials.)

Some singers have compared dinner-on-the-grounds to Christian communion, an extraordinary reinforcer of group membership across boundaries of time and place.

The memorial lesson just before Sunday's dinner invokes the spiritual presence of those who have passed on. During dinner singers may find themselves in the physical presence of the dead: when dinner is held outdoors it is often at the fringes of a graveyard, and many Southern singings take place on a church's annual cemetery decoration day. New singers are profoundly moved when they wander through a cemetery and see the surnames of local singers on stone after stone. Headstones and commemorative markers are sometimes engraved with lyrics from *The Sacred Harp,* musical notes, harps, or even bits of shape-note notation. (See Figures 8 and 9.) The juxtaposition of the memorial lesson and dinner-on-the-grounds encourages singers to place themselves within a much-widened Sacred Harp community, one that includes the new participant exploring the graveyard and the dead who are buried there.

FINANCES, RESOLUTIONS, AND ANNOUNCEMENTS

After lunch the arranging committee calls more leaders and breaks. At some point the finance committee takes up a collection to cover "minute

Figure 9: Gravestones featuring references to Sacred Harp singing. At left, an allusion to the "parting hand"; at right, detail from the grave of J. P. Reese, a prominent Sacred Harp composer and member of the 1859 and 1869 revision committees. (Photographs courtesy of John Plunkett.)

money"—the fee for publication in the minutebook—as well as the cost of building rental and publicity, if any. Per-day convention expenses may range from about $50 to well over $1,000, with higher numbers reflecting the rental cost of urban venues. Finance committees have been known to ask singers to contribute what they would spend for a family dinner at a fast-food restaurant. Indiana singer Samuel Sommers often tells the class, "It's a good thing Sacred Harp doesn't cost anything—because if I had to pay what this is worth, I wouldn't be able to afford it."

Singers spend generously to support the tradition. Average donation rates can surpass $15 per person—this on top of transportation costs and huge quantities of donated food. Donations in excess of expenses may go into a cemetery maintenance fund or an account to support future publicity and singing schools. Local singers sometimes insist on paying for visitors' hotel rooms if host housing cannot be found, and some singers have started nonprofit organizations to support conventions and give travel grants to students or needy individuals. The finance committee's exhortations—usually most intense at diaspora conventions, which tend to have higher expenses—draw on this whole structure of hospitality, commitment, and obligation.

As the end of the singing day approaches, the chairman asks for reports from the committees. The finance committee reports on whether expenses have been met; if not, the collection baskets will usually go around the room again. The secretary often gives statistics on the number of leaders, their places of origin, and the number of different songs led. The resolutions committee (sometimes replaced by the chairman) resolves to meet again the following year and usually gives thanks to God and the convention officers, along with those who have provided food, come a long way, donated the singing space, housed traveling singers, or otherwise contributed to the singing. The chair calls on singers to announce upcoming conventions or local singings; people observe that the road to this convention from their home area "runs in both directions," or that a certain singing "isn't very big, but it will be if all y'all come!" The class dissolves into its constituent parts as singers speak as representatives of their home regions. They speak from their places in different sections rather than coming to the middle of the square. Singers get irritable and shift in their seats during announcements, which can seem interminable and inelegant after the day's steady progress from song to song. People become detached and more aware of their physical fatigue, audible in the hoarse voices of those making announcements.

THE PARTING HAND

The chairman, sometimes accompanied by other officers, leads the "parting hand," the last song of the convention. The usual choice is a tune by the same name. (See Figure 10, Sound Example 3.) As with the first song of the day, after singing "the notes" the singers rise to their feet. While singing the words—usually just the first two verses—they walk around the room shaking hands and embracing, making a formal farewell before the bustle of the mass departure begins.

The text of "Parting Hand" is about parting ways, the passage of time during the singing day, the contrast of everyday duties with the pleasures of fellowship, and the divine presence in the square: "How loath we are to leave the place / Where Jesus shows His smiling face." Because this song is almost never sung at any other time, only experienced singers know the song well enough to fully partake in the parting hand and reproduce the sentiments of the text. Singers who have not been to many conventions remain tied to the printed lyrics; they will fumble with the words if they close their books and move around the square embracing people. Instead, they are left standing awkwardly in place holding their books, while others cry, sing, and hug all at once. Newcomers are partly excluded from the community of feeling, even as they bear witness to the "drawing bands" that might someday encompass them. When the song is over, the singers

Figure 10: "Parting Hand" (62), the last song of most Sacred Harp conventions.

PARTING HAND. L.M.

"But as touching brotherly love ye need not that I write unto you: for ye yourselves are taught of God to love one another." -- 1 Thes. 4:9.

Arr. - William Walker, 1835.

G Major John Blain, 1818.

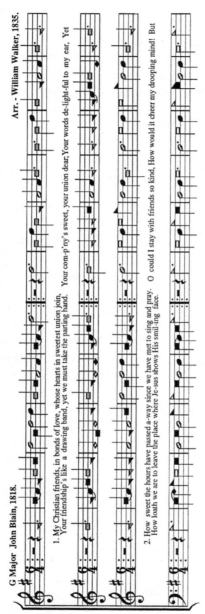

1. My Christian friends, in bonds of love, whose hearts in sweetest union join,
Your friendship's like a drawing band, yet we must take the parting hand.

2. How sweet the hours have passed a-way since we have met to sing and pray.
How loath we are to leave the place where Je-sus shows His smil-ing face.

Your com-p'ny's sweet, your union dear, Your words de-light-ful to my ear, Yet

O could I stay with friends so kind, How would it cheer my drooping mind! But

when I see that we must part, You draw like cords around my heart.

du - ty makes me un-der-stand That we must take the part - ing hand.

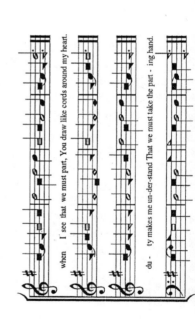

3. And since it is God's holy will,
We must be parted for a while,
In sweet submission, all as one,
We'll say, our Father's will be done.

My youthful friends, in Christian ties,
Who seek for mansions in the skies,
Fight on, we'll gain that happy shore,
Where parting will be known no more.

4. How oft I've seen your flowing tears,
And heard you tell your hopes and fears!
Your hearts with love were seen to flame,
Which makes me hope we'll meet again.

Ye mourning souls, lift up your eyes
To glorious mansions in the skies;
O trust His grace -- in Canaan's land
We'll no more take the parting hand.

5. And now my friends, both old and young.
I hope in Christ you'll still go on;
And if on earth we meet no more,
O may we meet on Canaan's shore.

I hope you'll all remember me
If on earth no more I see;
An interest in your prayers I crave,
That we meet beyond the grave.

6. O glorious day! O blessed hope!
My soul leaps forward at the thought
When, on that happy, happy land,
We'll no more take the parting hand.

But with our blessed holy Lord
We'll shout and sing with one accord,
And there we'll all with Jesus dwell,
So, loving Christians, fare you well.

hold still wherever they might be, bow their heads, and listen to the closing prayer. Then the room erupts into a flurry of collection of belongings,
rearranging of pews or chairs, and goodbyes. The physical arrangement of
the hollow square disappears almost instantly.

The prayers, memorial lesson, and parting hand are linked by their special status as signs of "respect for the tradition," as singers often say. Each
is led by a specially appointed person or committee and explicitly invokes
a sense of community through an emphasis on kinship, farewells, travel,
and reunions. Many singers feel the inclusion of these elements at a newly
established convention deliberately suggests an affiliation with and obligation to Sacred Harp practice in the South.

The Hollow Square and Senses of Place

Each singing, like each singer, has its own character and reputation in the
singing community. These are determined not only by the number and origins of individual singers who attend but by the past history of the singing
and by its location. The style and content of the formal spoken-word events
at a singing—the prayers, memorial lessons, and resolutions—reflect and
reinforce its character. On November 19, 2000, I attended the third annual
University of Chicago Anniversary Singing, whose venue and date have
varied from year to year. At this singing (as in the previous two years) the
chaplain and memorial committee talked about people rather than place,
emphasizing the role of travelers and of individual singers who had a strong
influence on the new singing and its young founding members. On January
14, 2001, I attended the seventeenth annual Chicago Anniversary Singing,
held the second Sunday in January and nearly always located at the Irish
American Heritage Center in Chicago. A singer told the class, "It's nice to
feel like we're beginning to have a home here." Even after seventeen years,
however, there is little to make the Irish American Heritage Center seem
homelike to Sacred Harp singers; it is a large building with many rooms,
one of which the Chicago singers rent out every year. There is no graveyard
nearby filled with singers, and Chicago's January weather is too forbidding to encourage the walks around an area that build an emotional connection to particular places. When the Chicago Anniversary Singing feels
like home, it is not because of the building but because of the singers who
are present and the characteristic sound environment that their particular
voices produce in the hollow square.

By way of contrast one might consider the Holly Springs Convention in west Georgia, which I attended for five consecutive years starting in 1999. At Holly Springs, formal and informal speech about the singing tend to revolve around the place itself. A memorial lesson at a place like Holly Springs might refer to people buried ten yards from the church door, people who occupied particular seats in the hollow square every year for decades, people who brought current singers to the annual convention as toddlers. Holly Springs is a location that invites nostalgia, a feeling that fills the gap between space and place and "insists on a nonarbitrary relationship between a particular place and people" (Sorensen 1997: 37). At the same time, like other hollow squares, Holly Springs is imbued with an "extroverted" sense of place; its relationships to *other* places are a key part of its own identity (Morley 2001: 441, following Massey 1995).

Georgia singer Richard DeLong, a high school teacher in Carrollton, has been attending west Georgia conventions since his infancy. His grandmother Dollie Hudgins began bringing him to local singings in the 1960s, and throughout his adulthood he has traveled widely to visit diaspora conventions and teach singing schools. When "Miss Dollie" died, he was asked to give memorial lessons for her wherever he went for a year (the prescribed memorial period). A lesson he gave at Holly Springs in 2000 described time, place, and people meaningfully conjoined:

> My grandmother didn't come here until late, late in her life, I think maybe fifteen years ago. And on the way home she said that she liked coming here because it reminded her of going to a singing when she was a little girl. The way the church was set up, the way it looked. And it brought back memories to her. And I learned from that. And now those of you who might not have known my grandmother have just learned something. You have learned how maybe a singing looked seventy, eighty years ago. . . .
>
> I counted yesterday twenty-four singers on treble, seventeen on alto, and eighteen on bass. I came here when not one of those would have been from anywhere but west Georgia or east Alabama. It would have been just as full, just as loud, but you know it's a difference. Every one of them sung from the heart. And when you had the whole room doing that, it seemed alive in a way that I cannot describe in words. And I see a lot of these old people still sitting here, and I can feel them. I feel Loyd Redding sitting right here. And when he keyed a song he meant business. And when he got started singing, you felt it. So it doesn't matter if you grew up singing Sacred Harp, or it doesn't matter if you've only been singing it a year. You'll be a traditional singer when you sing it from the heart.[23]

This lesson emphasizes the role of Holly Springs as a vessel for accumulated experience and historical lessons. DeLong places absent singers in the singing room, in the actual seats they once occupied, and in that sense the specificity of this particular place is important. Still, the specific collection of voices gathered by Holly Springs is even more important—especially the fact that they "sung from the heart." As I will discuss in Chapter 6, this ideology of sincerity is crucial to assessments of authentic Sacred Harp practice no matter where conventions are held. But singers looking for new convention venues seek out places they hope will gather traditional voices and *inspire* this kind of sincerity.

Places like Holly Springs tend to be considered the ideal for Sacred Harp singings, both acoustically and emotionally. Singing locations of this kind also exist in the North; diaspora singings at rural churches in Indiana, Wisconsin, and Minnesota have begun to produce a rhetoric of place distinct from what one hears at the Chicago Anniversary Singing or other urban venues. These sites can seem to exist at a remove from modernity. Some of them are part of history- or reenactment-oriented exhibits, like the churches at Murphy's Landing in Minnesota and Folklore Village Farm in Wisconsin. Their relatively remote locations enhance their distinctiveness; when participants at these singings describe their travels and bemoan their sleep deprivation, they invoke the circuit-riding preachers and old-time Sacred Harp families who traveled to singings by horse and wagon, covering much shorter distances but spending the same long hours on the road.

Lived connections to particular sites are tremendously important to many singers, and diaspora singers go to rural Southern singings in hopes of creating those connections. They seek out "real places," hoping to differentiate between authentic localism and "a place identity that corporate leaders or the mass media have arbitrarily assigned to a standardized, interchangeable, instant landscape" (Glassberg 2001: 118). Yet to a newcomer these rural churches—especially Primitive Baptist churches, which have no icons or decoration—could seem as generic and blank as the strip malls she passed on the highway. The difference comes in the attribution of authenticity: when all the unmarked dirt roads look alike, one blames *oneself* for not being able to tell them apart. If these end-of-the-line sites turn out to feel as interchangeable as airports, newcomers are driven to find and decipher marks of particularity: reading the gravestones, decoding people's song choices, finding out who built the chapel, how to drive there on back roads, and how to make the fried pies on the dinner table. After many years of intermittent Sacred Harp travels, Chicago singer Dean Slaton described the process of realizing how much local knowledge was required even to find some singings:

> [W]hen we used to go down there, you know we were just blissed out, people picked you up and you didn't have to memorize any streets or highways or nothing, it was just kinda like "Oh, somewhere out in the country," and all of a sudden you realize that all these people, there were fewer and fewer of them alive and willing and able to come and get you. And I said—finally it dawned on me, you gotta get instructions and memorize how to get there. You know when you're just the passive passenger you have no clue, it's just like "Oh, Wilson's Chapel, it's somewhere out there." But now I could take you there absolutely without fail, you know, I know exactly what streets, I know exactly the turns, I can get you there. . . . You know what I mean, it's passing to us now.[24]

The reward for taking on such obligations is a built-up sense of particularity, of dense experience, that compensates for the perceived impoverishment of other parts of the American landscape.[25]

But in another sense, the most crucial aspect of "place" in Sacred Harp transmission is the tradition's portability. While a small country church has many advantages, the basic requirement for a Sacred Harp singing is a hollow square of seats. Indeed, many lovely old churches have been passed over as singing venues because their pews were attached to the floor. The hollow square layout completely overwrites normal hierarchical seating structures in churches, creating new boundaries and margins to be filled in with another kind of experience. Singers profess to come to Sacred Harp seeking a remedy for alienation and placelessness. But the hollow square's portability keeps this localism from being strictly insular or defensive: singers have the tools and materials to reassemble a similarly-structured authentic locality anywhere, rather like the pre-fab house kits that Americans once ordered from catalogues. Their travels and their accumulated stores of local knowledge from different singing sites teach diaspora singers how their own hollow squares might be constructed and experienced as intensely local. Wherever a class assembles, the hollow square dramatizes the compensatory promise of "thick places" scattered through "the wasteland of thinned-out places" (Casey 2001: 409).

Leading from the center of the square is often described as the quintessential Sacred Harp experience. It constitutes a major opportunity to demonstrate one's competence in the tradition as well as one's willingness to make mistakes in public.[26] At the center of the square leaders may choose song, pitch, verses, and tempo at will, making a stylistic contribution to traditional practice. However, leaders are self-selecting; since new singers often lack the confidence to lead, there is a built-in mechanism of exclusion at work. Sacred Harp can afford to be all-inclusive in theory because only the initiated will regularly reach the center of the square and leave their mark on the tradition. Some singers describe having a kind of conversion experience at the center of the square, wherein they suddenly identify with the expressed ideals of the Sacred Harp community; others recount similar experiences but eschew the language of Christian conversion, instead describing an active choice to "surrender" or "be swept away" in collective sound and feeling.

In the seats around the hollow square, the ideology of equality among individual singers is reproduced on another scale to dictate equality among voice parts. The parts are separated, yielding a different effect than the popular folk music singing circle or drumming circle: most singers maintain loyalty to a particular section and develop personal ties within it. Songs with imitative entrances encourage leaders to acknowledge each part in turn; isolated entrances encourage singers to produce and listen for a sectional sound. The seating arrangement also complicates the gender divisions of typical four-part choruses: there are two mixed-gender sections (treble and tenor) along with two sections that are virtually always gender-segregated (alto and bass).

The alto section has an especially distinctive identity, due to its physical placement as well as its gendered quality. In churches, altos sit in the area ordinarily occupied by church leaders, either in chairs—displacing the preacher's lectern—or in the raised pews normally reserved for deacons or other important church members. (Since the tenor section is invariably the largest, it occupies the congregational seating that faces the pulpit, and altos must face the tenors.) Altos often have a clear view of the rest of the class and can interact without being seen by the leader, who faces the tenors most of the time. The result is a high incidence of inside jokes, whispering during songs, and a strong sense of sectional solidarity—more than once I have heard other singers teased for "carrying on like a bunch of altos." While being seated behind the leader's back might seem to be a marginalized, undesirable position, it puts the altos in the sightlines of everyone *but* the leader, where they can display a very public critique or endorsement of the leader's actions.[27]

Politically liberal singers often make approving remarks about gender equality at singings, observing that in certain segments of the Sacred Harp

population women play a secondary role in their own church services. Singing is a common outlet for women's expression even in religious circumstances where women's speech is restricted (cf. Patterson 1995 on Primitive
Baptist services); in this sense Sacred Harp is probably not an unusually lib-
erating experience for these women. Still, the fact that liberal singers *project*
this liberation onto conservative women certainly contributes to an egalitarian ideology. The perceived exceptional expressive freedom of Southern
conservative women at Sacred Harp conventions encourages singers who
might feel marginalized in everyday life, such as gay men and lesbians, to
experience a high degree of equality, independence, and community support in the hollow square.

While the hollow square does level the playing field in some respects, it
also structures status relationships within any given "class" of singers. The
most coveted position in a section is its "front bench," which faces directly
on the open center of the square where the leader stands. A front bench seat
provides an aural experience close to that of leading, with the heady feeling of being entirely surrounded by singers, and it permits intense visual
communication with the leader and other singers across the square. The
tenor front bench has a special responsibility to keep the class focused, both
musically and emotionally. The leader begins and ends facing the tenor
section; the tenor front bench vigorously beats time so that the tempo is
visible to all. Front bench singers are expected to sing at a high energy level
at all times, without sitting out songs, and ideally should not have to look at
their books much. In general, the front bench destabilizes the typical con-
ductor/chorus authority relationship. The leader's control over the singing
often depends on the authority ceded to him by the front bench tenors;
they pick up the slack to protect confused or incompetent leaders from
musical disasters, but they can also take over control of the tempo, number
of verses, and number of repeats against a leader's will. Front bench singers
can always see more of the square than the leader can. Surrounded on all
sides, a leader can feel more vulnerable than authoritative.[28]

Seating is open at a singing, but the second row may fill up faster than
the first. Singers defer to the most experienced, most competent, and most
"traditional"—measured by years, family, or origin—to fill the front bench
seats. At the Chicago Anniversary Singing there is always a front bench
seat open for Richard DeLong; if some neophytes have been foolish enough
to sit on the front bench, experienced singers will give up their seats to
DeLong or other high-status singers. Over the course of the day, courtesy
dictates that one give up one's front bench seat to another singer at some

point, and convention dictates giving it up to someone competent rather than leaving it open. This behavior creates a network of favors given and returned. Versatile singers of high status may simply end up moving from one front bench to another, not entirely of their own accord. Sometimes during a break or dinner someone picks up another singer's book and moves it to a front bench seat.

A primary goal of Sacred Harp singing is reaching the center of the square, with all that such an arrival implies. All of the traveling, all of the sound, and all of the feeling converge there. Experienced singers persuade family or strangers to come stand in the center while they lead, because "Once it gets ahold of you, it won't let go." People use the language of addiction or conversion in describing their experience in the square: "I was hooked." "I have to get my fix." "I was transformed." "It was my Sacred Harp baptism."

The hollow square is a portable focal point of emotional intensity, a mobile pilgrimage site, and the travels and repetitions that it engenders encourage singers to experience time differently (cf. Bohlman 1996). Wherever it is set up, the center of the square is the place closest to past and future generations of singers and the place where they communicate with one another. It relies on inwardly focused voices, eyes, and emotions to create an extroverted sense of place, a larger community crossing temporal, geographic, and mortal boundaries. (See Figures 11 and 12.)

As leaders enter the square one after another on a day of singing, or return to the same singing year after year, Sacred Harp singing experience can seem circular. One mixes up years, renditions of particular songs, and

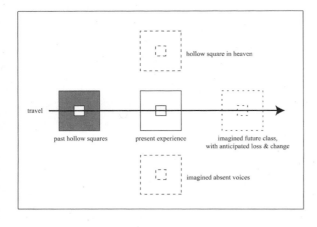

Figure 11: Some of the hollow squares one singer might experience in a single moment.

Figure 12: What it feels like to lead. An unsteady camera at the fringes of the square unexpectedly yielded an image of spiraling affective experience. All-California Convention, San Carlos, January 14, 2006. (Photograph by the author.)

different hollow squares. But memory accumulates nevertheless, along with its counterpart in the form of anticipation of loss. In prayer, memorial lessons, and informal speech, singers reiterate parallels between different cycles of time: the beginning and end of one's time in the square; the beginning and end of the day of singing; and the beginning and end of life. No sooner does one revel in understanding and forming a union with another's voice than one begins to fear its absence. Is it any wonder that the hope of a singing reunion after death becomes so prominent even in the minds of agnostics? To be caught in the suspension of the hollow square without anxieties of loss—it would be an appealing heaven for anyone who has ever been swept up in music.

3

"Well, You'll Learn"

TRANSMISSION, AFFILIATION, AND COMPETENCE

Sacred Harp singers in Chicago hold an Anniversary Singing every January, a celebration of their community in the mold of family memorial singings in the South.[1] It is a one-day singing, not a full weekend convention, and visitors face bitter weather; the class of a hundred or so is intimate compared to the Midwest Convention, Chicago's showcase singing in late spring. The Anniversary Singing always includes a Founders' Lesson, in which the original members of the local singing community are recognized by the class, and someone—usually Marcia Johnson—recounts the history of Sacred Harp singing in Chicago. In 1985 Johnson received a phone call from Hugh McGraw, then the president of the Sacred Harp Publishing Company, who had learned of their plans to join with a group of downstate singers and hold the first Illinois State Convention. At the 2003 Anniversary Singing, Johnson told the story this way:

> *Johnson:* So we decided that we would have a convention, the first convention in Illinois since the Civil War. I don't know if they had one *before* the Civil War! [*laughter*] It's true, we had this beautiful orange flyer, and we hear, I get a phone call [*interjections from others*], but somebody called and his name was [*imitating McGraw's Georgia accent*] Hugh McGraw. [*laughter*] And Hugh McGraw says, "Y'all are going to have a convention?" And I said, "Well, yes sir". . . .
> [*McGraw promised to attend, with other Georgia singers.*]

And we were thrilled, thrilled, and Hugh before we had our
convention, *sent us* the bylaws [*laughter*], the minutes, the songs
we'll sing, but that's when we met Richard [DeLong], that's when
Richard. . . . [*interjections*] Oh, and he said, "Do y'all sing the
shapes?"
[*interjections—apparently they did not*]
and he said, "Well, you'll learn." So I took Amazing Grace and
way late at night I'd study and I'd practice. . . . And I think that's
what we all did. . . . But we had just a wonderful convention, that
time, and believe me I would bore you to tears—
Judy Hauff: But two weeks later we were down South.
Marcia Johnson: Down South. . . . Judy was there, Ted Mercer,
founder; founder, come on up, Ted Johnson—
Ted Johnson: We were foundering![2]

A few years earlier, a small group of friends with an interest in folk music
had stumbled upon printed music from *The Sacred Harp* and tried singing
it together. But they had no experience with the ongoing Southern convention tradition. The encounter with Hugh McGraw is a key moment in the
founding narrative, the moment after which everything changed. Sacred
Harp became something separate from other folk music pursuits, and the
Chicago "founders"—who wryly claim the distinction of "foundering"—
became part of a network of affiliations and mutual obligations in a broader
singing community. As one Chicago singer told me, "I hadn't been singing
at our first Illinois State Convention for an hour before someone came and
said, 'You know, we have a singing at Holly Springs—'"

McGraw's casually authoritative "Well, you'll learn" established the next
phase of Chicago Sacred Harp history, when innocents abroad acquired
a new cultural competence through their contact with traditional singers. The Founders' Lesson always includes funny stories about their initial
gaffes. They didn't sing the fasola solfege. Judy Hauff declared there were
"about ten good songs in this book," as Marcia Johnson recounted in 2003.
Hauff brought a music stand into the hollow square at the first Illinois State
Convention, something that would look about as odd in the Sacred Harp
context as seeing the conductor of a symphony orchestra use a golf club for
a baton. During the 2002 Founders' Lesson, someone imitated the shocked
expression of the young Richard DeLong when, at that first convention, he
had dropped his arm in the typical downbeat leading gesture and no one

began to sing. The founders led "Montgomery" (189b), the tune DeLong had called that day. Afterward, DeLong stood and said, "It sounded a lot better today than it did then."

Recurring narratives like these show that there are complex status relationships in play at Sacred Harp conventions, where authority is claimed or ascribed according to singers' apparent competence as tradition-bearers. Status is a delicate matter, given the egalitarian ideology that underpins convention procedure: everyone gets a chance to lead, there is no performer/audience divide, no musical training is required, and no one is turned away from a singing. Regional groups are ill defined; there are no membership rosters, requirements, or dues, and organizational duties rotate mainly on the basis of willingness to work. Still, questions of authority bear exploring because they shed light on the system of affiliations through which singers transmit musical and social practices. When certain Chicago singers identify themselves as founders and establish an affiliation with Southern tradition, and when Richard DeLong confirms the claim both by his presence and with explicit verbal approval, a model for community social relations is on display.

*　*　*

In describing "traditional singing," singers and scholars emphasize birthright, community practice, and the hallowed folk principle of oral tradition, suggesting that traditional singers naturally sing a certain way because they grew up in an encompassing soundscape that is inaccessible to new adult singers. Sacred Harp has gained prestige as "one of the last remaining examples of authentic oral tradition in white American Protestant music" (Marini 2003: 74). Oral transmission is a familiar aspect of folk music mythology, often connected with assumptions about the isolation, purity, and antimodernism of folk traditions (Bohlman 1988).

In the Sacred Harp context, however, the division of the traditional and less traditional on the basis of oral transmission can be deceptive. There is a tunebook, after all, and it is neither a collection of transcriptions nor just a crutch for folk enthusiasts and musicologists. *The Sacred Harp* is an artifact of visual culture, a pedagogical tool, a symbol of tradition and change, and a repository for community decisions. Possessing a tunebook and knowing how to use it have always been the prerequisites of Sacred Harp competence, for nineteenth-century children at singing school as well as newcomers today.

A Brief Survey of the Sacred Harp Repertoire[3]

The 560 songs contained in the 1991 edition of *The Sacred Harp* are printed with composition dates from the eighteenth century to 1990. Many of the songs are arrangements of older hymn tunes or popular melodies. Singers most often divide the repertoire into three categories that reflect an increasing order of difficulty for leading: plain tunes, fuging tunes, and anthems. All three are indebted to English country parish music, a sacred song style that flourished in the eighteenth century, and Sacred Harp singers have continued to compose in these categories up to the present.[4] Plain tunes are homophonic; they are usually built from two symmetrical phrases that each set two lines of text. Whether pre-existing or newly composed, the melody line appears in the tenor part. Plain tunes are easy to lead because there are no separate entrances to cue; they are easy to sing because they are predominantly syllabic settings and move at a slower pace than fuging tunes. "Mear" (163b) is a popular plain tune; like many of its ilk, it is set to a psalm paraphrase by Isaac Watts. Vocal parts of similar contour and intervallic content are common in *The Sacred Harp*. (See Figure 13, Sound Example 4.)

Fuging tunes constitute the most distinctive genre in the Sacred Harp repertoire. Singers and American music textbooks alike associate them with early New England composers like William Billings—particularly when citing a connection between independent part writing and Sacred Harp's egalitarianism—but the style owes much to earlier English composers. These songs have a homophonic first section followed by an imitative chorus. They are typically sung faster than plain tunes—often at tongue-

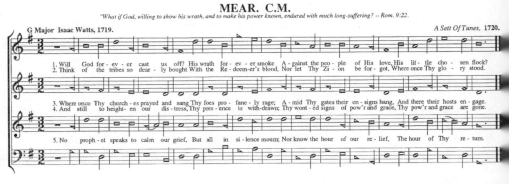

Figure 13: "Mear" (49b), a plain tune.

twister tempos with a driving rhythm, swinging eighth notes, and tapping feet—and may be quite vocally demanding. The tenor line is still considered the melody, but all four parts approach the same level of complexity.

"Save, Lord, Or We Perish" (224) is a popular fuging tune with a typical order and spacing of entrances. (See Figure 14, Sound Example 5.) Its composer, M. Mark Wynn, drafted the 1866 constitution of the Chattahoochee Musical Convention (founded in west Georgia in 1852). Fuging tunes offer leaders an opportunity to display their skill at spinning around to cue entrances, and singers enjoy the social interaction created by imitative dialogue across the hollow square. In "Save, Lord" the doubled tenor and treble parts create thrilling layers of parallel fifths and octaves when the four parts suddenly feature the same rhythm in measures 9–10 of the chorus. The C in the tenor part is raised a half-step to create a perfect fifth with the F# in the bass (a practice discussed below).

Figure 14: "Save, Lord, Or We Perish" (224), a nineteenth-century fuging tune by a Georgia singer.

Anthems are settings of nonversified Scriptural texts. They combine the qualities of plain tunes and fuging tunes, linking together homophonic, solo section, and imitative segments into a setting that lasts several pages and frequently involves tricky rhythms, short repeated sections, and changes of meter, tempo, and key. These songs are challenging to lead and to sing; because of their length, leaders often omit singing the fasola solfege before the words. Since anthems are led relatively rarely, many people don't know their parts by memory and must give up the pleasure of looking across the square at other singers. Choosing to lead an anthem demonstrates one's expertise as a leader but may also alienate a portion of the class; anthems consume time in which others could be leading, and a badly led anthem or one that is too difficult for the class may result in one of the rare musical train wrecks heard at Sacred Harp conventions. Nevertheless, anthems remain important as prestigious emblems of the complexity of Sacred Harp music and the skills of leaders and singers. Most are clumped together in pages 232 to 265 of the 1991 revision, reflecting pagination preserved from a shorter edition where they appeared as a virtuosic final section.

Anthems often have relatively simple, homophonic final sections that serve as a cathartic close to a challenging musical experience. At the end of Billings's "Rose of Sharon" (254), for example, fragmentary imitative entrances give way to a homophonic setting of a text that eloquently expresses the singers' relief at having reached that point intact: "For lo, the winter is past, the rain is over and gone." (See Figure 15.)

A fourth category of Sacred Harp songs falls into the "plain tune" group in terms of homophony and ease of leading but occupies different historical terrain. These songs—termed camp-meeting songs, revival songs, or spiritual songs—typically have several verses fitted to a single chorus, reflecting their creation or use in revival settings where verses were lined-out or improvised. They are well-suited to large crowds who are not singing from printed music or texts; verses can be added indefinitely, choruses are easy to learn by ear, and homophonic harmony parts can be improvised. Many songs of this type are printed in *The Sacred Harp* with arranger credit rather than composer credit. Camp-meeting songs have stood at the heart of the "white spirituals" controversy, since many revivals were sites of racial integration and mutual influence.[5] Here "Sweet Morning" (421), arranged by H. S. Reese in 1859, serves as an example of the genre. (See Figure 16, Sound Example 6.)

Many songs fall in the cracks between these categories, but this survey should provide a general sense of the diversity of the Sacred Harp reper-

Figure 15: Excerpt from "Rose of Sharon" (254–59). Note the difficult off-beat entrances in the sixth and twelfth bars, followed by a relaxed, swinging 6/4 concluding section.

Figure 16: "Sweet Morning" (421), a camp-meeting song.

toire in terms of historical origin, musical style, and performance difficulty. That diversity is not immediately apparent when a newcomer flips through *The Sacred Harp*; the tunes are not organized by genre, subject matter, composer, title, or date of composition. Their apparently random order was created by multiple revisions that added and deleted songs while preserving the page numbers of songs retained from the previous edition. Meanwhile, the shape-note notation and page layout in the 1991 revision make all songs seem more alike than different.[6]

Perceived difficulty, pacing considerations, personal textual preferences, and the memory of favorite musical moments guide leaders' choices far more often than composer or date of composition. The parameters of difficulty that are tied to the printed music include understanding time signatures; leading songs that start on an upbeat; changing tempo or time signature within a song; dealing with fermatas, repeat signs and first/second endings; finding one's starting pitch from the sounded tonic triad; and beating the printed time signature in "misbarred" tunes (e.g., sticking with

A solemn darkness veils the skies,
A solemn darkness veils the skies,
A sudden trembling shakes the ground.

He gives His precious life for you,
He gives His precious life for you,
For you He sheds His precious blood.

But lo! what sudden joys we see!
But lo! what sudden joys we see!
Je - sus, the dead re - vives a-gain.

Cherubic legions guard Him home,
Cherubic legions guard Him home,
And shout Him wel-come to the skies.

Figure 17: The chorus of "Morning" (163t) has a disorienting triple feel that can cause leaders to mix up their beat patterns.

a duple beat pattern in the chorus of "Morning" [163t]; see Figure 17). Singers make lists of tricky songs and ask how to deal with them in singing schools or at small local singings.

Authenticity, Oral and Written

In a review of the 1991 revision of *The Sacred Harp*, Ron Pen explained the practice's contemporary appeal this way: "The media that severed Americans from oral tradition and developed a national culture at the expense of indigenous local practice has induced a rootless and nostalgia-seeking generation to return 'home' to warm themselves in the glow of traditional community singing" (Pen 1994: 95). But Sacred Harp singing is itself a mass media phenomenon, the legacy of a progressive music education movement and a competitive nineteenth-century publishing industry. Shape-notes, also called "patent notes," served as both pedagogical tool and marketing gimmick.

Throughout the twentieth century, most young Southerners who learned Sacred Harp singing learned it in singing school, with book in hand. At most Sacred Harp conventions no one may lead a song that is not printed in the current revision of the tunebook. Many conventions were founded with written constitutions that formally adopted a particular book, staking out a position in the conflict half-jokingly referred to as the "book wars." Great rifts divided Sacred Harp singers when new tunebook revisions were not universally accepted. Competition among different shape-note tunebooks and later between the Cooper and Denson revision lines put the books at the center of controversies over community affiliations.[7] The annual convention of B. F. White's Southern Musical Association (Georgia, 1845–67) recorded a resolution forbidding leaders to "vary in rendering the music from the way it was written" (Cobb 1989: 131). From layout to added alto parts to page numbers, the printed music has always mattered.

Occasional exceptions to this rule still support the print culture of Sacred Harp singing. For example, a leader might distribute photocopies of a newly composed tune that could someday be included in a new revision of *The Sacred Harp*. This is permitted as a gesture of courtesy to composers and takes place at the discretion of the convention officers, typically at a pre-arranged time in the singing day. More rarely, a leader might ask the group to sing a favorite tune that is not printed in the prescribed revision. Some of the singers will oblige, singing the song from memory, but many others will sit silently (either from ignorance or irritation), rolling their eyes at sympathetic friends across the square and voicing objections in private later on.

As in all musical traditions, many aspects of performance practice do go unnotated. One need not stay long at a Sacred Harp convention to realize that not everyone is singing what's written. But the existence of a printed version places these orally transmitted elements in a particular context, one quite different from that of a strictly oral tradition. The tunebook has prestige as an artifact of American music history and Southern culture, and each new revision encompasses a new version of the canonical repertoire. Knowing when to deviate from the tunebook has its own prestige—particularly now, when there are so many new singers who want to learn to sound "authentic" and "traditional." Regional styles abound, reflected in complex ornaments, tempo, pronunciation, timbre, and changes to the printed notation. Alto parts are particularly variable; many of the printed alto parts were added to existing three-part settings at some point.[8] Versions of these parts have varied from one edition to the next, each leaving its residue in the memories of a generation of singers (and sometimes in their books, where singers have pasted in alternate alto parts).

The simplest ornaments are not recognized as changes to a printed song, but in most cases altering the printed pitches is. Some lifelong singers don't know they aren't singing what's written until a newcomer points it out to them; one New England singer ruefully told me, "Sometimes you see someone doing something especially cool and you scribble it down and then they look at the book and say, 'I've been doing it wrong all these years,' and you've lost it. I hate losing stuff like that."[9] In recent years, however, many are well aware of the discrepancy between their preferred version and the notation. Diaspora singers bring these local variations back to their own communities and gain authority from knowing "how it's done on Sand Mountain" or "in the Wooten family."

Orally transmitted elements of Sacred Harp performance practice have a special capacity to evoke authenticity. Jack Goody has asserted that a written text supplementing an oral tradition "quite rapidly . . . assumes authority over the utterance" (Goody 2000: 56), but this is not so obvious in a cultural context that privileges the remembered and the nonrecorded as the most authentic. The compelling sounds and sights of singing conventions, coupled with the baggage of "oral tradition" ideologies, have sometimes made a living tradition obscure a written one. But *The Sacred Harp* is not a historical relic or a sentimental keepsake for lifelong singers who learn by ear and know every note by heart. It has been revised at regular intervals by committees of singers who alter the available repertoire and decide what should and should not be explained in print.

The contentious matter of the "raised sixth" offers an illuminating example. Many Sacred Harp singers—including some lifelong Southern singers and new singers who aspire to a "traditional" sound—say that every tune printed in a minor key should be sung with a raised sixth degree, as in the well-known melody "Wondrous Love." Washington singer Karen Willard highlights this point by distributing an "Anatomy of a Sacred Harp Tune" handout to new singers. The sample tune is printed with a bracketed accidental for every sixth, with the annotation "traditional singers automatically and unconsciously raise the 6th note of the scale." Willard also supplies a sheet of supporting evidence in the form of nineteenth-century writing on accidentals by Ananias Davisson, William Moore, and B. F. White. With this sort of historical support, the raised sixth can be construed as a retention, an unconscious preservation of musical and cultural history in the voice of the folk.

But not everyone agrees that traditional singers "automatically and unconsciously" sing this way or that such claims further the ideals of traditional singing. Like the matter of *musica ficta* in early music circles, this issue is hotly contested. The crucial difference is that Sacred Harp singers have access to living "traditional singers"—and to the argument that lifelong singers who do *not* sing this way have been corrupted by exposure to

mainstream music. Some singers are frustrated by these arguments, finding in them a prescriptive ideology that would make traditional singing a
paint-by-numbers affair.[10] New singers' orthopraxic efforts to "follow the
rules" of traditional singing can lead them to apply raised sixths or natural
sevenths ahistorically and without regard to harmonic context.[11] One well-
traveled diaspora singer remarked that lifelong singers "would give me the
hairy eyeball if I consistently sang raised sixths that could be played on
a piano. . . . The problem is that the raised sixth doesn't happen because
people are singing in the Dorian mode. It is part of a larger phenomenon in
traditional singing whereby notes tend to bend toward centers of gravity in
the scale, particularly in minor."[12] Like many of the strict raised-sixth advo-
cates with whom she disagrees, this singer has a deep respect for Southern
tradition, historical practice, and the choices of tunebook revisers. But her
experience leads her to believe that "traditional singers are reluctant to support the efforts of newer singers to codify the oral aspects of the tradition,"
due to engrained reverence for the printed tunebook and a sense that the
complexities of oral tradition cannot usefully be codified. "It's not because
traditional singers can't hear, but because they can hear MORE that they
don't like to discuss the raised sixth. The subtleties involved make it very
hard to talk about."

All this dissent raises the question of how Sacred Harp revision committees have dealt with these issues in typesetting *The Sacred Harp* over
the years. Buell Cobb noted that in the 1911 edition of *The Sacred Harp* one
arranger "added a sharp [to one tune setting] at each point where the sixth
was notated. In so doing, of course, he was not altering the real tune but only
officially making the modification the Sacred Harpers insisted on in their
singing." But the 1966 revision committee, "reviewing the tunes for errors,
decided that the sharped sixth was not proper here and removed it" (Cobb
1989: 34). Some lifelong Georgia singers who had been active in the 1960s
suggested a reason for this decision in conversation with me. They felt that
singing the raised sixth was an error, a stigma of musical illiteracy that should
not be immortalized in print, and they spoke longingly of the days when
extended singing schools trained young people to be perfect sight-singers.

In general, the 1991 revisers maintained the practice of not adding raised
sixths to the musical notation. However, Garst's "Rudiments of Music" at
the front of the tunebook direct singers to sharp the sixth degree in minor
in every case. (See Figure 18.) To complicate matters further, the 1991 revision contains some new tunes written by contemporary composers, including several by Chicago singer Judy Hauff. Hauff always notates the raised

Traditionally, minor music is sung in the Dorian mode, with the sixth degree a half step higher than the natural minor notation indicates. The interval sequence is w-h-w-w-w-h-w, with half steps at degrees 2-3 and 6-7 (see Chapter IV, Section 4; and Chapter

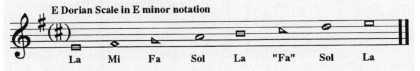

E Dorian Scale in E minor notation

La   Mi   Fa   Sol   La   "Fa"   Sol   La

VIII, Sections 13 and 14).

It is traditional to sing "Fa" at the sixth degree, even though the pitch actually corresponds to "Fi" (Section 20). The C♯ in parentheses in the key signature of the figure is understood but not printed in Sacred Harp notation.

Figure 18: Directions from the "Rudiments" on raising the sixth degree in minor.

sixth when she wants it. When one of her minor tunes *without* notated raised sixths is called, there is often some mumbling in the room as singers tell each other, "It's Judy's tune, she doesn't want them raised." Singer and composer Dan Brittain explained his position with respect to one of his own tunes in an October 2001 posting to discussions@fasola.org: "Cobb 313b was written as aeolian minor. When I heard the tapes made of the new tunes (done at Samford in Birmingham before the 1991 book was out), I realized most of the traditional singers had raised the second fa, (as they should have). It gives the tune a whole new feeling, and I love it. My strongest feeling is that the tradition is far more important than the note I put on the page. And if tradition says in minor you don't sing the sharped 7ths (even if marked) but you do sing the sharped 6ths (even if not marked), that's what you do."

The issue of what "tradition says" came up again when Terre Schill, a Texas singer, created a webpage containing .mus files for every song in *The Sacred Harp*, designed to assist singers in learning unfamiliar parts (http://users3.ev1.net/~amity/). Singers can use the site to listen to electronically generated versions of the songs while following along with the notation, transcribed as it appears in *The Sacred Harp*. The audio files present minor songs with raised sixths and naturalized accidentals (e.g., eliminating the occasional sharped seventh, which some singers consider untraditional and/or uncharacteristic of the Sacred Harp harmonic idiom). This prompted a discussions@fasola.org exchange between Schill and lifelong Alabama singer Henry Johnson:

> *Henry Johnson:* . . . Many, if not most, traditional singers in these parts (northeast Alabama), know what accidentals are, and sing them as written. Although there are singers everywhere who memorize the music, most of us can actually read it! Thanks for your efforts to promote Sacred Harp.
>
> *Terre Schill:* Hi Henry—On the accidentals/raised sixths issue—I surely do NOT have the credentials to make this decision without assistance, but because I am the one who did most of the transcription and put up the website it has fallen to me to do so [. . . .] Karen [Willard] wrote to me within a couple of hours after my posting volunteering to sharp the sixths and eliminate the accidentals, at least in certain songs. I had correspondence from others, too, both in favor and opposed. Meanwhile Berkley [Moore] has found some way to do so without it affecting the score. I then contacted every "traditional singer" I could get ahold of in a hurry and none of them could tell me for sure if they were raising sixths/singing accidentals or not (there is some sort of a moral there, I think. Most did not seem to believe this was too important. . . . I am still waiting for feedback from a few more). I next contacted some trained musicians with good ears who regularly sing in groups composed overwhelmingly of "traditional singers" in different parts of the country and asked them what they think they are hearing. What I am finding seems to be that for a lot of these songs raised sixths/ignored accidentals are less than universal, as nothing cultural ever seems to be absolutely consistent.[13]

Schill's response provides a window into the state of the raised-sixth controversy in 2004, after many years of off-and-on debate at singings, singing schools, socials, and on the fasola.org listservs. She and Johnson seem slightly at cross-purposes in their postings. Johnson addresses the treatment of notated accidentals, making the point that "traditional" singers are skilled music readers who respect the printed tunebook—an observation that undercuts the familiar story of oral transmission in an illiterate South. Schill's reply has little to do with music-reading, and she is well aware of the history of the raised-sixth controversy. She presents evidence about the diversity of contemporary practice in order to suggest that there is no need for a single correct and consistent form of "traditional" performance practice. On the website, she added the caveat "These files are not intended to be an entirely realistic representation of Sacred Harp songs as sung, but rather to be a useful learning tool. There is no substitute for attending singings to learn the 'culture' of Sacred Harp in practice."[14]

At most of the singings I have attended—even those with only a few singers per part—there is enough diversity of opinion or experience that there is simply a semitone clash every time the sixth scale-degree appears in a minor tune. This sound may itself be becoming "traditional"; some newer singers now think of this clash as part of the signature sound of minor tunes, the popularity of which is often ascribed to their dissonance.[15] This is one of many circumstances in which the complex interaction between concepts of oral and written traditions is plainly audible in the singing room.

Singing the Notes: Competence and Acculturation

Across the last century, the tunebook has played a changing role in the transmission of Sacred Harp singing as the practice has come to flourish outside rural Southern communities. As Philip Bohlman has observed in a study of pilgrimage, "Print media controlled by the group itself constantly restore the oral tradition . . . and empower it to express the group's own beliefs and ideological goals" (Bohlman 1996: 391). The process of revising the tunebook exemplifies such a restorative cycle. On another level, the tunebook's shape-note notation itself carries weight as an emblem of early American history; it marks this collection of songs as something different from, say, a volume of ballads transcribed by a folksong collector. Indeed, some newcomers are attracted to Sacred Harp more for its antiquarian tunebook/American history aspects than its oral tradition/folk-revival credentials.

For singers of all ages and backgrounds, musical memory and the acquisition of competence in the Sacred Harp sphere are channeled by the nature of shape-note notation as well as by convention procedure. The four shapes symbolize the particularity of Sacred Harp as opposed to any other singing tradition, and particularly as opposed to the seven-shape (Do–Re–Mi) gospel music that gradually diminished the number of Sacred Harp singers in the South (Campbell 1997). In recent years, new singers have used the notation to distinguish Sacred Harp not from gospel but from folk music; reliance on printed music clashes with folk-revival ideologies. Duncan Vinson recounts a singer's observation that "the dominant notions among folk revivalists were that one only needed an ear in order to sing and that reading music was too intellectual" (Vinson 1999: 25). At the same time, the special nature of shape-note notation keeps Sacred Harp from being immediately accessible to any music reader.

At the practical level of realizing the notation to produce song, the shapes require the development of a particular mode of music reading. Fluent shape-readers do not read one shape at a time, nor do they "memorize" long strings of individual syllables. Those who sight-sing rapid passages or "sing the notes" from memory are drawing on a lexicon of musical phrases made up of groups of shapes, groups that function like words in sentences (an analogy made by singing school teachers). This is an audible feature of the singing: rapid passages of shape-syllables are slurred together with particular notes receiving emphasis according to their importance in the shape of the phrase, just as emphasis shades the meaning of words in utterances. The distribution of shapes on the staff plays a role in cueing appropriate phrases from the lexicon: for example, in a major-key tune (immediately identifiable from the major triad sung by the person who is "keying") a large number of triangles (fa) on the top line of the staff in the tenor and treble call up stereotyped phrases for F-major tunes without requiring the singer to know keys or key signatures.[16]

Such practices bridge the processes of reading, remembering, and improvising; aural paradigms and notational cues interact as people "read" music (Treitler 2003: 38). At one New England singing I was sitting on the front bench when a leader called the song "Wondrous Cross" (447)—a relatively uncommon choice in that region—and led it at a fast clip. The man seated to my left tried to keep his head out of his book in order to perform his front-bench duty of interacting with the leader. While singing the fasola syllables, he reached the section that sets the words "All the vain things that charm" and accidentally sang "the notes" of a different song, "Morning Prayer" (411). (See Figure 19.) This kind of confluence is common in the Sacred Harp repertoire; each voice part has its own set of idiomatic phrases that tend to recur from song to song.

Every time a leader steps into the square, an interrelated system of cues draws on acquired competence and different modes of memory. The page number of the song and its position on the page (e.g., "48 on the bottom") call up past renditions. Experienced singers narrow down the options even before the leader calls a number: some leaders have a "sugar stick" (a favorite tune that they always lead if it hasn't already been called); some are known to be too inexperienced to lead long, fast, or difficult tunes; and some have a reputation for showing off by always choosing a long anthem or a little-known piece. The preferences of some leaders can be assessed based on physical appearance and regional accent even if they are not well known to the class; like many young newcomers from folk-revival back-

Figure 19: The final measures of the tenor parts of "Wondrous Cross" (447) *(top)* and "Morning Prayer" (411) *(bottom)*; 447 is in E-minor and 411 is in F#-minor, but the moveable-tonic shape-note notation renders key signatures redundant and demonstrates the songs' close resemblance when one "sings the notes."

grounds, I virtually always led minor fuging tunes until people began to tease me about it. More explicitly "musical" cues abound as well. Some keyers provide not only an appropriate triad but also the opening phrase (in fasola syllables) of the tenor part or its chorus. As the song progresses, more cues unfold: the shape-note "words" form syntactically appropriate longer phrases, "singing the notes" cues recollection of the verses, and the imitative entrances in fuging tunes cue one another. Experienced leaders also cue entrances, high notes, and notes of long duration in different parts. Singers look across the square, beat time together, and cue one another's parts with a hand gesture or a facial expression.

Every choice the leader makes points to her own experience and affiliations: her tempo, whether she beats two or four beats to the bar (the latter a feature of "new book" gospel and some Cooper book singing), how she observes printed repeat signs, how she cues in parts, whether she holds her book while leading, and of course her song choice. For the singers that compose a "class," each "lesson" conveys different cues as to appropriate musical and emotional responses and creates a link to other renditions.

Experienced Sacred Harp singers may know "the notes" to a given tune better than they know the words, and some rarely open their books during the course of the singing. Nevertheless, persisting in singing the solfege syllables before the verses helps maintain facility with realizing the notation at sight, and as new repertoire enters the tunebook this skill is invaluable. When the new compositions chosen for inclusion in the 1991 revision of *The Sacred Harp* were announced at a special singing convened for the purpose, the large group of assembled singers sight-read the entire new repertoire with impressive accuracy.[17] In so doing they "traditionalized" the new material, both through a sort of baptism in convention-style use and by adding unwritten markers of tradition like the raised sixth. The recently composed songs were written by fifteen Georgia and Alabama singers (twenty-three songs total) and seven singers from New York, Connecticut, Chicago, and Boston (fourteen songs total) (Bealle 1997: 267–68). In sight-reading these tunes the assembled singers took Sacred Harp's growing regional diversity in stride while also confirming the stylistic conformity of the new songs to older models.

"Singing the notes" has far-reaching effects on day-to-day singing practice and transmission. For newcomers, the notation tends to level the playing field among those with differing musical abilities. Matching a shape to a syllable is easier than worrying about locating "the right note" in some mysterious continuum of sound, and there are many voices to follow. A singer who cannot read music but has a good ear may have an advantage over an accomplished sight-singer trained in standard solfege. Those with perfect pitch are at a severe disadvantage, since songs are rarely keyed at the notated pitch level. One diaspora singer with perfect pitch told me, "My first trip South was in 1984, I was at the National Convention, and I could not sing. Because I had never learned to read music like most mortals. And it was never hardly ever in a key to which I could transpose."[18]

But those who do "read music like most mortals" can be just as confused by shape-note notation. Many simply refuse to sing the fasola syllables for a time. Meanwhile, fellow newcomers who cannot read music exploit the pedagogical qualities of the system and learn to read shapes fluently, though they still can't give the conventional letter names for the notes on the staff. Many such singers, including some lifelong singers, still claim they "can't read music," despite their flawless sight-singing of shape-note notation. Such remarks have perpetuated the idea that traditional singers really learn everything through oral transmission.

Shape-note notation makes Sacred Harp less accessible to newcomers in that it requires sustained effort and practice to achieve fluency. However, it can encourage participation in other ways. For singers who are not entirely comfortable with the texts to the hymns—most of which are explicitly Christian and many of which discuss death, hell, and the agony of Christ in frank terms—"singing the notes" of each tune serves as a kind of buffer for engagement with the words. In addition, because virtually all newcomers tend to flounder with the solfege, those who do not consider themselves "good singers" feel less self-conscious about singing out and making mistakes. I suspect that shape-notes also improve the retention rate for newcomers once they have achieved a certain degree of fluency—they have invested effort to learn a skill and they want to make use of it. At another level, of course, continued reliance on shape-note notation is what keeps *The Sacred Harp* in print.

Singers, academics, and local-color journalists alike have often compared shape-notes to a foreign language or an unintelligible babble. In a description of convention procedure, Buell Cobb writes that "Before the words are sung, the participants run each song through with its fa sol la's, to all appearances using their solmization like some unknown tongue to insulate and heighten their experience" (Cobb 1989: 2–3). Stephen Marini relies on metaphors of temporal distance to evoke foreignness; he describes a 1993 singing as being "ageless as the Alabama woods that gave it birth" and writes that "[w]hen all four parts sang their different lines in these shape-notes, syllabic cacophony ensued. Yet out of the syllabic babble emerged a soaring melody from the leads and primal harmonies from the trebles, counters, and basses" (Marini 2003: 74, 70).[19] John Bealle makes a more historically situated observation: following nineteenth-century reforms, "the shape note culture was now relegated to the South, its notation practically unintelligible to the northern singer" (Bealle 1997: 76). I would extend this point to suggest that rural Southern culture is often as inaccessible and unintelligible to new Sacred Harp singers as shape-note notation, partly because of the entrenched stereotypes that make new singers think they know what to expect. The process of learning to "sing the notes" is a process of acculturation, and often one of growing mutual tolerance.

Dealing with shape-note notation can be alienating, in a productive sense. It presents a kind of language barrier even to those who already read music, reminding them of the distinctiveness of this tradition and of the complex nature of cultural translation. As a shared skill, "singing the notes" binds experienced singers together and subtly restricts the participation of new singers. During the acculturation period in which newcomers gain competence with the notation and repertoire, they also learn social cues, official and unspoken etiquette, and how the print on the page differs from the music that is sung. New singers with strong voices and excellent reading skills could influence Sacred Harp regional styles very rapidly if they were not held back by the shapes; those who stay long enough to become competent shape-readers often deliberately hold themselves back in other ways, opening their eyes and ears to the subtleties of local practice. Shape-notes underscore the "stubbornness" of this unfamiliar music, in Walser's terms—"its insistence on a dialogic encounter in which its particularities matter" (Walser 2004: n.p.). The technical difficulties of reading shapes create a space for the development of mutually intelligible communication among people with widely varying religious, political, and moral beliefs.

Toward a Revisionist History of *The Sacred Harp*

The Sacred Harp is a teaching tool, propaganda vehicle, multivalent symbol, and transcendent canon all in one. In the Denson-book revision, line 179 of the original 242 tunes remain from the 1844 book, joined by 312 other tunes that have been composed in the intervening years or reprinted from other shape-note sources (see Table 2).[20] Tunebook revisers have the power to dismiss certain tunes from the active repertoire. The editors have recognized practical limits to the size of the book: leaders need to be able to hold it open with one hand and beat time with the other. The largest edition, the 1911 James revision, was considered impractically heavy, and thus in subsequent editions some tunes had to be removed if new ones were to be included. Choosing which tunes to remove is a touchy business, involving both the popularity of the tune in question and the feelings of the composer's living relatives, if any. It would be unthinkable to remove a song by a living composer. The 1991 revision process included statistical analysis of Sacred Harp convention minutes to determine which songs were led the least. Raymond Hamrick, a composer and member of the revision committee, told me that the near universal adoption and praise of the 1991 revision was a matter of both pride and relief for the committee members.

The existence of the tunebook relieves certain pressures of oral transmission. One need not learn the whole repertoire in a mnemonic order, for example, or worry about forgetting a song that is rarely sung. Then again, that song might be removed from the next edition, due to the revisers' emphasis on use-value. If people don't bother leading a song, it isn't worth keeping in the canon at the expense of possible additions, newly composed or old.

When a leader chooses a song he calls out its page number rather than its title. Many singers must flip through the tunebook only to find a song whose words and melody they already know—another practice that ties less experienced singers to the book. Twentieth-century revisers took care to preserve pagination as they made changes, printing a new tune on a deleted tune's page rather than adding all the new tunes at the end of the book. As John Bealle has observed, "The implication of page tracking . . . is

Table 2: **A Summary of Revisions to the Denson Book Line**

1844	242 songs compiled by B. F. White.
1850	102 songs added as appendix.
1859	74 songs added as appendix.
1869	Last B. F. White edition; 129 songs added, 49 removed, one page change.
1902	Cooper Revision.
1911	James Revision; 82 songs added to 1869 B. F. White edition for a total of 580; two page changes. (The Cooper and James revisions had different supporters and each has since been revised several times. The following editions are the successors of the James Revision.)
1936	Denson Revision; 41 songs added, 175 removed, 94 page changes, 446 songs total.
1960	103 songs added, 549 songs total.
1966	12 songs added, 22 removed (all of which had been added in 1960), nine page changes.
1971	All songs retained; one page change.
1991	1991 Revision; 60 songs added, 46 removed, 560 songs total.

Note: Of the original 242 tunes in the 1844 edition, 179 remain in the 1991 revision, together with 312 other tunes which have been composed in the intervening years or reprinted from other shape-note sources. (Adapted from Bealle 1997.)

a transcendent *Sacred Harp*, of which the actual revisions are but tangible manifestations" (1997: 150). The most current edition of *The Sacred Harp* always encompasses the entire available canon of tunes, with two hundred years of compositions and arrangements rubbing shoulders in no apparent order or hierarchy—just as the singers themselves interact, as some practitioners have told me.

While singers readily point out favorite songs, the active repertoire cannot shrink too much because of the rule against repeating a song within a singing day. During an April 2004 discussions@fasola.org exchange, Indiana singer Samuel Sommers offered one rationale for that practice:

> If a song gets done at a very fast speed and then later in a slow four beats, it might look like the later leader is setting the first one straight. Mr Barrett Ashley told a story of this happening many years ago at the Lookout Mountain Convention when two singers from families not on the best of terms chose to sing Montgomery. It took some diplomacy by the chair and his assistant to keep the first family from taking their dinner from its storage place under the back pews and going home early!

Not using the same song twice is a fine tradition, but it's not a law. If a child or a newcomer wants to sing something already used, no one is going to be offended. But I don't feel that tardiness or indolence should be offered as a reason to use a song a second time in one day. There are too many gems in the book.

As Sommers notes, exceptions are made for small children, elderly singers with memory problems, or special visitors (a journalist who only knows "Amazing Grace," for example). I have seen leaders in their nineties who no longer remember their children's names but can lead "the notes" and words of certain Sacred Harp songs from memory. If a song "belongs" to a singer who is present, especially an elderly person, she might be encouraged to lead her song even if it has already been called. But, generally, if a leader tries to repeat a number—owing to forgetfulness or late arrival—the class will reply, "It's been used." Roughly seventy to one hundred tunes are "used" in a full six- or seven-hour day of singing. This rhetoric of utility reinforces the idea that every page of *The Sacred Harp* possesses intrinsic value. Again, singers have drawn explicit parallels to the value of each individual at a convention.

Like the convention space and the seating arrangements, a leader's song choice indexes past experiences, improving singers' memory of their parts and creating a heightened emotional atmosphere—especially when a song is linked to a relative or a prominent local figure now deceased. An 87-year-old woman once poked me in the ribs when a leader called a number and whispered, "That's my brother's song, she's going to mess it up!" (She was correct: the leader faltered with the repeat sign.) Singers have strong memories of the favorite songs, favorite seats in the square, and distinctive voice qualities of past singers, all of which are linked to pages in the book. One could say the tunebook "functions as a portable graveyard," as Turner has written of family photo albums (1987: 150, following Sontag).

It is a cliché in Sacred Harp circles that this tunebook was second only to the Bible in ubiquity and status in nineteenth-century rural homes. Many old family portraits show the father and mother of the house each holding one of these essential books. (See Figure 20.) But as a physical object, the tunebook is not sacrosanct—certainly not as much so as a family Bible. Old editions may have sentimental or scholarly value, but at a singing virtually everyone uses the 1991 revision. Tunebooks are often left on the floor under pews, and in June 2001 I saw a lifelong singer kill a wasp with his book in an Alabama church. Still, singers do not treat the books as interchangeable; they rarely attend a singing without bringing their own copies, even when loaners will be available, and many tunebooks are filled with handwritten annotations. (See Figure 21.)

Figure 20: Isaac and Mary Rowe McLendon of Georgia in the 1890s. Isaac is holding the family Bible and a bottle of homemade communion wine; Mary holds an 1869 copy of *The Sacred Harp*. (Courtesy of the McLendon family.)

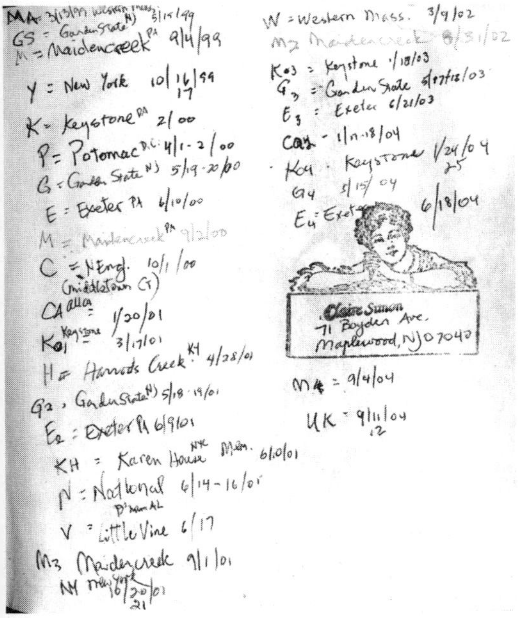

Figure 21: Annotations in singers' books. Top: Claire Simon's index for reading the coded references she writes next to individual tunes as they are led at a convention. Bottom: annotations by Virginia Douglas for "Ninety-Third Psalm" (31) and "Bethel" (27), using a similar coding system. Both women began singing Sacred Harp in New Jersey.

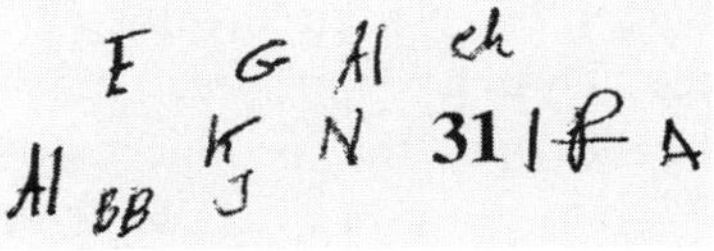

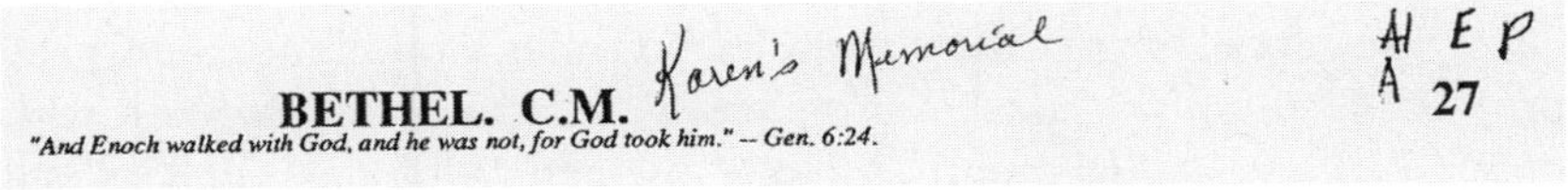

BETHEL. C.M.
"And Enoch walked with God, and he was not, for God took him." -- Gen. 6:24.

When the singing is in progress, the book functions as a symbol rich with potential. I have seen singers slam shut their books and their mouths at the same time, sitting out a song to express disapproval. A few times someone has deliberately dropped a book on the floor to protest a breach of convention etiquette. On the other hand, closing the book may signal one's competence and one's desire for total emotional engagement.

"Now You've Come to the Source"

The issues of transmission, competence, and affiliation that I have addressed thus far come together in the story of the Lee family, a Sacred Harp singing family from southern Georgia who have become something of a phenomenon in the national Sacred Harp community over the past decade. By the 1980s the Lee family considered Sacred Harp singing to be a local tradition that had died out elsewhere, though they knew related hymnody traditions continued in their own and other Primitive Baptist churches. They sang from an old edition of *The Sacred Harp* and had developed distinctive performance practices, including elaborate ornamentation performed at very slow tempos and a system of "walking time" according to the meter of the tune while leading. Sometimes a few people would sing the written harmony while standing at the center of three concentric circles of singers who droned the tonic and dominant pitches while walking in opposite directions. The Lees also maintained a close connection between their Sacred Harp singing and the practice of their Primitive Baptist faith, a connection that many in the national community do not observe so directly due to sectarian differences and an expressed ideology of pluralist tolerance.

Stories about the "discovery" of the Lee family have circulated among Sacred Harp singers all over the country for over ten years now. The version I present here is a composite of the variants I heard in the 1990s, all of which centered on the recording and circulation of a mysterious cassette tape. The story went like this: in the late 1980s, Jesse Roberts, an Atlanta Sacred Harp singer, stumbled upon the Lee family singers while looking for a church to join after a move to northern Florida. He was overwhelmed by the sound they produced, told some of his Atlanta singing friends about the family, and made a tape recording of their singing. Uncertain of how the family would react to the relatively secular and certainly very different stylistic approach of other Sacred Harp groups around the country, he proceeded cautiously: he labeled the tape "no copies" and shared it with only a few close singing friends. All were fascinated with the sound, as well as with the idea that any group of Sacred Harp singers could believe itself to exist in isolation. The tape gradually circulated through different areas of the country—Chicago, the Twin Cities, California, New England, and around the South—acquiring a certain mystique as it went along. Some copies were inevitably produced, but the recording was always shared in a private context, as special and sensitive material.

This isn't quite what happened, as it turns out. In fact, the tape had been made by the Lees themselves at a family occasion in the 1980s. A family member who attended college in Athens, Georgia, gave a copy of this tape to John Garst, a professor there. David Lee told me, "As I understand it, this is the tape that made the rounds up north. It was a tape of many of us singing around a dining room table (which was our way; we always stood around the dining room table for the sings held at someone's home). I have heard a copy of this 'underground tape' and recognized it as the one from Uncle Thomas's anniversary."[21] Meanwhile, David's cousin obtained a tape of the National Convention (recorded in Birmingham, Alabama) and gave it to David, who reports listening to it over and over. Family members also obtained and read Buell Cobb's book *The Sacred Harp: A Tradition and Its Music* in the early 1990s.

The typical narrative of the "discovery" of the Lee family does not include this exchange of media. Instead, it reproduces a classic fieldwork story, in which an outsider brings in modern technology to record and then circulate an exotic oral tradition. This narrative has its own earmarks of oral tradition; its formulas are familiar, and they may be recombined to suit different contexts and purposes. I should emphasize that the factual inaccuracies and simplifications in the basic narrative I recounted are the product of years of transmission, and certainly do not imply any misrepresentation on the part of Jesse Roberts, John Garst, or the other singers who interacted with the Lee family in the early 1990s.

Over a period of several years, a few experienced singers from the national Sacred Harp community went to Lee family singings in Hoboken, Georgia. To their relief, they were made very welcome. The Lees were delighted that Sacred Harp was not dying out, as they had long assumed, and religious differences did not seem to be problematic.[22] In the mid-1990s some Chicago singers organized a kind of debut for the Lee family, asking them to come teach a Sacred Harp singing school in Chicago to share their special performance practices with the wider community. The Lees agreed, and have since traveled to many out-of-state singings, participated on Internet discussion lists, and become full-fledged members of the national Sacred

Harp community. Diaspora singers make pilgrimages to sing with the Lees—"we do go as pilgrims there to that wellspring," a Minnesota singer wrote[23]—and like other lifelong singers, the Lees reciprocate by undertaking travels that have been compared to missionary work.[24]

The Lee family phenomenon strongly influenced Sacred Harp diaspora discourse and musical practice in the 1990s and thereafter. The homemade recording prepared the ground for their debut, and its near-clandestine circulation clothed the Lees themselves with a kind of esoteric authority. The family became instant celebrities, treated with profound respect. The singings they chose to attend gained status. If a Lee were present, he or she was always asked to perform one of the few special functions at a singing—delivering the opening or closing prayer, for example. In particular, the Lees were asked to deliver memorial lessons virtually everywhere they went. The purpose of the memorial lesson is remembrance of the dead and the sick, usually with some talk about the nature of the Sacred Harp tradition—and who better to perform such an office than the Lees, tradition-bearers *par excellence?*

I once wrote a paper on Sacred Harp memorial lessons and sent a copy of it to David Lee for feedback, with some trepidation. His response gave me pause: he thanked me for giving him insights into the tradition, because he had been acquainted with Sacred Harp memorial lessons for only six years. The Lees did not have memorial lessons at their singings prior to their involvement with the national community nor were they familiar with many of the other common-practice norms that have developed over the past century. Still, the mythology that has grown up around the Atlanta singers' near miraculous discovery, the mysterious bootleg tape, and the family's eventual emergence onto the national scene brooks no opposition. Like the Appalachian singers "discovered" by folklorists in the early twentieth century, the Lees have become quintessentially authentic. As one woman wrote to discussions@fasola.org, "I usually don't like the counting-out-loud, foot-stomping, or snapping of fingers during the rests. . . . Of course, if David or Clark[e] Lee is droning the count, I have no objection whatsoever. They could stand on their heads and lead with their feet, and the singing would be just great."[25]

Some consider the Lees to be the ultimate traditional Sacred Harp singers, despite the long gap in their involvement with the Southern singing community that has vehemently defended itself as practicing and defining "traditional Sacred Harp" for many generations. The Lees' apparent isolation has become the measure of their authenticity, and their commodification has served an essential role in producing that authenticity. This point is not lost on other Southern singing families, some of whom quietly resent being relegated to less-traditional status even as they acknowledge the musical talent and personal charisma of the Lee family. As one singer told me, "It's putting some other families' noses out of joint."

When I raised this issue with David Lee, he responded that he cannot understand "what they would have to be jealous of. We have changed to be like them because we admire them and look up to them so much. I can't see that we have supplanted them or usurped them in any way. Why anyone would think we were special is more than I can know. I suppose, on an intellectual level I can understand it, but we have never felt that we had anything to share with the others besides our love and respect for them."[26] But the veneration of the Sacred Harp diaspora is a force to be reckoned with. The Hoboken annual all-day singing has swelled to become one of the largest Sacred Harp gatherings in the country, drawing several hundred singers a year, an exceptional number for a one-day singing. The Hoboken singing uses the Cooper book, but because of the Lee family's reputation it draws large numbers of Denson book singers—a fact that is plainly audible at the singing. There is frequent discord in the alto section, as experienced Denson book singers neglect to look down at the Cooper books in their hands.

I first visited the Hoboken singing in March 2002. All day Saturday the assembled class observed typical convention procedure; the sound and style of the proceedings were much like those at any other large Sacred Harp convention that draws singers from distant states, except for notably slower tempos on some tunes. But the highlight of the Lee convention was reputed to be an evening meeting at Mars Hill Primitive Baptist Church, where the Lees and other local church members would sing from Lloyd's Hymnal, a Primitive Baptist hymnbook that contains words but no musical notation. Previous visitors described this event as the apotheosis of Sacred Harp singing, pure oral tradition in a worshipful atmosphere with no preacher—the last a crucial point, since many of the visiting singers would not have been comfortable in a Primitive Baptist church service.

Upon attending the evening singing, however, I discovered that in practice many singers continued to rely on printed notation rather than trying to learn tunes or ornaments by ear. There were no official song leaders, but a member of the Lee family collected requests for songs; virtually all the hymns requested were those sung to tunes printed in *The Sacred Harp* (as the visitors knew from listening to tapes of the Lees). Singers whispered *Sacred Harp* page numbers and song titles to one another so they could sing a tune or harmony part that they already knew. It was the *idea* of a purely oral tradition that appealed.

The plainest churches, most isolated regions, thickest rural Southern accents, and most evidently "oral" or "improvised" practices have enormous appeal to many new Sacred Harp singers, from the North and South alike. Their nostalgia suddenly seems less like a fantasy of privileged moderns and more like a celebration of places that really exist in America, places that can transport them back to an earlier time to interact with simple, friendly, naturally musical people. In this context it is no surprise that some singers refer to a visit to the Lees as a pilgrimage—nor that by now some use the same word with an ironic bite, rolling their eyes at a worshipfulness they view as overly pious and pretentious. These latter singers have never suggested to me that the Lee family has deliberately cultivated such a following; to the contrary, they express sympathy that the family must deal with a flood of pilgrims and they worry that some of these visitors are indulging in a kind of fetishism.[27]

Oral traditions possess some prestige in America today, but it is prestige grounded largely in nostalgia. Orality continues to serve as a marker of otherness, anachronism, naïveté, and irrationality.[28] But lifelong Southern singers have every reason to confirm and actively perform some of the positively valued aspects of this stereotype complex. It brings them respectful recognition, and it might help to perpetuate regional musical practices that have proved of little interest to many of their children and grandchildren. As David Carlton has written of another prominent singing family, "Plane-hopping northerners and urbanite southerners are willing to travel to remote Sand Mountain and drink from the well the Woottens and their fellow keepers of the tradition have protected over the decades" (Carlton 2003: 58).

Moreover, the unnotated aspects of Sacred Harp singing can serve as both an attraction for visitors and a protection from them. Like singers who cannot "sing the notes," those who have never sung with "traditional singers" are recognizable from their performance practice and do not receive authority in the community. In some cases "oral" elements that could easily be notated are deliberately withheld, like the raised sixths that were once printed in *The Sacred Harp* but removed in the next revision. David Lee himself did not attempt to represent ornaments when he transcribed his family's version of "I Walked Abroad" for a new collection of shape-note tunes. After he and Clarke Lee sang the song with New England singer Aaron Girard in March 2002, David Lee said, "Now you've come to the source, now you've drunk from the fountain."

Lee's half-joking remark bears a family resemblance to Hugh McGraw's "Well, you'll learn." It is a self-aware claim of competence, authority, and good will toward an eager student. Lee knew that Girard had learned the tune from a tape, and recalls that "[N]obody else that we asked had ever heard that tune. So when we got the chance to sing it with Aaron, knowing that we were the only ones that could . . . we did it to continue, by extension to him, our weak efforts to repay the Sacred Harp community at large for all they had done for us."[29] In some ways this family's Sacred Harp history is more like that of the Chicago singers than those of other Southern singing families. They were a small group singing in isolation and inventing local practices to suit their own interests and needs. "We didn't involve anyone else in the universe," Judy Hauff said in the 2003 Chicago Founders' Lesson. "No, it was like coming up from an atomic blast," Marcia Johnson replied.

It is a peculiar paradox that the Lee family's isolation from the flourishing, continuous tradition of Southern Sacred Harp singing has made them paradigmatic exemplars of "traditional singing" to so many new Sacred Harp practitioners. But their "oral tradition" had tremendous appeal, supported by recorded renditions of songs so elaborately ornamented that singers could scarcely recognize familiar tunes from *The Sacred Harp*. A music that had become familiar was again rendered tantalizingly alien. Furthermore, the Lees' status as a family tended to evoke ideas of organic purity and natural musicianship. Geography, too, played an important role: Hoboken, a small town in the rural South, is a perfect pilgrimage site.

Like the Chicago singers, after they were "discovered"—and made their own discoveries—the Lees learned the norms of convention procedure, began holding conventions, and traveled to the conventions of singers who came to Hoboken. They have participated in the community's many written traditions, contributing songs to new collections of shape-note music, submitting convention minutes to the annual minutebook, and posting on the Sacred Harp listservs. They have made several recordings of their family singing style for preservation purposes, acknowledging that sustained contact with the national singing community will likely alter local practice. And Johnny Lee has joined the editorial committee of the Cooper revision of *The Sacred Harp*, forging yet another relationship between oral and written tradition in Sacred Harp transmission.

The Perils and Privileges of Oral and Written Transmission

In a group discussion held as part of a series of Sacred Harp singing schools in Western Massachusetts in the winter of 2001, an experienced New England singer suggested that the printed music "is about one hundredth of one millionth of what actually goes on. You can't, you can't reconstruct it out of genetic materials, from, I don't think, from the notation, because that's not the music, it's just sort of ink. . . . [I]t's 99 percent traditional, and . . . the notation is just sort of a mind-jogger."[30] His point is well taken, and it is an important thing to emphasize if one is interested in promoting Southern singing practices in Northern folk-revival communities. After all, if one could reconstruct the tradition from notation, one wouldn't need to travel, learn from lifelong singers, or otherwise participate in the national community. Contemporary scholars, and some singers, have often asserted that "it is ultimately not the printed page that is important in the singing" in order to emphasize that "there are everywhere glimmers of a living oral tradition in the Sacred Harp" (Cobb 1989: 44–45). When we consider the cultural authority that the category "oral tradition" now carries, these are not surprising claims. But one must take care not to underestimate the role of the written tradition when considering a musical community that recognizes composers, performs an explicit vocal representation of the notation before the words of every song, and experiences schisms based on publication rights and editorial choices.

The Sacred Harp tunebook valorizes rural Southern culture—so often stigmatized and stereotyped—while seemingly rendering that culture duplicable by urban folk revivalists, reenactment hobbyists, and early music choirs. But the intersections and contradictions that connect oral and written tradition provide a safeguard against facile and superficial acquisition of Sacred Harp practice even as the ready availability of the tunebook encourages its dissemination. A newcomer can find the tunebook in a library, read the "Rudiments of Music," practice realizing the shapes at home, or even sing all the voice parts with friends or family members, but she cannot learn certain markers of traditional practice without going to singings. All the singers will be carrying the same oblong tunebook, but their accents, ornaments, and gestures will testify to their origins and influences—as does each new revision of *The Sacred Harp,* at a slower rate of change. In the latest revision the tune names with colonial New England and nineteenth-century Southern resonances—"Boylston," "Concord," "Shawmut," "Alabama," "Georgia," "Newnan"—have been joined by "Wood Street" and

"Granville" (places in Chicago) and "Natick" (modern New England). Ted Mercer of Chicago has tunes called "Sheppard" and "O'Leary" in the 1991 revision, the first named in honor of a prominent Alabama singer and the second for Stephen O'Leary, the Chicago singer whose California wedding to Mary Rose Ogren inaugurated the California Convention.[31]

Steven Friedson has characterized tradition as "the recurrence of the possible" (Friedson 1996: 2). The Sacred Harp tradition is possible largely because it is portable: it developed in transit and effectively promotes its own recurrence. While singers acknowledge and seek out wellsprings of oral tradition, eager to "drink from the fountain," their practices constantly reiterate the importance of the tunebook: something that can be carried, cited, marked up, revised, and put in the hands of a newcomer anywhere as a tangible proof of Sacred Harp's musical distinctiveness and historical substance. *The Sacred Harp* and the annual convention system have engendered a sense of cyclical, cumulative singing experiences, in which each page acquires its own set of associations for individuals and local communities. As singers ascribe traditional authority with their musical choices, they inscribe layered memories in their books.

4

"Speaking May Relieve Thee"

TEXTED EVENTS AND EVENTFUL TEXTS

The Sacred Harp is full of stories about travelers, strangers, journeys, and death—compressed portraits of human uncertainty, anxiety, and isolation. Sacred Harp singers have made the book a traveling companion for over 150 years, and they use its Christian language to tell their own stories and articulate their hopes and fears. The book says, "I am a stranger here below" and asks "Oh, is there anyone like me?"[1] It defiantly asserts: "I'm glad that I am born to die . . . and I don't care to stay here long."[2] On another page, it gently acknowledges the frailty of that conviction: "Death is the gate to endless joy, and yet we dread to enter there."[3] It expresses bitter fears that "pleasure only blooms to die,"[4] then turns to say that "pleasure tunes my tongue."[5] Many times over it says, in different forms, "Farewell, vain world, I'm going home; I belong to this band, hallelujah."[6] These lines are like cables drawn taut across the hollow square, across the gap between loneliness and belonging, the joys and terrors of travel, fear of loss and hope of gain. They pull across the square and vibrate in the tense throats of singers; they pull across years of experience and bind certain moments together into memory books encompassing joy and mourning.[7]

Leaders don't always choose songs for the sake of their texts, and a given text means different things to different people, but sometimes a leader draws the class into his interpretation. One year at Holly Springs an elderly Texas man named Kelly Beard remarked that he had thought he might never make it to Holly Springs again; then he led "All Is Well" (122), with its poignant lines about resignation to death:

What's this that steals, that steals upon my frame?
Is it death, is it death?
If this be death, I soon shall be
From ev'ry pain and sorrow free.[8]

At the Midwest Convention in 2001, a local singer named Jerilyn Schumacher led "Morning Sun" (436), an upbeat major fuging tune with grim lyrics:

Your sparkling eyes and blooming cheeks
Must wither like the blasted rose;
The coffin, earth, and winding sheet
Will soon your active limbs enclose.[9]

She made no comments, but many of the singers present knew she was dying of cancer. Her friends sat on the front benches a few feet from her gaunt figure as she led; they sang hard and loud, a grueling and bittersweet experience. A year later, in the same room, the memorial committee read her name on the list of the deceased. When we sang "All Is Well" at that convention I thought of Kelly Beard; the man beside me leaned over with a catch in his throat to say he remembered singing the same song with Jerilyn.

When people ask how non-Christians can get anything out of Sacred Harp texts, these kinds of stories come to mind. For Christian singers, of course, the texts relate to a whole other world of personal narratives, especially in the realm of crises or confirmations of faith. In either case, such stories form another collection of repeated texts that singers cite to make sense of past experience and prefigure the future. Narrative "emphasizes retrospective intelligibility" (Rosaldo 1989: 132); these Sacred Harp stories not only explain how songs make sense but suggest how they might *always* have made sense—like messages only waiting to be decoded—and therefore how newer singers should expect them to become meaningful in the future. The songs in *The Sacred Harp* and the stories repeated at singings and on the road constitute a shared repertoire of expressive means in which each singer's vocabulary continually accrues different inflections.

Sacred Harp singers communicate, and inevitably sometimes miscommunicate, in their choice of song. At a convention they have few other opportunities to address the whole group, unless they are presenting a memorial lesson or wish to test the patience of the class by talking during their leading time. Outside of formal convention proceedings they continue to use songs to get points across: they cite snatches of text in conversation, or accomplish the same thing indirectly by humming part of a tune or referring to a page number. For some singers any two- or three-digit number has a message-in-a-bottle quality: phone numbers, license plates, gym locker combinations, and highway exit numbers all bring songs to mind. As Minnesota singer Martha Henderson reported to singings@fasola.org,

> It's strange how numbers take on a different significance when you have been singing Sacred Harp for a while.
>
> I was in Wal-Mart today, waiting to return something. You take a number and wait your turn. Number 64 was up on the scoreboard that they use to keep track of whose turn it is. Suddenly I thought, "64—Nashville!" and I heard the tune in my mind. . . .
>
> It's a strange feeling, standing there amid a crowd of people I don't know, who have no idea that Sacred Harp even exists—or driving down the freeway among all those cars, looking at all the numbers on the signs—hearing tunes in my mind, and knowing that I'm the only one there who can hear them. I feel both lonely and privileged—sometimes one more than the other, sometimes both at once. How wonderful it is, then, to go to a singing and be once more among people who, if they see the number 64, are just as likely as I am to hear Nashville in their minds. . . .
>
> It's like having a photo album with me all the time, on signs, price tags, everywhere. The numbers remind me of absent friends.[10]

Singers reading the collection of lines in the first paragraph of this chapter will also be reminded of absent friends. They will hear the music as they read the words—maybe just the melody line of their own voice part, maybe a particular person's voice, maybe a whole class at a convention. Some can unwind stories from each of these lines, as though my brief citations were loose ends to spools of thread that spin freely on the axis of memory.

Singers are extraordinarily articulate about their Sacred Harp experience and what it means to them, being accustomed to accounting for their commitment to the tradition. Diaspora singers constantly try to explain Sacred Harp to friends and family. Lifelong singers must field questions from newcomers and sometimes craft longer presentations for singing schools. Traditions of rural Southern storytelling and preaching contribute to the proliferation of Sacred Harp narrative styles; when I interviewed older Southern singers, they often came prepared with well-worn and well-polished anecdotes that they unpacked from single statements or song texts in the manner of Scriptural exegesis. Finally, the fact of singers' ideological diversity, the long hours they spend traveling together or hosting one another, and the fundamental tenets of mutual tolerance and "leaving politics at the door" combine to encourage the development of singing-oriented discourse: in many social situations Sacred Harp itself seems to be the only safe topic for conversation.

Faced with a wealth of recurrent themes that are constantly remixed, revised, and resolved into new images of identity, commitment, and conviction, I will employ an analytical mode indebted to just such repertoires of anecdote and exegesis. Narrative performance makes "events grow texted," as Kathleen Stewart writes (Stewart 1996: 181). I will pursue this point while also keeping its mirror image in view: that texts grow eventful, perhaps song texts most of all.

Texted Event: "I Know Where You Learned to Sing!"

I can point to a single moment when I realized how entrenched my local singing attachments had become. A few weeks after moving from Chicago to Massachusetts, I attended the 2000 session of the New England Convention in Middletown, Connecticut. Things proceeded more or less as I expected—until a leader on his way into the square took a starting pitch from a pitch pipe. With a visceral shock of indignation, I immediately shut my book and sat out his lesson. At that point I recognized myself as a Chicago singer.

As I sat with my book and wondered when I had become so dogmatic, I remembered my sense of gratification the first time a singer pinned a regional identity on me. The first time I met Paula McGray, she was sitting next to me on the tenor front bench at the Young People's Singing in Nashville in 1999. Paula was from Massachusetts; she assiduously worked Southern Sacred Harp singings into her frequent business travels.[11] She had a powerful voice and I had to work hard to hear my own. After a couple of songs, she gave me a sidelong look and said, "I know where you learned to sing!" To Paula, I was plainly a Chicago singer. I had learned as much as I could from a young man named D.J. Hatfield, who in turn had emulated Chicago singer Ted Mercer and Georgia singers Richard DeLong and David Lee. D.J. had also listened to homemade tapes of certain Southern singings over and over, tapes given to him by Midwestern singers who felt his voice was too heavily influenced by a particular New England style; he had loaned those same tapes to me. Paula could trace this history of influences in my timbre and ornaments, though I had been singing Sacred Harp in Chicago for only two years. Paula's assessment of my voice provided me with a singing home, a family style. Having been recognized as a Chicago singer, I began to identify as such, and leaving Chicago came to represent a great personal loss.

The following year, as I tried on my new identity as a singer from Cambridge, I felt disheartened. I missed the Chicago singers and the set of ideals we explicitly and implicitly shared, the community cohesion betrayed by timbre and ornaments, the family style. Above all, I missed feeling my voice was recognized and understood by other singers, as Paula had recognized it in Nashville. Chicago and New England are not closely linked in the Sacred Harp diaspora.

The Chicago singers had their differences; even the most idealistic newcomer could never see them as a monolithic tradition-bearing entity. In the 1980s their local group experienced schisms over the question of allegiance to Southern traditional singing (as opposed to a folk choir, old-time, or early music model), and differences of approach and allegiance remain today. But Chicago singers also had a base of integrative experiences that had produced fairly consistent local norms. The labor of hosting two large singings a year, the Midwest Convention and the Chicago Anniversary Singing, required coordinated decision-making and commitment from local singers. Enthusiastic new singers like myself were soon asked to serve on convention committees, paired with people who could teach us the subtleties of arranging or giving a memorial lesson. Experienced singers gave new singers important responsibilities, helped them travel to Southern singings where they would be recognized as Chicago singers, and recounted local history to them in the form of the Founders' Lesson and less formal narratives.

Boston-area singers were comparatively fragmented. The New England Convention rotates between Massachusetts, Vermont, and Connecticut on a three-year cycle, so there is no year-to-year continuity of convention officers or hosting responsibilities. Some area singers barely tolerated the convictions and practices of local organizers, and some avoided local singings entirely, only seeing their fellow local singers at large conventions. I spoke with several singers who traveled widely to out-of-state conventions but rarely attended the weekly singings in Newton organized by the "Norumbega Harmony" chorus. A newly established weekly singing at Boston University operated for many months without any crossover with the Norumbega Harmony singings or third-Sunday Charlestown singings, although some of the BU singers made trips South during this period.

From the perspective of singers I interviewed in the South, the Midwest, and on the West Coast, the singing communities in Vermont, eastern Massachusetts, and Connecticut seemed to revolve around a few core groups of folk-revival choirs led by charismatic men with formal Western music training, men like Larry Gordon (Village Harmony, Word of Mouth Chorus), Stephen Marini (Norumbega Harmony), and Neely Bruce (Wesleyan choral groups). Similar groups exist around the country, but they are especially common in New England, home to the early "tunesmiths." Marini himself notes that "New England at first developed a regional pattern of Sacred Harp singing based not in local communities but rather in performance groups specializing in *The Sacred Harp* and early New England hymnody" (Marini 2003: 83). These choral groups typically approach Sacred Harp as a participatory musical tradition, but they do so with an emphasis on historical reenactment and performance for an audience. They give concerts and produce professional recordings. They differentiate between open singings, public workshops, and closed rehearsals. In concert programs, CD liner notes, and other forms of print media they often refer to their repertoire as traditional early American music without reference to current Sacred Harp practice (see Chapter 5).

These practices have led to uneasy relations with Southern traditional singers and the diaspora singers who identify with and emulate them. These people take exception to the claims of authority, ownership, or first-mover status made by some New England singers—those who "have never sung in the South, so they have little idea that the tradition is in fact Southern, rather than an early New England tradition that was simply forgotten since 1800 or so," as a Boston-area singer complained.[12] Diaspora singers likewise take issue with the suggestion that, in Marini's words, "Just as New England singers sparked the first Sacred Harp revival in 1976 by organizing the first annual convention in the North, twenty-five years later they are pioneering the next phase of that revival by creating the first viable regional network of local singings outside the South" (Marini 2003: 84). What might constitute a "viable regional network" is a matter of debate in the national community.

I myself first encountered songs from the Sacred Harp in a folkish New England context—at my progressive high school in Vermont, where the weekly community "Sing" relied heavily on folk-revival repertoire. When I first moved to Chicago, I told people I'd learned to sing in New England; even when I didn't, my vocal style and favorite songs betrayed my background to experienced Chicago singers. But as I began attending conventions in the Midwest and the South, I learned that citing an affiliation with New England singers would not earn me much credibility. Indeed,

New England singers often downplayed their regional affiliations when I encountered them at conventions in other parts of the country. They preemptively established themselves as dissenters in their home scene and complained that too few of their fellow singers recognized the importance of travel.

After my move back to New England, these discourses of affiliation, recognition, and disavowal resolved into my refusal to sing in the key of a pitch-pipe. It took a return to New England—for which I had felt nostalgic longings in my first years of Sacred Harp singing in Chicago—for me to recognize the fulfillment of Paula's prophecy. She knew where I learned to sing, and it wasn't in New England.

Eventful Text: "Speaking May Relieve Thee"

The New England Sacred Harp scene has suffered from some of the same divisive circumstances that afflicted the California singing communities discussed in Chapter 1 (see Herman 1997), but with an intensity born of local historical awareness. The long tradition of folk-revival shape-note singing in New England, along with historical and geographical links to early shape-note composers, gives many New England singers a sense of ownership that does not rely upon a connection to Southern practice. While singers in places like Chicago "may have been more inclined to 'trust the tradition' than to invent themselves as the consequence of regional history" (Bealle 1997: 210), singers who imagine New England as Sacred Harp's homeland need not imagine themselves as part of the obligation network of a South-based diaspora. Some of these singers resent the authoritative manner of people who have "been South" and who come back full of instructions on authentic traditional practice. These conflicts of authority can result in an undercurrent of irritation at local singings.

At one local Boston-area singing in 2002, the progression of leaders was interrupted by a debate over whether the sixth should be raised in a minor tune by Billings that appeared in a new shape-note compilation. In New England, the question of what would be "historically authentic" performance practice in Billings's day had as much weight as what Southern singers would "naturally" do when faced with an unfamiliar minor song. Singer A, usually a strong advocate for raised sixths on traditional grounds, used historical evidence to come down on the side of natural sixths in this case. On the ride home, another singer was frustrated by the apparently arbitrary nature of evidence-gathering in such arguments, feeling that Singer A had simply been "flexing" for the sake of appearing authoritative. I could only speculate that since this particular song had not been "traditionalized" as part of the Southern Sacred Harp repertoire, Singer A had concluded that the next most authentic thing would be to do what Billings would have done.

Some diaspora singers have the same visceral reaction to this kind of argument that I had to the pitch pipe in the hollow square. Of course, these reactions are partly a matter of personality; some find such discussions annoyingly pedantic in any sphere. But others might gladly participate in these debates on the discussions list while finding them infuriating at a singing.

Massachusetts singings are especially prone to conversation in the square because of their "free call" leading system. At local singings I have attended elsewhere, people usually take turns leading by going around the room—no one is "arranging," but there is an orderly progression. Singers are expected to have a number ready when their turn comes. In the "free call" system anyone may call out a page number at the end of a song.[13] While some praise this system as being more dynamic—because it encourages people to lead "when the spirit moves them" and to react to the previous leader's choice—it also slows the momentum of a singing and decreases the number of leaders. There are gaps between songs as people try to defer to shy leaders, and discussions grow out of these gaps.

But why shouldn't people talk in the square? Is it that important to get through as many songs as possible at a three-hour monthly local singing? There are singers on all sides of this issue, and some find social and intellectual stimulation in debating performance practice across the square or recapping old controversies for the benefit of new singers. But those whose stomachs clench at such discussions attribute their reaction not only to a desire to spend more time singing, but also to the ethos of a separation of spheres around which so much Sacred Harp discourse and practice revolves.[14] They have internalized this ethos to the point of embodied response; in Bourdieu's terms, their "practical belief is not 'a state of mind' . . . but rather a state of the body" (Bourdieu 1990: 68). These singers become frustrated when others transgress the boundaries that mark off time for singing and time for discussion. They are outraged when singers bypass the repertoire of expressive means at their disposal, the opportunity to speak through one's choice of song. Singers resent being held captive by storytelling when they could be bringing their own thoughts and expressive impulses to the practice of singing, sometimes against the grain of the leader's intentions.[15] As the dictum to newcomers goes, Sacred Harp is not listeners' music.

Respecting this separation of spheres requires active conflict-avoidance at conventions. Participants treasure the noncombative atmosphere and guard it carefully. As David Lee wrote to me,

> I do live in the same world as everyone else and I participate fully (current entertainment, news of the day, voting, culture wars, etc.) but that is a completely different part of me. . . . My church and my singing are "above the fray" of common life. . . . I am certain that my own ideas of right and wrong will be quite different from that of many of the people that I sing with around the country, but I'm sure that applies to us all. I have told a couple of people that I only have a relationship with them through Sacred Harp. Without that we wouldn't be friends, indeed we wouldn't even be acquaintances. If I ever leave Sacred Harp singing or if they do, we won't have anything else in common. . . . I subscribe to what I heard another Sacred Harp singer say one time: "What it would take for a fellow Sacred Harper to hurt my feelings would bring blisters on a wash pot."[16]

Another singer, who identified herself as politically liberal, told me that she felt certain a few of the people she sang with were extremely conservative, racist, homophobic, "could be even KKK types," but if they were going to singings they couldn't be all bad—and, she noted with humorous pragmatism, if they were going to singings they didn't have time to be "out burning crosses." Using a similar line of reasoning, some Christian singers hope that any exposure to Christian traditions will somehow impact nonbelievers for the better. Other singers evince tolerance through building personal relationships that transgress their usual norms: for example, they might condemn or mourn homosexuality as a sin in private conversation but show tremendous love and support for the gay singers they know personally. Singers who view such behavior as hypocritical tend to self-select out of diaspora conventions. Those who remain prioritize "leaving politics at the door" over taking an activist or proselytizing stance at singings.

On rare occasions the hollow square does become a venue for explicit political ideology. At the 2002 Georgia State Convention a longtime New England singer—who had recently moved to Georgia and was already well traveled in the South—put out leaflets on chairs advocating an end to the "war on drugs." Several other singers who held disparate views on this issue instantly collected them up again. Putting out leaflets appeared to be this singer's response to being taken to task for speaking about the matter during his lesson at the Western Massachusetts Convention two weeks before (when he had connected his comments with the song "Liberty" [137] and

the lines "No more beneath th' oppressive hand / Of tyranny we groan"[17]).
Clearly, distributing print matter was still viewed as crossing a line. He was
not called to lead until the second day of the convention, when he led "The
Christian Warfare" (179) without further comment. At another convention,
at which I was not present, a local preacher who had been asked to deliver a
prayer made remarks that implicitly condemned some young singers from
New England who were transgressing local norms for church apparel: some
women were wearing casual pants and men were wearing jewelry. A few
prominent local singers—who probably adhered to these norms personally,
at least in church—reportedly walked out during the prayer to support their
visitors. Stories about the unusual events at these conventions circulated
widely at socials, on car trips to singings, and in conversation at breaks during other conventions, but despite their broad circulation, these narratives
themselves remained in the sphere of private discourse. The events they
describe did not appear at all in the lengthy, glowing reports of these same
conventions that were posted to singings@fasola.org.

Like David Lee, most singers try to keep such "culture wars" issues out
of the singing room. But sometimes conflicts internal to the singing community arise at a convention. At the 1999 Southern Wisconsin Singing,
for example, some tension developed between singers from Minnesota
and downstate Illinois. Over the previous few years the dates for the Minnesota and Illinois state conventions had tended to conflict, splitting the
broader midwestern Sacred Harp community between the two singings.
The Illinois State Convention was run by a small group of downstate singers and was an important part of the Chicago singing community's founding narrative; it was Chicago's "Well, you'll learn" convention, predating
the establishment of the Midwest Convention and the Anniversary Singing
in Chicago (see Chapter 3). But the Illinois State had grown small; it was
far from major airports and couldn't promise the fun of a big city weekend
for distant visitors. The Minnesota Convention was a relatively new, very
strong Twin Cities singing whose organizers had not yet settled on a stable
date formula. Resentment surfaced when some singers thought that Minnesota organizers were choosing dates that would be most convenient for
high-status Southern visitors at the expense of the smaller but older Illinois
State Convention. Chicago and Wisconsin singers felt torn between supporting old friends at the more intimate Illinois State and going to Minnesota, where they could enjoy a very strong convention, catch up with the
distant singing friends it would attract, and promote exchange with their
own conventions.

During dinner at the 1999 Wisconsin singing, which took place six weeks after the two state conventions had fallen on the same weekend, several independent discussions developed around this problem. A few Minnesota singers noted that *they* had not been included in the process of choosing their state's convention date; another said pointedly "We'll talk about it later." When the singing reconvened, Ted Mercer of Chicago chose to lead the tune "The Grieved Soul" (448b):

> Come, my soul and let us try
> For a little season,
> Ev'ry burden to lay by,
> Come and let us reason.
> What is this that casts thee down?
> Who are those that grieve thee?
> Speak and let the worst be known?
> Speaking may relieve thee.[18]

Mercer had also cited this text in a posting to singings@fasola.org shortly after the two conventions, as part of an exhortation to the two scheduling committees to communicate with one another and find a way to eliminate the date conflict in future. Thus those who subscribed to the list, including most of the singers from Minnesota and Illinois, were positioned to interpret his choice of tune as a strong reminder of his written comments.

"Speaking may relieve thee" is an eventful text for me, with an ironic cast in my memory. It marks a point when a singer demonstrated how to make a point *without* speaking in the hollow square. This text makes an appeal to reason and, in Mercer's usage, points to the long-term insignificance of such community skirmishes—the injunction "speak and let the worst be known" and the prediction that "speaking will relieve thee" together suggest that airing the details of a conflict will reveal its triviality. But Mercer's own example definitively locates such talk-therapy outside the hollow square. Making points through song choices might be considered less rhetorically forceful than speaking directly, but it addresses the competing demands of conflict-avoidance and individual agency by according interpretive power to the class. It capitalizes on music's "untalkability," the quality that allows for "a heightened looseness of reference, and personal and group appropriation" (Turino 1999: 249). After all, Mercer might have just felt like singing 448b after dinner that day. No doubt many people didn't think twice about his choice.

In its humor, subtlety, and invitation to complicity, this rendition of "The Grieved Soul" seemed to put contentious debates about convention dates, raised sixths, and leading style in their place: a place removed from the singing. Using songs in this way preserves the ritual fabric of the convention without denying the existence of conflict. Singing can be a form of sounding resistance, but it need not demand a response.

Texted Event: "These Folks Really Get Into It"

In the summer of 1999, after two years of encountering tactful misgivings whenever I told singers that I'd first encountered Sacred Harp in New England, I listened with surprise as lifelong Southern singers at the National Convention in Alabama heaped praise upon a new Massachusetts convention they had attended a few months before. The Western Massachusetts Sacred Harp Convention first took place that March, and I began to hear a lot about it by June. The Alabama singers told me that this was a traditional-style convention, that there were an amazing number of young people in attendance, and that these young people seemed to be the ones responsible for the "traditional" qualities of the singing.

This new breed of college-age singers in Western Massachusetts assuaged an anxiety that had been growing among diaspora singers in the 1990s. The New England folk choirs and college groups attracted young people to shape-note singing, which everyone agreed was wonderful, but what were these young people learning about traditional Sacred Harp practice? Very little, according to many singers I spoke to in the late nineties. My own experience in Chicago suggested that young people might be very enthusiastic about traditional-style conventions, which seem to exemplify the ideals of cultural authenticity through egalitarian community music-making that form a large part of the folk-choir attraction in the first place. But who would teach the New England young people traditional practice? It was a worrisome issue for the singers I knew.

The Western Massachusetts Convention showed that some of the New England young people had indeed learned something about Southern practice and were subsequently unsatisfied with the existing Sacred Harp scene in New England. Establishing a new annual convention is a major gesture of self-representation. New conventions are publicized nationwide via word of mouth, the Internet, mailings, and the minutebook. The local community has to find an appropriate space, coordinate rides and housing, feed a crowd that may number in the hundreds, and make every visitor feel welcome. They are also incurring an obligation to attend some of the home conventions of their visitors, which can require significant expenditures of time and money. After the convention, gossip and reports to Sacred Harp newsletters or the fasola.org lists provide feedback on the quality of the event and affect future attendance. The founding of the Western Massachusetts Convention was no minor undertaking, and many singers speculated that it was a deliberate act of disassociation from the existing New England Convention.

The Western Massachusetts Convention sprang from years of regular local singings in the Amherst-Northampton area. Here too the singing community revolved around a few charismatic individuals, but with a different ethos from the folk-revival choirs. The most prominent of these local organizers was Tim Eriksen, a gifted singer with a master's degree in ethnomusicology and a performance history that joined punk music and traditional ballads.[19] As Chicago singer Ted Johnson posted to the singings list after his first visit to the Western Massachusetts Convention,

> [A]side from demographic and geographic factors—plus all the hard work that always has to get done—building up a new singing scene seems also to depend on some particularly energetic or charismatic character being around to help spark the mixture (a mixture that in this case had been around for about ten years). If you think about the various SH-singing regions, you can tick off in your mind different people who have performed this function. In the case of Western Massachusetts, it just might have been (Cordelia's Dad's) Tim Eriksen (who could probably have gotten a singing going in a desert). He lives in Minnesota now, but the mixture he and others left behind is really cooking. I mean, these folks really get into it. Some even get to shaking. (As one observer said, you half expect someone to start speaking in tongues. So they are some serious singers.)[20]

This posting not only praises Eriksen's charismatic organizational abilities but draws attention to a much-remarked attribute of many Western Massachusetts singers and leaders: their participation is so emotional and physical that it can seem closer to the trance traditions of charismatic churches than the tightly controlled, masterful leading style of Southern lifelong singers who grew up in the singing-school tradition. Some visiting singers are taken aback by this local style—"shaking" and "speaking in tongues" suggest an inward-directed transcendent experience rather than an outward-directed concern with the group experience of the whole hollow square. But as Johnson implies, their sincerity as "serious singers" is unmistakable, even if its charismatic aspect is not universally praised. (I will return to the issue of local aesthetics and performative approaches to leading in Chapter 6.) The singers in this area manifest visible signs of the intense physical effects that virtually all long-term Sacred Harp singers describe, among them the trance processes catalogued by Judith Becker: "emotional arousal, loss of sense of self, cessation of inner language, and an extraordinary ability to withstand fatigue" (2004: 29). As a group, Western Massachusetts singers are exceptional in their outward display of these effects; they rock back and forth in their seats, look skyward or shake their heads while leading, and stamp their feet.

Tim Eriksen, his bandmate Cath Oss (from the punk/folk ensemble Cordelia's Dad), and a few other young New England singers built up close relationships with certain Southern singing families, relationships that were publicized by word of mouth and through postings on sing-ings@fasola.org. The convention organizers also made a series of choices that clarified their affiliations and loyalties. They deliberately differentiated themselves from Boston-area Sacred Harp singing by adopting the title of "Western Massachusetts Convention," even though there was no "Massachusetts State Convention." They actively recruited Southern singers, going to great lengths not only to demonstrate gratitude for their presence but also to give them opportunities to exert their influence. They coached local singers on how to produce appropriate and sufficient food for dinner-on-the-grounds, something that had been a problem at other New England conventions. They included prayers in the convention proceedings, although observant Christians were probably a minority among the attendees, and they instituted a traditional-style memorial lesson. Finally, they submitted an account of the proceedings to the annual minutebook. The protocol and format decisions made manifest in the minutes, from prayers to committee members to arranging choices, told knowledgeable readers how this local singing community placed itself in relation to Sacred Harp practice in the South.

The second Western Massachusetts Convention, in March of 2000, was as well-received as the first. That spring I heard many singers in the Midwest and South make pointed comparisons between the fresh new upstart convention in Western Mass and the established New England Convention (then twenty-five years old). An eerily consistent routine unfolded when I told Sacred Harp friends around the country that I would be moving to Boston in June of 2000: first, many wrinkled up their faces and made sympathetic remarks about the divisive atmosphere I'd have to face in the local singing community. Then they brightened and made comforting gestures when they remembered that the Western Mass singers would be within driving distance. The Western Massachusetts Convention generated so much goodwill among visiting singers that even when attendees reported on "mistakes"—like a sign over the treble section indicating it was for women with high voices, when male trebles are a prized component of Sacred Harp's harmonic texture—they employed the generous rhetoric of "Well, they'll learn." Similar perceived lapses of protocol at the New England Convention were the subject of irritable pronouncements on its "deliberate isolationism" and "stubbornness." They were read as *refusals* to learn, denials of the narrative of conversion to Southern traditional practice.

When communities host conventions, locals are often outnumbered by out-of-town visitors. The first Western Massachusetts Convention drew many of the same singers as the New England Convention. Yet somehow the core organizers articulated a distinctive local identity as they pulled together singers from the connected and contested spheres of the long-standing New England Sacred Harp scene. In the following years they continued to make careful choices in their self-representation, from holding a series of singing schools in the weeks leading up to their convention to producing a CD that testifies to the style of their singing. Most importantly, local organizers articulated and promoted themes of obligation, respect, and integrity as key attributes of convention behavior. At the final pre-convention singing school in March of 2001, they enjoined new singers to lay claim to these ideals in a broad-ranging discussion of expectations for the upcoming event:

> *Eliza Cavanaugh:* One thing I regret, well one of the things I regret, from the first Western Mass convention, which was the first convention that I was part of hosting, was that I wasn't paying close enough attention to the things that were happening that weren't being said in the leading. Like, I could follow if somebody wanted to lead something straight through. But if there was something that was happening that was a little different from how I was used to doing it, that was just kind of getting communicated, I was sort of resisting doing it. So I would say that mostly for the new people, to just like pay attention to how it's happening even if it's different from what you're used to, and go with what's happening in the room.
>
> *Singer 2:* Could I say that that's one of the great things about conventions, because you get your group and you get the Montclair group and you get the Vermont group, and they're all doing

a little bit different things, and that's—to me that's one of the glories of the convention format, is because we're not doing it our own stick-in-the-mud way. And I think every individual group has their own sort of habits that they get into, but then to see how others are doing it, I think that's one of the glories of the convention. . . .

Singer 3: At the New York Convention it was put this way in the singing school: that there's a healthy tension between honoring the leader and honoring the tradition. As a leader when you get up to lead you want to honor the tradition as much as you can, and as a class you want to honor the leader as much as you can. And so the tension is a good thing.

Tim Eriksen: As long as the tradition doesn't become a sort of abstract thing, with a capital T—just because then it's not—it's a sort of rhetorical tradition.[21]

Over the course of the singing school, Eriksen reinforced the ideal of respectful hospitality: local singers should respect a visiting leader's wishes and local leaders should respect the abilities and inclinations of the diverse assembled class, without anyone getting hung up on pedantic claims about tradition "with a capital T." This group had obviously had this kind of discussion before, and their revisiting of these points demonstrated a conscious engagement with the question of what a convention should be and accomplish. Even a singer who found this discussion "a little Sunday schoolish, like preaching to the choir" still conceded, "You can't fault them for insincerity. They can seem a little over-earnest out there, but at least they really think through what they're doing."

Like the Chicago Founders' Lesson, the discussions at the singing school established a coherent set of local ideals. But to maintain and develop this local integrity on a larger scale, the Western Massachusetts Convention would have to become a particular kind of destination in the hierarchy of interconnected spaces that make up the national Sacred Harp community. I began to see how this might happen on the drive to and from this same singing school.

Paula McGray and I were traveling with Sally House, who had come from Rhode Island and picked us up in Boston on her way to Amherst. It was a long trip from Rhode Island to Amherst, especially considering that a big convention would be held in the same area the following weekend. But Sally was still deciding whether she would be at the convention. Her daughters Karen and Kelly were two of the core members of the group that established the Western Massachusetts Convention; the minutebooks show the three women leading together at the first two conventions. Karen had died very suddenly in the summer of 2000, and Sally wasn't sure she felt able to participate in the third convention without her.

Sally talked casually about other subjects and took tissues from Paula from time to time. The two women traded stories about the deaths of their parents and grandparents. Then Paula began telling stories about death and Sacred Harp singings. She described her sense of shame when she had cried at a singing after her mother's death, and how another singer had approached her and told her she was doing exactly the right thing in the right place. She told about a widowed Southern lady who kept stopping on the way to a singing, sure she was going to turn back, but finally made it into the singing room because she knew her husband would have wanted her to be there—moreover, Paula said, the trauma must have been much greater than the lady was letting on, since Southern women express themselves in accordance with a very delicate and subtle social structure. She was sure she would never know the full implications of surface actions at Southern singings.

To me, it seemed that Paula was saying that it was impossible to predict what would happen at an emotionally charged singing, and perhaps even impossible to interpret what had happened after the fact, but that nonetheless Sally might do what Paula had done: first cry and feel ashamed, then learn she was in the right place, and finally identify with Southern women and their perceived deep reserves of emotional strength. Most importantly, Paula was suggesting that the Western Massachusetts Convention could be the site of such a transition. Sally House need not "go South" to experience the family reunion of living and dead that takes place at traditional singings; she did not have to seek out vicarious experience. Diaspora singers, including Paula, have often expressed great disappointment that they cannot seem to share the Sacred Harp experience with their families. Paula was reminding Sally that she had had the great luxury of singing with her children, and that the Western Massachusetts Convention could be a family memorial singing for Karen—something few Northern singers can hope for. By drawing on Sacred Harp narrative themes of hospitality, family, death, and obligation, Paula appraised the Western Massachusetts singers as a moral community and allied them with Southern traditional singing. She modeled appropriate ethical action on what she perceived as Southern cultural norms—stoicism, generosity, humility, and kinship ties—and she cited Southern singing stories with the aphoristic force of citing song texts. Paula was offering Sally a collection of narrative tools with which to prefigure her experience of the convention, should she choose to attend.

There was a striking contrast between the kind of efficacious grieving experience Paula was mapping onto the Western Massachusetts Convention and the memorial aspects of the New England Convention held a few months earlier. Susan Garber, a longtime core member of the Connecticut Sacred Harp community, had died a few months before the 2000 New England Convention. There was a memorial lesson at the convention, but it consisted only of a reading of the names of the sick and deceased, with no further commentary. What some attendees read as an austere, respectful and egalitarian remembrance—a lesson that did not single out any individuals for special attention—struck others, especially regular travelers, as a slight to Garber. Here was a case of speaking too little in the square, passing up an opportunity for "Speaking may relieve thee," and failing to put Garber in her place: back in the square to be mourned.

Eventful Text: "I Belong to This Band"

Up to this point I have focused on the way experiences accrue to individual songs—the "photo album" of page numbers that singers like Martha Henderson describe. But this is not all I mean by "eventful texts." A song can be a vessel for associations with friends and memories of different renditions, but no song begins as an *empty* vessel. Sacred Harp texts were written over the course of several centuries; while almost all of them are Christian, they are doctrinally inconsistent, historically particular, and they speak to experience in different voices. Even Christian singers cannot have a straightforward faith-based relationship with all of them. For textual and musical reasons, some songs gather experience differently than others. They can delimit or transgress the borders of an individual's ideological comfort zone, and they can prefigure an experience instead of merely storing and transporting it.

Singers agree that Sacred Harp can afford relief from grief, anxiety, and feelings of alienation, but their explanations for how and why this effect is accomplished are less consistent. Some suggest that all group singing can be similarly efficacious, referring to the embodied experience of singing open harmonies, feeling the blend or clash of timbres, and moving in rhythm. Words are beside the point, though eighteenth-century psalm paraphrases may hold some literary interest. But others find this stance incomprehensible. One singer wrote to the singings listserv, "Sacred Harp without the words and traditions is called 'solfege.' That doesn't make it unworthy of time and effort, because after all, music is still the expression of heart and soul. Music is a wonderful discipline, and a terrific academic exercise. But how much richer and fuller our experience is when we join mind, heart and voice to worship our Creator in music and in words!"[22] Many people are baffled as to why non-Christians would want to sing Sacred Harp texts or how they could feel comfortable doing so.

On the whole, my experience suggests that singers who truly come "for just the music" and manage to keep the texts pigeonholed as historical curiosities are rare. A deepening relationship to song texts over time—sometimes grounded in anxiety and internal conflict—is a near-universal aspect of Sacred Harp experience regardless of religious affiliation. One West Coast singer described this process in an interview with me. We had been discussing the memories she associated with Judy Hauff's tune "Granville" (547), which were event-focused rather than text-related.

> KM: Do you ever have a text just kind of resonate with something that's going on in your life? Or is it more the opposite direction, like with Granville, when you sing the song you associate it with another event when you sang the song?
>
> Singer: I would say more the latter, but I think I do think about the words a little more. I mean, I'm softening up to the words. I haven't been—I've kind of ignored the words, out of necessity.
>
> KM: Out of musical necessity [i.e., to concentrate on reading the music], or ideological necessity?
>
> Singer: Ideological necessity, but I'm leaning more towards not ignoring the words.[23]

Non-Christian singers often remark on this gradual "softening up" as something surprising and hard to account for, especially with respect to texts they once found alienating or even embarrassing. Consider the following lines:

> I'm not ashamed to own my Lord
> Or to defend his cause[24]

> Ashamed of Jesus! just as soon
> Let midnight be ashamed of noon[25]

> Let those refuse to sing
> Who never knew our God[26]

Such direct professions of faith and allegiance to Christianity "feel strange in my mouth," one singer said. There is no Credo recitation at a Sacred Harp singing, but a text like "I'm not ashamed to own my Lord" can feel like the same thing, even with the buffer provided by "singing the notes." Perceiving a shortcoming in one's own sincerity or authenticity of feeling can be a painful experience.

Even Christian singers may not be exempt from this discomfort; some are indeed "ashamed to own their Lord" in social contexts where Christian rhetoric is closely associated with particular political stances. When I began a new weekly singing at my university, several of my folk-music-loving recruits expressed discomfort with the texts and asked me if anyone ever changes the words or writes new non-Christian songs in this style. I initially assumed that these singers were uncomfortable because they were not Christian themselves, but it turned out that some were regular church-goers. They just didn't consider themselves the same kind of Christians as those who would normally sing these texts.

Paradoxically, this sense of alienation, embarrassment, or hypocrisy can be exacerbated by a singer's experience of genuine, intense emotion at a singing. Some singers feel that by using Sacred Harp as an emotional outlet they are taking advantage of a tradition not rightfully theirs. Hugh Thomas, then a graduate student in Chicago, described this feeling in his 1999 survey response:

> I like, but am also somewhat disturbed by, the way that one can put a lot of emotion into singing. I like it because there are very few activities in our culture where we get together and it's appropriate to, for instance, shed tears, and no one feels self conscious about it, and no one would ask about it. On the other hand, I think part of why it disturbs me is that I feel like I'm putting my feelings into something where they don't really belong. . . . I guess I feel like for a traditional singer, with standard Christian beliefs, it's possible to connect up your grief or whatever to the words of the song, and not feel like you're smuggling something in surreptitiously.

This discomfort with "smuggling" one's own concerns is fairly widespread among newer singers, particularly when there is not a straightforward link between their personal beliefs and the hymn texts. As Thomas wrote, "[S]inging really invites you to involve yourself in the feelings of the song, but I'm not entirely comfortable doing that, because I don't share the religious beliefs of the writers of the songs."

For some people, certain texts touch a nerve due to personal history. An Illinois survey respondent observed, "Many harp singers who did not grow up in the tradition . . . seem to have chosen this kind of musical experience as a reaction against some musical or religious or other personal background that they experienced as 'stifling' their feelings, voice, expressiveness." This is particularly true of the sizeable group of gay men and lesbians who sing Sacred Harp, both inside and outside the South. These singers, and others who feel themselves to be marginalized by or alienated from mainstream religion and culture, can be troubled by texts that manifest an explicitly exclusionary sentiment. One gay singer cited the text to "Melancholy Day" (419) as an example:

> Death, 'tis a melancholy day,
> To those who have no God,
> When the poor soul is forced away
> To seek her last abode,
> In vain to heav'n she lifts her eyes,
> For guilt, a heavy chain,
> Still drags her downward from the skies,
> To darkness, fire and pain.[27]

This song reminded him of an oppressive, guilt-driven, threatening form of Christianity that he had long since rejected.

But some singers who have experienced exclusion, repression, or emotional trauma identify these texts as *The Sacred Harp*'s greatest asset. Like Jerilyn Schumacher, whose own body was "withering like the blasted rose," they choose to "speak and let the worst be known." For them, textual content can channel emotional release without any anxiety about smuggling in their own troubles. These singers have discovered a place for themselves in the singing community.

After a certain point, singers know enough songs to access the pleasures of the musical experience—looking up from their books, following the nuances of the leader's style, adding vocal ornaments—but they may not know other participants well enough to feel that they are sharing that experience in the right way. Singers who find emotional solace and musical satisfaction in Sacred Harp but do not feel a strong sense of community sometimes fear they are abusing the privilege of participation in the tradition. But in time many of these same participants seem to pass through this in-between stage and experience a major shift of perspective. The quasi-conversion narratives that I have collected from singers suggest that this transition involves two intertwined processes: an individual actively identifies with the Sacred Harp community and finds a way to make Christian language personally meaningful.

Sacred Harp texts are full of questions, drawing singers into a community of uncertainty rather than placing them at the margins of a community of belief. Songs like "Mear" (49b), which expresses doubts and fears in the first person plural rather than singular, can be especially effective:

1. Will God forever cast us off?
His wrath forever smoke,
Against the people of His love,
His little chosen flock?

5. No prophet speaks to calm our grief,
But all in silence mourn;
Nor know the hour of our relief,
The hour of Thy return.[28]

The private anxiety of lines like "Is there anyone like me?" or "What will become of me?" is different from the collective anxiety of "Will God forever cast us off?" but the juxtaposition of these kinds of texts in the hollow square encourages "a simultaneous perception of solitude and multitude" (Hatfield 1997: 17, following Baudelaire). When private troubles are expressed publicly and collectively—when two hundred people sing "Is there anyone like me?"—one becomes inclined to identify with fellow singers. A flyer for one annual singing made this point by reproducing the tune "Jackson" (317b), which includes the lines "I am a stranger here below" and "Oh is there anyone like me?" The song is captioned, "Don't be a stranger! Come join your Sacred Harp family for the McWhorter Memorial Singing." (See Figure 22.)

Over time, singers come to feel it is appropriate to bring their own concerns to a singing, whether or not they are openly expressed. They fit songs to their own lives and pass private worries through the mouths of the assembled class out into the resonant room. One of the most moving examples of an active use of such a text during my fieldwork years came in the months after September 11, 2001, when "Granville" (547) was called over and over at the singings I attended. (See Figure 23.) The song's plaintive second verse, written by Isaac Watts in 1719 and set by Chicago singer Judy Hauff in 1986, became newly eventful during this period:

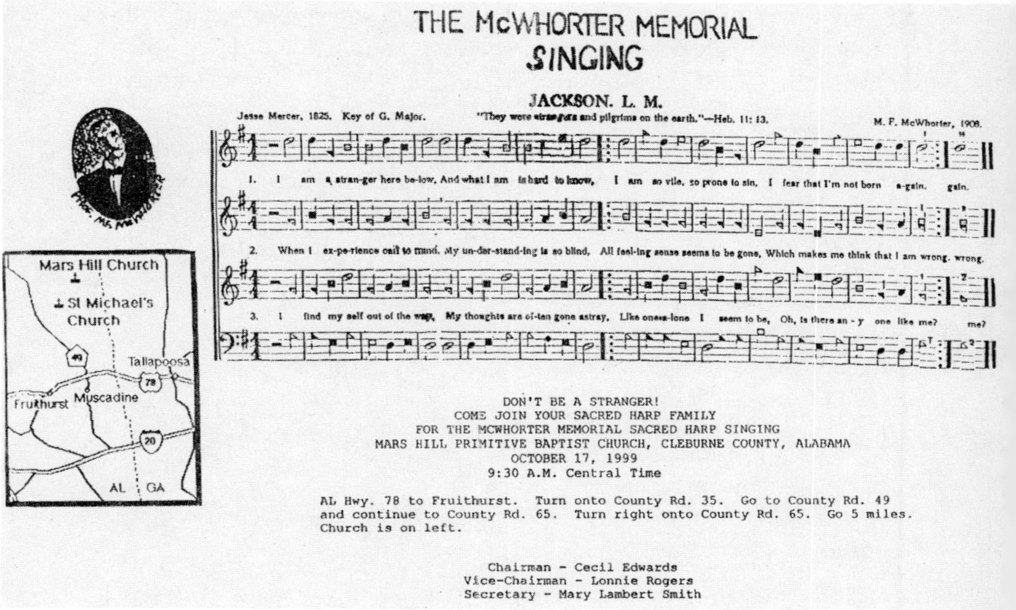

Figure 22: "Don't Be a stranger!" The song "Jackson" (317b) was composed by M. F. McWhorter in 1908; here its first-person account of loneliness, doubt, and alienation becomes part of an invitation to honor McWhorter's family by participating in their annual memorial singing. (Courtesy of Teenie Moody.)

> Lord, while we see whole nations die,
> Our flesh and sense repine and cry;
> Must death forever rage and reign?
> Or hast Thou made mankind in vain?

These words gather a community of agonized human witnesses. Hauff's setting, with its extraordinary leap to the song's highest pitch on the word "rage," galvanized singing communities in their capacity as mourners in the fall of 2001. Its new embedded history became and remains a site of identification for singers. In a visual parallel to this galvanizing experience of community, Massachusetts singer Chris Noren created an image of the New York skyline out of Minnesota singer Tom Mitchell's Sacred Harp photographs to use as the cover of his compilation *September Psalms*. (See Figure 24.)

When it comes to explicitly Christian texts, one common strategy employed by non-Christian singers entails the creation of a meta-narrative

Figure 23: Judy Hauff's "Granville" (547), a 1986 song that now embeds memories of September 11, 2001, for many singers.

Figure 24: Chris Noren's cover image for a tunebook he compiled to commemorate the events of September 11, 2001, and raise money for survivors. (Noren 2002, reprinted with permission.)

in which "Jesus," "Jerusalem" or "home" stands in for the Sacred Harp community itself. The practice of singing itself effectively takes on the role of a loving redeemer, the same role that Jesus plays for their Christian singing companions. The text of "Beach Spring" (81t) exemplifies a theme of acceptance that holds great affective power for singers:

> Let not conscience make you linger,
> Nor of fitness fondly dream,
> All the fitness He requireth
> Is to feel your need of Him.[29]

For people who view themselves as "wayfaring strangers," weak and alone, the idea that acceptance is there for the asking—that the only qualifier for belonging is an expressed need to belong—seems as dumbfoundingly generous as the offer of "free grace" does to born-again Christians. As the same metaphors are performed over and over, they come to be self-fulfilling prophecies: in acknowledging and accepting these textual offers of acceptance, singers come to depend on Sacred Harp for support.[30]

Flexible interpretations of texts permit singers with diverse beliefs and experience to relate to Sacred Harp in personally meaningful ways, and that relationship develops over the course of a singer's experience. Because experienced singers explicitly describe this process—in personal conversation as well as in formal contexts like the memorial lesson—newer singers can actively learn strategies to reconcile their surface discomfort with or disassociation from certain texts. The stories of other singers prefigure their own experience, leading them to formulate allegorical interpretations, to link a tune with a friend who leads it rather than to its literal meaning, or simply to wait for the predicted shift in understanding to occur.

This process is not unlike the experience of Christians who wait to "feel a call" before they become members at the church they have attended for years (cf. Patterson 1995). In general, the practice of creatively interpreting Sacred Harp song texts—along with seeing Sacred Harp page numbers everywhere, as in Martha Henderson's Wal-Mart example—bears a strong resemblance to Christian fundamentalist approaches to Scripture. Some liberal-identified singers have credited this practice with altering their perception of Bible-based fundamentalism. Where they previously viewed fundamentalists as performing static, passive, literal readings of the Bible, their Sacred Harp experience leads them to view such readings as potentially active, creative, and empowering (though they remain opposed to the political conclusions drawn through these interpretations).

In a 1999 singings posting, Henderson provided an elegant metaphor for her own altered perspective on the words and their religious content:

> Ten years ago, I came to Sacred Harp for the music. There was no audition (I always liked to sing but felt I had no voice) and the tunes are beautiful. But over a period of years, I found that the words began to mean more and more to me. Now, I think that singing Sacred Harp just as music, without at least some connection to the words, takes the heart and soul out of it. It becomes shallow—very pretty to listen to, but with no substance, like sunlight glancing off of water, or like a mirror that reflects back to us only what we care to see in it.[31]

This account sanctions the experience of finding something unexpected, challenging, troubling, or distressing in Sacred Harp texts—not only passive reflections of what a singer has already brought to the song or cares to see in it but also unpredictable and uncontrollable responses. Songs become windows rather than mirrors.

A memorial lesson given by Chicago singer Marcia Johnson suggests how this can come to pass. At the 1999 Chicago Anniversary Singing she performed a complex exegesis of the word "band," beginning from the text to "Ragan" (176t):

> Farewell, vain world, I'm going home,
> I belong to this band, hallelujah.
> My Savior smiles and bids me come,
> I belong to this band, hallelujah.[32]

Johnson referred to the band of singers present with her at the singing, the metal bars around her mother's sickbed, the corresponding band she felt tightening around her heart—an oblique reference to "Parting Hand" and the line "You draw like cords around my heart"—and the band that included singers past, present, and future. The bands of obligation drew them together, obligation not only to meet but also to separate: as the closing tune "Parting Hand" says, "But duty makes me understand that we must take the parting hand." "Belonging" is not usually described as an emotion, but statements like "I belong to this band" fit Reddy's definition of emotive utterances; they clearly serve Johnson and others as "instruments for directly changing, building, hiding, intensifying emotions" (Reddy 1997:

331).[33] (Another of Johnson's lessons, from the 1999 United Convention, may be heard in Sound Example 7.)

The density of reference here, the slippage from one "band" to another, illustrates the condensed affective potential of song texts. In memorial narratives these texts are "fitted with new histories" as mourners reframe them to meet new emotional needs (Briggs 1993: 952). Part of this reframing depends upon the qualities of the spoken voice as it alternates with the singing voice. By midday on the second day of a convention, one's vocal cords can be as tight as the cords that draw around one's heart. Memorial speakers are usually hoarse; the cracks in their voices signify the authenticity of physically manifested emotion. Singing as loud as possible for hours on end simulates the physical effects of grief, and the memorial lesson converts that simulation into reality—the grain of the speaker's voice bears witness to the truth of her words. Back at home, too, singers experience their worn-out voices both as tokens of loss and as the physical proof of an authentic experience.[34]

It is worth emphasizing that both songs and memorials are referred to as "lessons," unlike prayers, resolutions, or other spoken-word elements of a singing. Song-text exegesis and memorial lessons are linked emblems of social unity; they use language to demonstrate its own inadequacy compared to song. Thomas Turino asserts that linguistic efforts to account for profound musical experiences are bound to fail, that "When people shift to symbolic thinking and discourse to communicate about deep feelings and experiences, the feeling and reality of those experiences disappear and we are *not* satisfied" (Turino 1999: 250). Yet that very lack of satisfaction lays the ground for profound experience. By establishing a world of loss, anxiety, uncertainty, and inadequate expression, these narratives intensify the satisfactions of singing.

Texted Event: "A Family in Practice"

Sally House did attend the 2001 Western Massachusetts Convention. The memorial lesson at the convention repeatedly returned to the death of her daughter Karen, who had been buried in the cemetery at Liberty Baptist Church in Henagar, Alabama, a Sacred Harp stronghold. The loss of such a young and well-known singer brought a binding gravity and maturity to this very young diaspora convention, catapulting it to a new level of felt authenticity and community cohesion.

Before Karen was mentioned at all, local singer Eric Morgan asked Richard DeLong to speak about the passing of his great-uncle Jack. This decision to give precedence to remembrance of a lifelong Southern singer conveyed tremendous respect for the Southern tradition and gratitude for DeLong's attendance, and DeLong acknowledged it by bringing Karen House into his own lesson:

> Last year at this convention, one of the people that we sang for was my grandmother. And this year at this convention one of the people we sing for was her last living brother. He was buried a week ago yesterday. 89 years old. He lived a long life. But you—if you don't know it, you're never ready for it. It doesn't matter if they're 89, or 109, or 39. It doesn't matter. It's the same impact. . . .
>
> I know, of course, in the hearts and minds of many here today, Karen House—she's crossed my mind numerous times, and I know there are many others that she's constantly on their mind. When you lose someone very very close to you, people mean well. And they'll come up and give you all kinds of advice. Some of it's very good, some of it's not so good. But you smile and endure it and hug their necks and shake their hands—and some of you have heard me say that I believe the best piece of advice that I got about my grandmother: this woman sat me down and she said, People will tell you that you'll get over it. But she said, I'm going to tell you the truth: you won't never get over it. You won't never get over it for the rest of your life, but you will get different. And that has meant a whole lot to me. . . .
>
> I don't think there's a day that goes by that I don't think about Sacred Harp. Because it—you can't help it! It gets down in the innermost part of you, and you get to love the people, and you love what we do and you love coming together, and my grandmother when she knew she was getting in bad health, and before a big singing would happen at home, I told somebody yesterday: a month before the singing was going to happen, she would go to worrying if she would be well enough to go to the singing. A month! And I hope I—she would say, I hope I can go one more time, just one more time. And we'll be like that. Because the same passion that I've seen my Uncle Jack get up and lead with, at 89, you'd think he was going to fall over, he was so feeble. I've seen his eyes roll back in his head in ecstasy in the square. It was all over him. And he loved it with all of his life, like many of you do.
>
> And I've seen that. I've seen that here, at this convention. I've seen you get up here and you don't even—you're just *lost*. Because you love it so much. And with that comes the love of these people we get to know, and friends, family, and sometimes they're even closer than family. So we'll sing 65. [leads "Sweet Prospect"][35]

DeLong's lesson paid Karen House the honor of comparison with his own family, acknowledged the shock of loss and the exhaustion of the obligation of mourning, and ascribed authenticity of experience to the Western Massachusetts singers—earned through their demonstration of "the same passion" he saw among Southern singers. Like most of the core Western Massachusetts organizers, DeLong was a generation or two younger than many of the lifelong singers he sang with in his home community. His statement "And we'll be like that" skipped over the fact of his much longer singing experience—dating from infancy rather than college—to make this generational connection and enjoin the young singers around him to share his feelings, his commitment, and the promise of being "even closer than family."

Eric Morgan repeated and extended several of DeLong's points as he gave the general lesson for the dead, rearticulating the themes of duty and family while continuing to defer to DeLong's authority as a traditional singer.

> The other night I was laying awake, nervous, knowing fully that there was no possible way that I could be poetic enough to properly do justice for those who we are going to sing for. And as I lay there I started thinking, and the words "brothers and sisters" came into my mind. I started thinking about that, and the various contexts in which that exists. And we use those terms in church to address one another, and there's a doctrinal reason for that, but it does more than that. It brings people together as a family, in practice, and not just the idea of a family. And as I started thinking about those terms in *this* context, here, brothers and sisters, the faces of those dear to me in this valley, and all across New England, all across the Northeast, all across the country, back home, those faces started popping into my mind. And I thought, we really are a family. Not just the idea of a family, but a family in practice. We come together, we sing together, we're brought together by the bonds of love and fellowship, and we are required to do what families do, and that's to pay honor to those who've gone before. . . .
>
> Let me just say when that became absolutely clear to me, this notion of family, was on a night in June, I had a message on my machine from Cath, to call her back. And I called her back, and she told me that Karen House had died. And I cried. And I didn't know Karen as much as I would have liked, I wasn't around in the early days when Tim and Bradford and Kelly and Cath and Jeff and you all were figuring this stuff out, creating those bonds. But I cried. And I cried because I felt a connection to Karen not unlike that that I have to my own sisters, to my own family. And that became very real to me, and I thought it only fitting that we pay tribute to her in song, as we do.
>
> Brothers and sisters, I want us to remember that we do have this family, and it's from this family that we can come together and take comfort in

these times of loss. We can come together and find strength in these times, we can find solace and consolation. And I'll quote Hebrews, chapter 2, here, "and it's for that cause, for which I'm not ashamed to call you brethren."

Morgan's lesson, like DeLong's, made Sacred Harp the site of bonds that may be even closer than blood connections because they are so actively practiced and explicitly acknowledged. His acknowledgment of his own brief tenure in the local area made it clear that the Western Massachusetts singing community was produced by travelers as much as by rooted insiders—by new travelers like the college students and venerated older ones like the convention's Southern visitors. This local community's collective identity emerged not from blood ties and matching vocal timbre but from the intersection of many narratives, many self-fulfilling prophecies, and many travels. The Western Massachusetts Convention became what its singers needed it to be: a place for asserting difference, honoring tradition, and grieving, a place where strangers are made into family.

"Western Mass" became an eventful convention, much like an eventful text: an assembly with its own character and experience-gathering qualities, its associations, its galvanizing moments of grief, love, and conflict. The memorial lesson in 2001 had something of the quality of the Founders' Lesson in Chicago, where DeLong's benevolent presence was also a regular feature. At the much younger Western Massachusetts Convention, DeLong gave the class his blessing by acknowledging the genuineness of their experience and intent. He and Morgan established the guiding metaphor of family relationships that was so literally borne out in the tragedy of Karen House's death and, at future Western Massachusetts conventions, in the joy of her sister Kelly's marriage, Kelly's husband's commitment to singing, and the birth of two children. Tim Eriksen and his wife, the ethnomusicologist Mirjana Lausevic, also had two children during this period; they brought them back to Western Massachusetts singings regularly even after moving to Minnesota. Through these events, this new convention was overwritten with the narrative of family. The Western Massachusetts singers allied themselves with particular communities of the living and dead, and they deliberately set out to form new ones. "Required to do what families do," they joined with strangers to travel, make music, eat, and mourn.

Events become texted in the telling and retelling, as songs become eventful over years of singing and conventions gather guiding narratives that prefigure experience. In this way "Oh is there anyone like me?" becomes "I belong to this band," "I'm a long time traveling" becomes "I'm on my journey home," and "the idea of a family" becomes "a family in practice." The questions, injunctions, exhortations, and professions of faith that pass through the mouths of the class create ways "to sing the things that cannot be said," as Paul Robinson wrote to the singings listserv.[36] Kelly House described this process in the prayer that ended the memorial lesson for her sister: "Dear God, when all we can see is despair and grief, you hear our voices crying in the wilderness, and you turn them into harmony." When speaking provides no relief, singing might render the unspeakable bearable.

5

"A Strange Land and a Peculiar People"

MEDIATING LOCAL COLOR

"Sacred Harp singings can transport you back to an earlier century," the title of a 1980 newspaper article promised—a promise with a hundred years of precedents.[1] By 1904 Southern journalists were already regularly referring to Sacred Harp singing as "old time" music and pushing its origins back to murky antiquity. A 1915 article referred to "the shaped or buck-eye notes, which have not been in general use for nearly 200 years," placing the heyday of shape-notes about 80 years before their invention.[2] The 1980 article moved the start date back even further, claiming that "'Sacred Harp' has been around since the 1500's and longer."

Sacred Harp singers often echo the spirit of these claims, comparing their travels to certain singing venues to trips back in time. They drive down twisting country roads that become narrower and turn to gravel to reach one-room churches. They park near rows of nineteenth-century gravestones, some decorated with Confederate flags, and emerge into moist summer heat that pulses with the swell of unaccompanied voices. "I felt like I'd gone back two hundred years, to the old revival meetings on the frontier," one seasoned diaspora singer told me of her early experience at rural Southern singings. "I was overwhelmed just by the sound, a weirdly compelling sound. Old, and authentic, like it got into my bones." Another compared his first impressions of the rhythmic pulse of the singing to "tribal chanting," especially on the singing of the shapes—"like the nonsense syllables, you know, in the old Native American recordings." "It's a primitive sound, or primal," someone said. "I love it that it's so primitive." Another singer winced.

Today's singers need not look far to find reminders that they are not at a nineteenth-century camp meeting, even after they stop chatting by rows of parked cars and enter the confines of the singing room. There are the tunebooks themselves, of course, printed in 1991 or later. There are the tape recorders (and now minidisc or flash recorders) that singers have hung on nails in the wall or discreetly placed under chairs. In 1987, a *Houston Chronicle* writer marveled that "Elderly men and women wielded enormous cassette recorders—the boom boxes or ghetto blasters favored by teen-agers—and taped the proceedings."[3] More and more singings are being recorded with professional-quality microphones, which can crowd the internal corners of the hollow square or extend from the fringes on booms—recordings sometimes destined for personal archives, sometimes transferred to CDs at a nominal fee and sold to raise funds for a local convention. Lifelong Alabama singer Amanda Denson described receiving tapes of conventions in the mail from Hugh McGraw when she was living overseas: "And when the mail would come, if there was a tape in it, I had a tape deck in my kitchen, and I would put it in and the children's daddy told the children, if they would start to ask me something, he would say, 'Just don't try to talk to her for about forty-five minutes because she won't hear you.'"[4] At many singings at least one person has a video camera, either for occasional handheld shooting from a seat in the square or set up on a tripod in a corner to record the entire convention. Photocopied flyers cover tables at the edge of the room; they provide basic instructions for beginners or advertise other conventions. (See Figures 22 and 31.) Singers wave cardboard fans printed with funeral home advertisements or radio station call numbers (Figure 25). Some people make their way to the ends of twisting dirt roads with directions and maps downloaded from www.fasola.org (Figure 26). After the singing, singers post reports of the event to Sacred Harp listservs within days or even hours.

The Sacred Harp diaspora could not exist without modern media, just as the regional networks of Southern conventions in the first century of Sacred Harp singing could not have existed without a mass-produced tunebook. The national community comprises close-knit local groups of singers with a high degree of awareness of the activities of other groups in far-flung parts of the country, an awareness achieved not only through reciprocal travels but also through the production and circulation of media. Singers represent themselves and communicate among themselves in every media format currently available. Setting aside the tape recordings, CDs, videos, and minutebooks that circulate coast-to-coast, there are also personal,

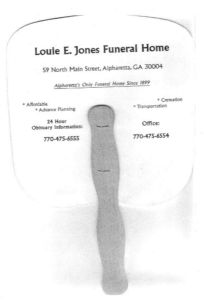

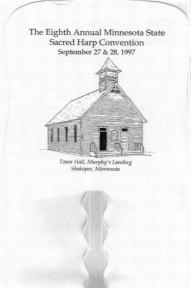

Figure 25: Cardboard fans used by singers to keep cool, beat time in their seats, and remember past conventions. Top: front and back of a fan supplied by a Georgia funeral home. Bottom: a fan commemorating the 1997 Minnesota State Convention and advertising the virtues of its venue, a historic building with acoustics like those of a small Southern church.

Figure 26: "Drive north on Interstate 59 from Gadsden. Exit east onto Alabama Highway 68, at Exit 205, toward Collinsville. Turn right, south, on U.S. Highway 11. Look for the sign to the church at mile marker 211. There is often a flea market meeting on Saturdays between mile markers 212 and 213, which you will want to pass." Map and directions to the Lookout Mountain Convention in DeKalb County, Alabama, provided at www.fasola.org/maps.

local, and regional Sacred Harp–related webpages—many centrally accessible through links on www.fasola.org—which contain enormous archives of photographs, mp3 recordings, and digital video clips. Folk festival posters, newspaper listings, newsletters, new tune compilations, cookbooks, and promotional mailings are in constant production, along with goods like printed T-shirts, tote bags, and aprons sold to benefit conventions.[5] Singers write press releases that attract reporters to conventions; they post the resulting articles to the fasola.org lists with commentaries and disclaimers about the accuracy of quotations.

Electronic and print media extend the range of existing vehicles for the transmission of practice, affiliations, and ideology. The conventional media that transmit performance practice in the hollow square include memorial lessons, vocal ornamentation, and regional accents. Accents heard on recordings, usually audible only when the leader calls a page number, convey a lot of information about the recorded convention; in an article that surveyed Sacred Harp–related media, David Carlton referred to "the opening strains of 'Exhortation' (called in the crisp midwestern accent of Chicago's Connie Karduck)" as a way of signaling the diversity of the class at this Alabama convention (Carlton 2003: 62). On another recording, a midwestern singer might call out a page number in an adopted Alabama accent; a Western Massachusetts singer on the road to a convention listens to it on a CD ordered from yet another singer's website.

The traveling habits and documentarian impulses of Sacred Harp singers parallel some old and new norms of ethnographic fieldwork. Most prominently, searches for the ancient, exotic, primitive, and out-of-the-way are still very much alive and meaningful for some Sacred Harp singers, who are a little disappointed when one year the end-of-the-line Georgia church has suddenly acquired air conditioning and indoor plumbing. Such disappointment is not limited to urbanite newcomers; lifelong Southern singers from prosperous farming families have also made nostalgic remarks to me about the changeover from outhouses to in-house facilities, while conceding that the latter are far more comfortable for the aging relatives they are helping up the new ramp to the church door. But newer singers, whether from the North or South, tend to express the greatest anxiety about the implications of these changes—in part because they are concerned about their own impact. One Illinois singer described going to a Southern singing where "There must have been ten of us or something, and about twenty-five people from Minnesota. Well it wasn't an Antioch singing anymore. The alto benches were all Northern. Syble [Adams] never got to sing. And when tons of you go, that's what happens to the singing."

Fears about dilution nag at some singers until they either travel to fewer Southern conventions altogether or seek out singings other outsiders haven't found yet—both to assure themselves that such singings still exist and to add a supportive but not overwhelming vocal presence that might prolong a dwindling convention's lifespan. Like the New England singer I quoted in Chapter 1, their goal is "to be either the only foreigner there or one of so few foreigners that it doesn't muck up the sound." The idea that some singings remain isolated provides consolation to new and lifelong singers alike, especially as lifelong singers make the compromises required to participate broadly in the Sacred Harp diaspora. As David Lee wrote to me, "There are many more of us down here that other people do not know about. . . . You would have to move down here to live and go around with us to meet and sing with all of them. What I'm saying is that, though some of us have changed, the heart of our old tradition is still alive in various out-of-the-way places. And that, somehow, gives me great comfort."[6]

Among Sacred Harp singers (as with academic ethnographers) the quest narrative of end-of-the-line searches has generated friction with two newer discourses: the discourse of guilt over polluting or exploiting a pure tradition that I have just discussed, and a discourse that suggests the idea of a pure tradition is grounded in paternalistic nostalgia and runs counter to the spirit and history of Sacred Harp singing. Singers have used all available media to construct and represent their own positions with respect to these three ideological approaches. They negotiate their difference not only through choices in the hollow square but through mediating efforts to promote and preserve the tradition. At the same time, they often downplay or undermine the value of modern media: singers use a medium to demonstrate its own failings, just as they make the spoken component of the memorial lesson demonstrate the expressive shortcomings of speech. Singers' representations of Sacred Harp often have an antimodernist thrust, privileging face-to-face communication and oral transmission of tradition. In earnest or with deadpan irony, they regularly reproduce the nostalgic and nationalist themes of local-color journalism that were so crucial to the invention of the rural South as a cultural region.

"Our Contemporary Ancestors"

The post–Civil War rural South, particularly the coal-bearing mountain regions, underwent the same colonizing procedures that Gayatri Spivak describes as characteristic of Third World nations: "Transportation, law, and standardized education systems were developed—even as local industries were destroyed, land distribution was rearranged, and raw material was transferred to the colonizing country" (Spivak 1988: 287). The raw materials that were transferred from the rural South to urbanizing, industrializing America consisted not only of coal and timbers but also of culture: an otherness both fascinating enough and familiar enough to be extremely marketable, not only commercially but ideologically.[7] Inhabitants of geographically and politically isolated areas within America—mountains, swamplands, dense forests—played and still play the role of "living ancestors," a people caught at an earlier stage of social evolution. Sacred Harp has long been featured in these stories of anachronistic rural Southern culture. Journalists have repeatedly asked and answered the sort of question posed by a 1964 writer (addressing Sacred Harp in Texas): "What is this precious musical commodity, and who are the vintage Americans who preserve it?" (DeLaughter 1964).

The discipline of anthropology has been discovering "living ancestors" for a long time, populations who seem to exist outside of time for the education and delectation of self-consciously modern people.[8] Rural white Southerners have had a more specialized role to play, representing not just humanity's living ancestors but *our* living ancestors, when *we* are genuine (implicitly, white) Americans with colonial roots. Kymlicka's definition of culture "in the widest sense" provides both a pertinent analysis and an object lesson: "we can say that all of the Western democracies share a common 'culture'—that is, they all share a modern, urban, secular, industrialized civilization, in contrast to the feudal, agricultural, and theocratic world of our ancestors" (Kymlicka 1995: 18). Feudal (and feuding), agricultural, and theocratic are all epithets that have been applied to isolated rural white Southern communities by those attempting to fix their simultaneous difference from and kinship with a modern, urban, secular, industrialized American mainstream.[9]

Since the late nineteenth century the main themes of "local-color" journalism on the Southern mountain region have remained remarkably consistent, so much so that Batteau has described them as "archetypes that prefigured not only the control but the very existence of the region as singular entity" (Batteau 1990: 10). The earliest local-color work in the region couched the ubiquitous tale of "discovery" in scientific terms, borrowing the anthropometric language of contemporary anthropology. Will Wallace Harney took this approach in his 1873 article "A Strange Land and a Peculiar People." He condensed primitivist and nationalist tropes in a taxonomy of racial characteristics: "The natives of this region are characterized by marked peculiarities of the anatomical frame. The elongation of the bones, the contour of the facial angle, the relative proportion or disproportion of the extremities, the loose muscular attachment of the ligatures, and the harsh features were exemplified in the notable instance of the late President Lincoln" (Harney 1873, reprinted in McNeil 1995: 48).

William Goodell Frost's famous 1899 article "Our Contemporary Ancestors in the Southern Mountains" uses this same paradigm of scientific investigation, framed by a remarkable account of tourist subjectivity:

> It is a longer journey from northern Ohio to eastern Kentucky than from America to Europe; for one day's ride brings us into the eighteenth century. Naturally, then, these eighteenth-century neighbors and fellow countrymen of ours are in need of a friendly interpreter; for modern life has little patience with those who are "behind the times." We hear of the "mountain whites" (they scorn that appellation as we would scorn the term "Northern whites") as illiterates, moonshiners, homicides, and even yet the mountaineers are scarcely distinguished in our thought from the "poor white trash." When we see them from the car window, with curious eyes, as we are whirled toward our Southern hotel, their virtues are not blazoned on their sorry clothing,

nor suggested by their grave and awkward demeanor. They are an anachronism, and it will require a scientific spirit and some historic sense to enable us to appreciate their situation and their character. (Frost 1899: 311)

Subsequently, Frost clarifies the distinction between the "poor white" and the "mountain white," claiming that the former has been "degraded by actual competition with slave labor" while the latter has been isolated from interracial relations (1899: 316). Along the same lines, he asserts that the "rude dialect" of mountain whites "is far less a degradation than a survival" of Saxon speech (1899: 313).

These accounts of rural Southern life persistently deny that the people in question are the writer's cultural contemporaries; they refer to backwardness, anachronism, and celebrated "survivals" of earlier historical periods.[10] Charles Morrow Wilson entitled a 1929 article "Elizabethan America" (Wilson 1929), while John Fox Jr. admonished readers, "First, last, and always, however, it is to be remembered that to begin to understand the Southern mountaineers you must go back to the social conditions and standards of the backwoods before the Revolution. . . . They were loyal to the Union for one reason that no historian seems ever to have guessed. For the loyalty of 1861 was, in great part, merely the transmitted loyalty of 1776, imprisoned like a fossil in the hills" (Fox 1901, reprinted in McNeil 1995: 143).

Fox's work also used the "Southern mountaineers" to further a xenophobic political agenda. Like Frost, he linked geographical isolation with racial purity: "Americans to the core, they make the Southern mountains a storehouse of patriotism; in themselves, they are an important offset to the Old World outcasts whom we have welcomed to our shores; and they surely deserve as much consideration from the nation as the negroes, for whom we have done, and are doing so much, or as the heathen, to whom we give millions. . . . It is only fair to add, however, that nothing that has ever been said of the mountaineer's ignorance, shiftlessness, and awful disregard of human life . . . has not its basis, perhaps, in actual fact" (Fox 1901, reprinted in McNeil 1995: 143). His turn back to negative stereotype reinforced the urgency of civilizing this great American asset, who were fortunately also "naturally capable, eager to learn, easy to uplift." Three-quarters of a century later, Horace Newcombe located this same attitude in popular television programs like "The Beverly Hillbillies" and "The Dukes of Hazzard," observing that "The real viciousness of these views . . . is that mountain people and Southerners are not considered part of the adult population of the country or of the culture" (Newcombe 1979–80: 160).

As scholars of Appalachian cultural history have shown, the population derided as hillbillies and squirrel-eaters have from time to time been called upon as the standard-bearers for American racial purity, family values, and old-fashioned God-fearing religion—or, depending on whom you ask, for aesthetic authenticity, the "simple life," spirituality, and ecological stewardship.[11] The stereotype seems infinitely malleable and therefore infinitely politically useful. Both liberals and conservatives have attributed an emphasis on community (or clannishness) and rugged individualism (or ignorant xenophobic backwardness) to rural Southerners, as explicitly American values or as selfish provincial prejudice.

The Local Color of Sacred Harp

Like these writings on Appalachian culture, a century of local-color writing on Sacred Harp singing has consistently emphasized the Americanness, the historicity, and the strangeness of the practice, contributing to its image as quintessentially homegrown, authentically ancient, and compellingly exotic. A 1972 article in the Sunday magazine of the *Atlanta Journal and Constitution* provided a genealogical history for Sacred Harp that mirrored the American melting-pot narrative, from immigration to intermarriage to the shaping influence of the regional landscape:

> The music is not gospel rock, spirituals, *a cappella* chorales, old camp meeting songs, or Gregorian chants, although the 'sound' of Sacred Harp is all of these and more. Born in England, then married to the folk music of the Appalachians and 'Southernized' on the plains of Georgia and Alabama, Sacred Harp survives as a distinctive American art form. Supporters are largely rural, middle-aged and older. However, many urban young people are "digging" Sacred Harp today with an enthusiasm their parents show for butter churns and cane-bottomed chairs, and its ranks are swelling with folklore scholars and academicians. (Byron 1972: 60)

More recently, on the opposite coast a *Palo Alto Weekly* journalist conflated nationalist and primitivist discourses as adroitly as Harney did in 1873, assessing a California Sacred Harp convention as "folksier than folk music, certainly more accessible than jazz. And these poetic hymns were being sung in churches throughout the land at the same time Jefferson and his revolutionary cohorts were discussing the finer points of life, liberty and the pursuit of happiness. Mom's apple pie couldn't be more all-American. And yet, the four-part shape note hymns are about as familiar to the average American as Maori tribal chants" (Hayde 1995: 15). Here a gathering comprising mainly white, upper-middle-class Bay Area singers gains the cachet of what Erlmann has termed the "myth of world music," which is based partly in the conviction that "autonomous, uncommodi- fied forms of musical practice still thrive in some places," including "in the heart of Western consumer societies" (Erlmann 1996: 474). Writers who view Sacred Harp through this lens generally assess the singers as either unselfconsciously anachronistic—the living ancestors angle—or deliber- ately antimodern, perhaps with an escapist edge.

When journalists visit rural convention venues, their reportage almost invariably reproduces the end-of-the-line narrative I sketched at the start of the book and in the introduction to this chapter. In a 2002 *Carrollton Times-Georgian* article about the Chattahoochee Convention (in west Georgia), a brief gloss of Sacred Harp history leads into the archetypal arrival scene:

> Apparently, this style of music originated in New England and spread around the eastern part of the United States during the 19th century. As America grew more sophisticated in its musical tastes, Sacred Harp became outdated. But here in the southeast, where things move a little slower and we tend to be a little behind on trends, shape note singing kept a firm foot- hold and the tradition stayed alive.
>
> We drove to the end of Cross Plains Road and found ourselves on a gravel road. Then we spotted the little brick chapel, standing proud atop the crest of a gentle hill. From the looks of the sea of cars parked around it, Sacred Harp was alive and well in Carroll County. We parked and started up the long grade. It was still early morning. The air was quiet. Up in a big oak tree, a single "Katy-did" was warming up for its first performance of the day. Then the singing started. Now, I have to tell you, I've been in a lot of churches in my life. Heard and sung many fine inspirational songs. But I've never heard singing like this. It was powerful, like shouting. It pushed under the doors of the little brick chapel and rolled like a wave down the long hill. We were pulled up by the strength of it.
>
> I stood for a moment, unable to move from the spot as I listened to the sound of rejoicing voices unafraid in the strong company of each other. They came to the end of their song and I followed Rhonda and her mama up the rest of the hill and into the clean white door of the old chapel.[12]

The writer, Mimi Altree, is self-consciously Southern and local; she describes getting directions to the convention through "a few queries to the Carroll County grapevine." But even so, the singing seems powerfully unfamiliar to her. Her description of hearing the music from outside the church is a common element of journalistic accounts of Sacred Harp singing, often coupled with the admission that the writer arrived late owing to difficulty finding the way. The disembodied sound that "pushed under the doors" is overwhelming, paralyzing, a force of nature—it "rolled like a wave down the hill."

Consider a contemporary journalistic account of a diaspora convention. Describing the 2001 Minnesota State Convention, Cathy Taylor writes, "Entering Murphy's Landing September 28, I heard the singing some distance down the dusty road from the 1870 town hall. The sound wasn't elegantly enunciated and modulated, like modern choral singing. It was a ferocious full-volume nasal snarl with something of New England about it, and something of the South. Vowels narrow and intense, every consonant hammered home, it was the noise of a whole people busy being born."[13] Again, the disembodied mass of voices is heard at a distance and has a visceral impact; its antimodern timbre hammers at the writer from down the road. But its traits are attributed not to local hidebound habit but American history writ large: "something of New England" and "something of the South," a culturally-integrated nation "busy being born."

Altree embeds her Sacred Harp convention in the regional landscape much more specifically than Taylor does. But while Altree spends a few sentences on Sacred Harp history, she does not situate the Chattahoochee Convention historically. This seems curious given that her article is about the 150th annual session of the oldest continuously meeting Sacred Harp convention, an intensely historicized event that was promoted as such at singings around the country well in advance. The "sea of cars" would have been far smaller any other year. John Plunkett, an Atlanta singer, had been working to organize the commemorative activities for this convention for two years; he enlisted me to compile and edit a historical sourcebook for the sesquicentennial (Miller 2002). He also sent out press releases to area newspapers, which may well have been the impetus for Altree's article. At breaks in the singing, John and I were signing copies of the sourcebook and selling them to benefit the convention and cover the expenses of preparing for so many visitors. But even in this atmosphere of historical self-consciousness and media promotion, Altree attributed the size and strength of the convention to the unsophisticated, conservative tendencies of the South, always "a little behind on trends." She wrote as though the "firm foot hold" of shape note singing had never faltered for a moment since the nineteenth century.

An article on the 2001 Missouri Convention sets the scene in a fashion by now familiar—in "a white country church . . . time stood still for an eclectic group of singers who practice an archaic form of music known as Sacred Harp"[14]—before describing the history of the Sacred Harp revival in Missouri:

> While the music eventually died out in New England and the Midwest, it was passed uncorrupted from generation to generation in Primitive Baptist and other churches in the deep South. When a revival of interest in Sacred Harp music began around 1983 in places like Chicago and St. Louis, it was the Southern harpers who eventually showed the newcomers how to sing it full bore.
>
> "We had been struggling along on our own," said [Gary] Gronau, another founding member of the St. Louis Shape Note Singers.
>
> At first, the members passed around barely legible photocopies from the original tunebooks, met in attics and basements, and tried their best to conjure the magic the printed matter only hinted at. Then, it occurred to Gronau to seek out those who had grown up in the tradition, in much the same way blues fanatics had scoured the Mississippi delta seeking links to Robert Johnson and other masters.

This narrative closely resembles that of the Chicago Founders' Lesson, which also emphasized a period of isolated "foundering." It veers sharply away from that account in that it credits the St. Louis singers with initiating a kind of treasure hunt for traditional Sacred Harp singing, as though lifelong singers were just waiting to be found. In a singings posting, with the subject line "Falsely accused," Gary Gronau wrote, "[N]ow that postings have directed everyone's attention to it I am even more mortified than when I read the article myself. . . . [I]t refers to comments, allegedly by me, that I most emphatically DID NOT MAKE. Specifically it imputes to me a seemingly vainglorious claim that it was somehow my original idea to travel south ("to seek out those who had grown up in the tradition"). I neither said nor implied any such thing and I hope that those who know me (and who know that I was a relative late-comer to southern travels) will just naturally assume that the attribution is false."

This article and Gronau's response demonstrate how media representations of Sacred Harp tend to articulate points about status, regional hierarchies, and identity politics that are rarely made explicit at singings. The stereotyped language and historical glosses of local-color journalism exist in counterpoint with singer-produced media, from fasola.org postings to convention flyers to full-length documentary videos, which also articulate and sustain narratives of authenticity and authority.

Circulating Authenticity

The Sacred Harp diaspora's "discovery" of the Lee family, singers who met the standards of authenticity-seekers to an unprecedented degree, illuminates the role that sound recordings and the fasola.org lists have played in shaping relationships across the singing community. As I discussed in Chapter 3, many singers first encountered the Lees in much the same way that folk music enthusiasts encountered Sacred Harp in general in the 1950s and 1960s: through the circulation of a recording. During the folk revival, the recordings were often collections like Harry Smith's *Anthology of American Folk Music* (Smith 1997 [1952]), which included a few Sacred Harp songs mixed in with music performed by groups like the Cincinnati Jug Band, the Sanctified Singers, and the Carter Family. These anthologies led some people to seek out albums devoted exclusively to Sacred Harp, like the Lomax recording of the 1959 United Convention (Lomax 1960). In contrast, the recording of the Lees that circulated around the country in the 1990s had been made by the family themselves. It traveled exclusively through personal affiliation networks rather than commercial distribution or library collections.

Such "cassette culture" stories have become ubiquitous; recording technology is now relatively cheap and accessible to vast numbers of people worldwide (Manuel 1995). Paradoxically, the timeless, premodern character that has long been attributed to orally transmitted music has actually been reinforced by modern technology. A recorded performance is trapped in amber and isolated from its contemporary social world in a way that no "folk community" ever has been. Recording makes it possible for a performance to acquire a place in modernity through reproduction and distribution in endless new contexts while the original performance remains essentialized as premodern, authentic, and fundamentally distant—lost to true understanding. The recording can become a portable trace of authenticity, a simulacrum that evokes nostalgic guilt; like a cicada shell, it perfectly delineates the contours of the living thing that has always already gone.

But this quality does not prevent particular recordings from developing performative life histories of their own, constituted in use. Modern media are easy to circulate and difficult to control, unstable in meaning and "prone to wander."[15] The Lee family made the anniversary singing tape themselves, but retained control of neither its circulation nor the story of its production. Many still assume the tape was made by a sympathetic outsider who recognized the value of preserving this sound and brought recording technology to an oral-transmission community.

Once the Lees began to travel to distant singings, however, they gained the power to recontextualize the recording, using their unsought celebrity to particular ends. In discovering the Sacred Harp diaspora and accepting the mantle of tradition-bearers, they gained the means to transmit their special performance practices and core beliefs about the religious nature of Sacred Harp singing to a large and receptive community. While diaspora singers were initially most interested in hearing and perhaps learning to replicate the *sound* of Lee family hymnody, the family members who traveled and taught singing schools were far more intent on transmitting their spiritual understanding of the tradition. David Lee has consistently emphasized his awe of other singing families and denies his family's ability to teach other singers anything, even in the North. As he wrote to me,

> When Ted Mercer asked me about teaching a singing school in Chicago, I was startled by the request and told him so. I told him that I didn't see there was anything we could teach them about Sacred Harp singing, rather I thought they could teach us a great deal. . . . [A]fter much thought over the next few weeks, [I] told Clarke that we would go and just try to show them (the Chicago people) the faith-based side of our tradition. . . . As it happens, that is the thrust of every "singing school" I have taught anywhere since then. Of course, I include stories about family, details about our traditional exercises in Sacred Harp, and so forth. But, primarily, I try to share the love and the faith of our tradition.[16]

Conversations with David have made it clear that any other approach would have connoted an expression of vanity that is anathema to his family's faith. With the egalitarian paradigm of fellowship in mind, he can continue to protest, "Why anyone would think we were special is more than I can know."[17]

The Sacred Harp diaspora was revitalized by the authenticity it ascribed to these singers, imagined as devout believers from an unbroken family line hidden away in a secret pocket of the rural South. The abundant good will and tolerance the Lees demonstrated as they encountered different branches of the national community also helped to perpetuate the mainstream Sacred Harp ideology of egalitarianism and mutual respect among those of different religious beliefs. In a poignant chapter of both the Lee mythology and of their personal lives, the Lees became martyrs to this cause: in 1995 and 1996 members of the family were expelled from their Primitive Baptist congregation for participating in worship with outsiders. As John G. Crowley described these events in an online Baptist journal, "Since no Crawfordite church has carpet, the Lees were soon called on the planks about their participation in semi-religious sings, patronized by agnostics on the one hand and heretics on the other. . . . One Lee clearly expressed the effect of these events. When expelled from the church where his family has worshiped since the 1820s, he arose from his seat and left the meetinghouse singing *Liberty* from the *Sacred Harp:* 'No more beneath th' oppressive hand/ Of tyranny we groan/ Behold the smiling, happy land/ That freedom calls her own'" (Crowley 2004).

David Lee's account to me was less colorful. He downplayed the role of singing in the rupture, noting that his congregation was already experiencing discord before this issue arose. But he emphasized the importance of a Sacred Harp recording and book in encouraging him to accept an invitation to an outside convention in the first place:

> By the early '90s, I was dissatisfied (along with most of the rest) and, therefore, was already desiring something better by the time the invitation from Alice Bejnar [to attend a Florida singing] came. Having been introduced to the Sacred Harp community through the Birmingham tape and through Buell Cobb's book, I immediately went to the Tallahassee sing to see if there was anything there for me. . . . [W]e were so warmly received, I felt as though I was back in the loving atmosphere that I had enjoyed through my church and my family for all my earlier life. After I began attending these Sacred Harp sings, some of the brethren in the church decided to take action against me for what they perceived as abandoning the church.[18]

Subsequently, David, his parents, and his cousin Clarke Lee were expelled from their church. After a period of visiting other area churches, they became members at Mars Hill Primitive Baptist Church.

To the best of my knowledge, the story of this rupture became the subject of public Sacred Harp discourse for the first time with the Crowley article, which a singer posted to both fasola.org lists in July 2004. An earlier scholarly article had stated that "At home, the Lees have been thrown out of their church because of their 'new style' sacred harp" (Sommers 2000: 35)—a less than ideal summary, since the church dispute was focused on participating in worship with nonmembers rather than on musical style—but this article was not cited on the listservs. Until the 2004 posting of Crowley's article I had only heard the expulsion discussed in private conversations among singers. People seemed to assume it was privileged information, even as it became close to common knowledge—like the spread of the anniversary recording, this piece of the Lee story gained symbolic importance through controlled distribution. But in fact David Lee was quite forthcoming (as he has been with other scholars) when I asked how he would feel if I wrote about this sensitive subject in an academic article (Miller 2004a). The Crowley article predated mine; after it was posted to the discussions list, singers began to post questions and comments about the rupture and about Primitive Baptist associations in general, which they addressed not to members of the Lee family but to the list at large. Once again, certain media and forms of inquiry effectively skirted the boundaries of appropriate Sacred Harp public discourse and brought potentially sensitive topics into play through a back door.

Members of the Lee family have actively managed the representation of their singing tradition as scholars and distant singers have taken an interest in it. The ethnomusicologist Laurie Sommers observed, "By the time I first interviewed David and Clarke in winter of 1997, they had become quite sanguine about who they were and what made their tradition different: I was treated to the most articulate, reflective, and eloquent first interview I have ever recorded" (Sommers 2000: 44 n. 12).[19] In general, singers and scholars often assume that the expressive capacities and interpersonal skills of the family have developed from their time teaching singing schools and fielding endless questions about their family tradition; after all, they are imagined to have lived a life of almost monastic isolation before their national debut. Sommers notes, "A man now in his mid-forties, David grew up without radio, television, or motion pictures. This remarkable isolation is dramatized by the fact that he bought his first television in 1997, and that was only to play videos of sacred harp sings" (Sommers 2000: 34).

It is reasonable to conclude that the family became more articulate about their approach to Sacred Harp when they were constantly asked to discuss it, but an emphasis on the family's isolation in "a folk region in the classic sense of the word" (Sommers 2000: 33) has occluded their prominent role in business and community affairs. David Lee confirmed that he did not take part in "worldly entertainment such as TV, radio, movies, local fairs, rodeos, dances, music parks, or anything of the sort" while growing up, but he has hardly led a life isolated from mainstream society. When I asked him what business his family is engaged in, he replied,

I own a wholesale commercial lawn equipment distributorship for the southeast U.S. and a local retail lawn equipment dealership. I also own a leasing/floor planning company which provides financial services for dealers and end users of commercial lawn equipment. Daddy started the wholesale business in 1984 but later sold out to me.

Daddy was previously the executive manager for a couple of area credit unions and I was project manager for a heavy equipment contractor. We have both been in office/management positions throughout our lives. I served on the local school board for two terms before giving it up to devote more time to our business. During his time with the credit unions, Daddy served on numerous national boards around the country.[20]

With or without a TV at home, a long career in the business world has contributed to David's ability to speak articulately to large groups and to manage his family's image in the Sacred Harp diaspora, local media coverage, and scholarly writing.

Tollie Lee, David's uncle, often posts messages to the fasola.org lists. Marked individuals are much less marked on the Internet: visible and audible otherness seems readily effaceable for those with versatile writing skills. But Tollie Lee has chosen to emphasize his audible otherness—his rural Southernness—to the point of ironic self-caricature. A May 2000 posting to singings@fasola.org, in response to an announcement about a Western Massachusetts Cooper book singing, provides a rich example:

Good going and Gracious speed. I do personally wish you the best in all your attempts at Sacred Harp. We will be praying that your singing will be abundantly blessed from an all wise and all powerful creator. Let the voices reach the roof top of the upper skies and all the hearts be filled with gladness.

hope to see yall soon
frum de lower side uv de okofanokee bad land tremblin' urth,
jest let ebber wun be soothed wid de oilll of gladness
love to all
Tollie
ps sing on::: and on::::[21]

Tollie Lee's ability and willingness to perform this kind of code-switching are an example of the way stereotyped subjects co-opt the terms of stereotype to reinvent their self-representation (Ching 1997). His shift from the gracious, formal style of a respected mentor to spelled-out Southernness brings out the performative character of his participation in the community.

At the same time he engages creatively with the cyberspace issues raised by Barbara Kirshenblatt-Gimblett: "What is the nature of presence in a disembodied medium? Of performativity in a typographic medium?" (Kirshenblatt-Gimblett 1996: 23). There is a more subtle joke embedded here as well; most readers are likely to assume "bad land tremblin' urth" refers to the apocalyptic Southern preaching style Lee is quasi-parodying, but in fact "land of trembling earth" is the translation of the Seminole word "Okefenokee," the name of the wetlands area where the Lee family lives.

Tollie Lee is a Primitive Baptist preacher, and his postings often draw on that rhetorical genre to extraordinary effect. After the 1999 Tri-State Convention, held in Alabama, Lee posted an account of his experience to singings@fasola.org. Such reports are the main subject matter of the singings list, along with announcements of upcoming singings and major events in the lives of singers. Like local-color journalism, they often include details of the long trip to reach the venue, impressionistic descriptions of the power of the singing, and praise for the local specialties on the dinner table. At some point the writer makes special mention of a few local organizers or particularly impressive leaders, with the caveat that he is bound to have left someone out. Tollie Lee's 1999 posting incorporates all of these generic elements into a tour de force parody of improvised Baptist preaching:

> Twas a singing we went to
> In tha South of Alabama,, ah convention it's called by
> name. tri State.
> Some came early some were late
> To tha singers a notable date
> Plenty of food for every plate.
> By spirit that tis tha plate
> Just one day convention
> with plenty of attention
> Sacred harp was tha menu
> Fla was represented By Floyd and Pat
> John E and Aubrey, Janet. Alice and Tor
> Bob and Lois from Oca LA,, FA So LA
> Mi—canopy sent Les Singleton
> last and least Tollie and Ramona from Callahan.
>
> Georgia, had David and Clarke Lee, their wives Kathy and Julie and Clarke's
> kids. Bro Johnny and, Delorese filling in the seats of base and treble. Ala-

bama turned out many. Nall, Jones. Smiths and Spurlocks,, Olivers. Frank-
lins, Adams. Aplins,, and several more in laws and names that I have not
learned them all yet. From Minn, Jim and Kitt Pfau, Martha, Tom Mitchell
and others who were important to our singing.

The little place called Travelers Rest
Is akin to the blue bird nest
She sits in a secluded spot
A ways in the country side
Singers can sing and ride
Upon the joys of a moving tide
Voices rose and fell as tha breeze
An consoled our very being
Tha lil' town of Samson not far away
made me think of strength that day
He represented power in his might
And voices led by beautiful light
Some water in tha form of tears
Flowed and helped away the fears
Nevah can Ah hint at tha matter
For myself was humbled at first
When Bill ask me to lead the three songs
No. 84, 108 top and 129
For is their manner for someone to do aft. Morn.
Devotion My heart was so full I thought I'd burst with emotion . . .
A sweeet relief arrived and I survived
all glory to our MAKER!!
Dinner on the table outside was a special treat.
Some of us sang several by request from the Lloyd Hymnal
Afternoon was another treat. John E ask me to stand with him and sing
    319 Religion is a Fortune,,, Lord only knows and the feelings that
    overcame,
John's face was like a flame,, some time will maybe tel ya why that is so
    special to me.

WE are lightered knot buddies. A lighter knot is a piece of very fat pine
wood that will explode into flames when touched by a spark of a match.
So will two hearts sing when properly led by a MAster of Assemblies.

hope ave not bode ya ta much with our lil conv.
Yall member nxt yeah it:ll be in Bohoken Ga
on tha Sat, fore tha thud sun in oct 2000

Sincerely want to thank all who came and sang and listened and th cooks
who were blessed to prepare all the wonderful tasty food. If any went away
hungry it wud bee theah own fault!!!!!
sing on::
And LUV to All ,, Tollie[22]

This posting recalls the work of scholars of Appalachian religion, who have
painstakingly transcribed and analyzed this kind of improvisatory preaching and prayer (Titon 1988, Patterson 1995, Tyson, Peacock et al. 1988).
Primitive Baptist preaching often employs formal devices like rhyme and
complex verbal rhythms in the course of unpacking Scriptural references.
Lee's posting came complete with creative use of punctuation and line
breaks to reproduce the effect of marked pauses and to distinguish rhym-
ing sections from "prose" sections. He converted the usual laundry list of
names in Sacred Harp convention accounts to a Scripture-like litany that
includes internal rhyme (e.g., "Johnny and Delo*rese* filling in the *seats*"—a
rhyme only accessible to readers who know how to pronounce "Delorese").
He performs exegesis of the idiom "lighter knot," explaining its etymology
in a "prose" aside and then converting it into a Scripture-reliant metaphor
for the experience for singing together—a metaphor conveniently flagged
with "<allegory>," like an HTML tag. All in all, Tollie Lee's posts infuse
the listserv with an alternative and highly distinctive form of local color.[23]
His style leans toward parody—today no scholar would transcribe a rural
Southern accent with dialect spellings, as in "hope ave not bode ya ta much
with our lil conv."—but never quite drops over the edge into irony because
it incorporates so many signs of sincerity.

Tollie Lee's postings encapsulate erudition within parodic exaggerations
of Southern dialect, a stereotypical marker of ignorance. He developed
this writing style in correspondence with "a fellow from Ohio that started
teasing us (and Tollie in particular) about southern ways," as David Lee
explained—"This fellow is also a southerner at heart and began emailing to
Tollie and me using this imagined southern vernacular. We all thought it
was funny and Tollie ultimately started using this manner when posting to
the website. Probably for the very reason (though most likely subconscious)
that you mentioned: poking fun at stereotypes."[24] One of the things that
make Tollie's postings funny is their representation of an improvisatory

tradition in faux-transcribed form in a high-tech medium. The fact that he also manages to integrate all the genre conventions of local-color journalism and listserv convention reports into his "sermon" postings makes them even more effective.

Those who recognize such subversive gestures sometimes experience a flash of guilt, a sudden unflattering self-awareness. Is it all right for them to laugh when Tollie Lee performs a stereotype, when they know (and he might know) that all their lives they have laughed at parodies of Southern accents? As one singer told me, "I always thought I might feel unwelcome at a singing in the South because wouldn't they be a bunch of ignorant Bible-pounding Baptists, prejudiced all kinds of ways and ready to consign me to Hell for being a liberal agnostic Yankee? I've spent a lot of time kicking myself over that, because obviously I was the prejudiced one. My horizons are a bit broader now." I have heard variants of this kind of "blind but now I see" confession from singers of all political stripes. Such guilty realizations can be quite pleasurable, in that they reinforce singers' confidence in their own good intentions and the inclusive nature of the Sacred Harp community.

Tollie Lee's postings do not merely hold up a mirror to an essentializing gaze. When Lee writes to offer encouragement to a new Northern singing—"I do personally wish you the best in all your attempts at Sacred Harp"—he subtly reinscribes an established ideology: that Southern traditional singers are in touch with the essence of Sacred Harp, while newcomers make laudable but imperfect attempts in that direction. New singers are much appreciated, and perhaps even crucial to the continuation of the tradition, but will always be "visitors" to some degree. The minutes of the 1999 New England Convention include two comments with similar undertones that were made by Southerners when they were called to lead: "Gary Smith 569b (Gary graciously commented that he was glad to have 'come home' to New England where Sacred Harp singing began). . . . Hugh McGraw 413 (Hugh offered a few words about the first time he visited the north to sing from the Sacred Harp and expressed gratitude that the tradition is being kept alive here)" (Sheppard and Ivey 2000: 210–11).

Gary Smith's remark might at first seem to cede authority to New England, but he is known for his dry humor; as noted in the minutes, the "gracious" character of his comment already established his status as a Southerner, and at many other Northern conventions he has remarked on how glad he is "to be back in Northern Alabama." The fact that these comments were recorded at all suggests that the convention secretary was sympathetic to the Southern tradition and its claims on diaspora singing. Minutes do not usually include remarks made by leaders during their lessons, and these are the only such comments that appear in the 1999 New England Convention minutes.

Many lifelong Sacred Harp singers have the regional accents and mannerisms that might in other circumstances cause them to be read as Southern "white trash," as I discussed in the Introduction. In the Sacred Harp context they have participated in their own transformation into keepers of sacred cultural wisdom. Northern singers now turn to Southerners—not only lifelong singers, but any singer with a Southern accent—as leaders in a search for a fulfilling lifestyle. Hugh McGraw, Richard DeLong, and the many Southern singing families whose members agree to teach singing schools in the diaspora have at least tacitly self-identified as authorities on Sacred Harp, in part by enlisting their own Southernness as evidence. They enhance their markedness rather than concealing it, converting the Southern accent into an emblem of moral and intellectual authority and an instigator of liberal guilt. As singing-school teachers, convention organizers, and ordinary singers alike, Southern singers have taken their authenticity on the road. They have turned nonsynchronicity into cultural capital, and they have done it in the process of maintaining what they consider to be the essential characteristics of their different regional traditions.

Rivers of Delight: Sacred Harp as Folk Hymnody

There is one commercially released Sacred Harp recording that might be considered a counterpart to the Lee family tapes, in terms of distribution and influence in the national singing community: the 1979 Nonesuch recording *Rivers of Delight: American Folk Hymns from the Sacred Harp Tradition*. On this album Larry Gordon and his Word of Mouth Chorus affiliated themselves with traditional Sacred Harp singing, although their performance sounds very different from contemporary Southern Sacred Harp. Like other vocal ensembles of its ilk, Word of Mouth performed "a wide variety of traditional as well as medieval and Renaissance music"; founded in 1971 and based in Vermont, the chorus also had strong connections to Bread and Puppet Theater, a progressive political theater company (Gordon 1979). Two articles of cultural common knowledge made it reasonable for Word of Mouth and other folk-revival or early music choirs to present their Sacred Harp sound as traditional: first, that "American folk song" lies in the public domain, free for the taking; second, that the rural

South constitutes a legitimate source of raw materials for export and transformation, whether such materials consist of coal, old-time music, homespun cloth, or "family values."

On sound recordings and in folk festival programs, "American folk hymnody" is the most persistent genre category for Sacred Harp singing, at least since the label "white spirituals" fell by the wayside. Classifying American sacred song traditions can be difficult for ethnographers, historians, record producers, and even singers. Christian texts have long been sung both within and outside of church services, and some of these songs have close musical, textual, and performance-context relationships to secular genres like narrative ballads. The "folk hymnody" label solves the classification problem by creating a catch-all category for sacred-texted polyphonic songs that have not been confined to formal worship contexts and which are thought to have connections to Old World or early American traditions (whether or not the composers are known). "American folk hymnody" is a sufficiently flexible category to accommodate the tastes of people who identify as fans of folk music, Christian music, or early American music. Moreover, folk hymns constitute a repertoire of "traditional music" that Americans with no particular ethnic affiliation can claim as their own, regardless of their actual experience within a continuous musical tradition.[25] Defining Sacred Harp as American folk hymnody rendered it accessible to the wave of folk-revival enthusiasts who discovered it in the 1960s and 1970s. *Rivers of Delight* remains a preeminent exemplar of this "folk hymnody" paradigm.

A first reading of the album notes for *Rivers of Delight* suggests that the Word of Mouth project was laudably respectful of traditional Southern singing. The bulk of the space is given over to the remarks of Buell Cobb, then and now a respected Sacred Harp singer and historian. His detailed account of shape-note history—the New England tunesmiths, the nineteenth-century singing schools, the peculiarities of the notation—lends credibility to the recording. Cobb's description of contemporary performance practice is relatively brief: he alludes to the hollow-square seating formation, mentions that "each singer has an opportunity to come before the 'class' and lead a 'lesson'—a song or two of his choice," and sketches the musical style: "The characteristic sound of Sacred Harp singing is comprised of several elements: the surging beat, the intonation of the singers, the minor-modal melodies, and the open harmonies" (Cobb 1979). This is dry and technical compared to the force-of-nature descriptions I discussed earlier; it reads as authoritative rather than impressionistic, giving the recording scholarly heft. Since Cobb eschewed adjectives in describing the traditional "intonation of the singers," the uninitiated folk music enthusiast could conclude that the Word of Mouth Chorus exemplifies that intonation—in other words, that Sacred Harp sounds quite a lot like a historically informed Renaissance choral ensemble, only in English and with a bit more rhythmic drive.

Larry Gordon provided a more personal note on behalf of the Word of Mouth Chorus, which I reproduce here in its entirety:

> Many of us first sang Sacred Harp music together in 1971. In the years that followed, we found ourselves more and more drawn to this music, with its strength and spirit, and its raw Americanness of expression. In April 1976, a group of Word of Mouth singers traveled to the Georgia State Singing Convention and were profoundly impressed by this and several subsequent direct experiences with the ongoing Southern shape-note tradition. We were moved by the deep fellowship among the participants, a fellowship that reached out to include us, bridging vast boundaries of age, culture, politics, and religion. Moreover, the singing itself—the rhythmic drive, the unrestrained quality of the voices, the sheer power of the sound—permanently altered our approach to Sacred Harp music. We like to regard Sacred Harp as a live tradition which can be the vehicle for a very special sharing among singers of all ages and abilities. In our area, people have begun once again to create new songs using this idiom, as well as new texts reflecting some of the concerns of our present-day lives. (Gordon 1979)

After a few "direct experiences," the Word of Mouth Chorus felt qualified to produce a recording claiming membership in the tradition, even to the extent of placing some newly composed songs squarely within the Sacred Harp repertoire. Gordon legitimizes Word of Mouth Chorus performance practice by describing their musical pilgrimage to Georgia—indeed, the very name of the chorus suggests a special attention to oral tradition. He suggests that the New England singers were accepted into the tradition by its official gatekeepers, who "reached out to include us." Georgia singers who were present at this particular convention confirm this claim, with a different spin; they have told me that the New England singers were specifically invited to attend—like the Chicago singers some years later—because Southern singers were concerned about their ignorance of traditional performance practice. But Gordon's more utopian account of how Sacred Harp fellowship extended itself to encompass visitors minimizes potential conflicts over who represents traditional singing and reinforces the perceived Americanness of Sacred Harp, which can bridge "vast boundaries of age, culture, politics and religion." The tradition becomes a democratizer, a fire beneath the melting pot.[26]

If the Sacred Harp tradition is all-inclusive, then almost anyone is qualified to represent it. It is within this frame that New England singers could freely "create new songs using this idiom" and situate them within a discourse of American tradition. Gordon acknowledged that Southern singers were engaged in an ongoing tradition, yet he obliquely situated the Southern tradition in the past. His chorus's newly written texts reflected "the concerns of our present-day lives," making a strong contrast to Cobb's closing statement that Sacred Harp is "a music and a tradition that have remained virtually unchanged since pre–Civil War days." The juxtaposition presents traditional Southern singers as an anachronism, living ancestors who are available for consultation on traditional American folkways if revivalists choose to seek them out.

Considering the content of the album notes, the extent to which the Word of Mouth performance style diverges from contemporary Sacred Harp practice is striking. To begin with, the chorus is made up of an exclusive group of semiprofessional musicians, not a democratic jumble of "singers of all ages and abilities," a fact which flies in the face of conventional Sacred Harp ideology as expressed by Gordon himself. The vocal style falls within the limits sketched by Cobb—the melodies are modal, the harmonies open, the rhythm fairly marked—but a comparison to contemporary recordings of Sacred Harp conventions reveals the accommodating vagueness of these terms. Western Georgia and eastern Alabama conventions recorded in the 1970s present a group sound that is heterophonically ornamented and features distinctive timbres among the voice parts (Sound Example 8, "I'm On My Journey Home" [345b]). Singers forgo clear enunciation of individual words in favor of large-scale phrasing and flow, with words running together just as the solfege do. Faster passages are sung with marked "shuffle," a rhythmic quality akin to swing (Sound Example 9, "The Golden Harp" [274t]). But the Word of Mouth rendition of "Evening Shade" (209; Sound Example 10) is as perfectly blended and smooth as an early music choir's performance of a Palestrina motet, with carefully pronounced words, no dynamic variation to emphasize phrasing, and no "shuffle" on the eighth-note fuging entrances. Their "Cowper" (168; Sound Example 11) has something closer to the volume, timbre, and attack of contemporary Southern singing, but here the quarter-note fuging entrances are as consistent as a jackhammer; like the legato, perfectly even eighth-notes of "Evening Shade," these precise staccato entrances lack dynamic contour and tend to obscure large-scale meter. Compare the Word of Mouth rendition of "Cowper" with a recording from the 2002 Chattahoochee Convention in west Georgia (Sound Example 12).

Rivers of Delight also features peculiarities of arrangement. For example, it would be an extraordinary occurrence for any Sacred Harp tune to be sung with only the tenor and bass parts, as is the case for "Idumea" on this recording (47b; Sound Example 13), or with a new part entering at each verse, as with "North Port" (324; Sound Example 14). These renditions give Sacred Harp a high and lonely sound—closer to the isolated, eerie, soloistic sound that characterizes Appalachian ballads in the popular imagination. But the success of a Sacred Harp convention is often measured by the number and volume of its participants: the sound is loud and full. It is the music of a large and active community, not an isolated mountaineer or an accomplished solo singer. Sacred Harp singers sing slow, minor-key, death-oriented hymns as loudly as fast, cheerful ones—many of which are also about death, since the Christian tradition marks it as "the gate to endless joy" as well as something to be feared and mourned. On "Evening Shade," the Word of Mouth singers make death a *sotto voce* affair.

An "American folk hymn" should represent American ideals, and Gordon describes a tradition that seems to fit the bill—egalitarian, tolerant, welcoming. He does not mention the fact that the vast majority of the singers at the Georgia convention were white Protestants. The album notes do not engage with the religious meaning of the texts; the word "Christian" appears only in reference to the tunebook *The Christian Harmony*. Cobb downplays the religious aspect, intentionally or not, by writing that "[T]hey join voices in selections from the oblong song book, some of which are folk melodies that had been passed down for generations before they were given sacred texts . . ." and that "Some of these anthologies . . . spawned non-denominational groups devoted exclusively to a particular song book and the perpetuation of its tunes and singing style." While these observations are entirely accurate, without further context the reader might conclude that the religious content is something of an afterthought. Such a conclusion enhances the "Americanness" and accessibility of the tradition: it is still all-inclusive, even if the texts are Christian. But of course the life-long singers that the chorus encountered in Georgia were inclusive only in the sense that they didn't turn unbelievers away. Singers who are uncomfortable with Christian song texts, prayers, or memorial lessons are not accommodated by all-encompassing fellowship; they self-select out of the singing community. The Georgia State Convention organizers didn't strive to use alternate names of God, nonspecific names for a divine presence, or gender-neutral language.

Closer engagement with the religion question makes "American folk hymnody" a problematic category. If Sacred Harp is not simply folk music—with all the murkiness of origin and ownership that such a classification implies—but a spiritually oriented practice maintained primarily by white southern Protestants, then it does not support the ideology of an all-inclusive American folk tradition. If this is "raw Americanness of expression," what definition of "American" is implied? If one acknowledges Sacred Harp's complex history—not as something trapped in amber "since pre–Civil War days," but as a changing tradition embedded in regional religious practice—one might conclude that it neither represents all Americans nor belongs to any American who happens along. But *Rivers of Delight* does present Sacred Harp as folk music, something that belongs to everyone, a useful tool in the construction of an American identity liberated from the complex trappings of religion, region, and race. The Word of Mouth Chorus could release *Rivers of Delight* with no disclaimers addressing their stylistic divergence from traditional practice precisely because Sacred Harp seemed to be theirs for the taking.

It would be easy enough to let this story fall into a standard genre: another tradition appropriated by well-meaning outsiders in the service of a culture and a music market hungry for authenticity. My analysis certainly fulfills many of the requirements of such a narrative. But the Georgia singers never behaved like passive victims of cultural appropriation. In the wake of the Word of Mouth Chorus visit to Georgia, Hugh McGraw persuaded many Southern singers to attend the first annual New England Convention in the fall of 1976, bringing Southern convention practice and singing style with them. As Bealle relates,

> In years to follow, a chartered bus from the South has made regular appearances at each new northern convention. . . . It is difficult to overstate the extent to which this gesture has influenced local singing in northern areas. Not only did it demonstrate the extraordinary commitment of southern singers but, by lifting the quality of the singing to unimaginable heights, it left on local groups a considerable burden to continue meeting these raised expectations. (Bealle 1997: 196)

Many singers now contextualize *Rivers of Delight* within the pre-history of the national diaspora: an often lovely-sounding example of "foundering," of harmless and naïve folkie efforts to join a tradition the chorus hadn't come close to understanding.

The affectionate condescension such singers lavish on this album poses a formidable comeuppance to remarks like "We like to regard Sacred Harp as a live tradition." As Paul Sant Cassia has observed, in a sense inauthentic or mediocre folksong performance makes authentic folk music possible; it "leaves a gap in the construction of [folksong] for it to be 'rediscovered' outside such contexts as 'authentic performance'" (2000: 290). In the late 1990s, when Sacred Harp singers of my acquaintance introduced me to this recording, no one mentioned the album notes or the title's claim to represent "the Sacred Harp tradition." Instead, they warned that the singing was "prettified," "much too clean," or sounded like "generic Balkan choir singing." But these same qualities had made this recording compelling to folk-revival fans in the early 1980s, and several singers credited *Rivers of Delight* with inspiring them to find out more about Sacred Harp singing. John Bealle performed a statistical analysis of Sacred Harp minutes that clearly demonstrated the influence of what he called the "*Rivers of Delight* corpus" on diaspora singing; this corpus "represents only 19 of 560 songs in the book," but national minutes show these songs being led at an increasing rate between 1979 and 1984. They were statistically over-represented even beyond these increases at the first Illinois State and Midwest Conventions in 1985 and 1986 (Bealle 1997: 263–64).

Many singers still use this recording when they try to interest friends and family in Sacred Harp singing. Recordings of actual Southern conventions are generally considered to be much less accessible and appealing to the uninitiated, and they can have deep emotional resonance for the experienced. Singers want to shield them from listeners who tend to hear them as "primitive" music at best and more often as monotonous, too loud, unintelligible, and out-of-tune. *Rivers of Delight* "is like a gateway drug," someone once quipped to me; "most people can't handle the hard stuff right away." Along these lines, a 2001 *St. Louis Post-Dispatch* article on the sixteenth annual Missouri State Convention ends with some recommended recordings: "The St. Louis Shape Note Singers have recordings of some of their conventions available. They give an accurate idea of the sound (foot-stomping and all) but they aren't going to be to all tastes. For many listeners, a professional recording, using professional singers, will be a better choice. . . . [F]or something between the authentic and the polished, consider 'Rivers of Delight: American Folk Hymns From the Sacred Harp Tradition.'"[27]

Singers confirm this music critic's assessment of *Rivers of Delight* as "between the authentic and the polished." They continue to recommend it as a more accurate representation of contemporary practice than the "early music"–style recordings of the New England shape-note repertoire by groups like the Boston Camerata and Anonymous 4: *Rivers of Delight* at least nods to the ongoing Southern tradition.[28] But, singers hasten to add, even the Word of Mouth album "isn't traditional singing." Recordings like this one are a form of appropriation, but appropriation that demands repayment and engenders obligation. After making a claim to a stake in the Sacred Harp tradition, folk-revival singers could hardly turn away the visits and the criticism of their "living ancestors," who took a chartered bus right over the "vast boundaries" that separated them from contemporary New England.

In the following decades diaspora organizers actively lobbied for the "Southern bus" to visit their conventions; if they succeeded, they often advertised the coming visit in advance. (See Figure 27.) The longtime organizer of these bus trips, a retired Alabama teacher named Ruth Brown, died in May of 2003 at the age of ninety-two. Her passing prompted memorial lessons that brought formal attention to the importance of Southern travelers and their support of diaspora conventions. In one such lesson, given in Seattle, Karen Willard compared genuine Southern singing to heaven; she credited Ruth Brown with bringing "living ambassadors of the tradition" to earthly conventions outside the South:

> In C. S. Lewis's book *The Great Divorce*, the main character is allowed to travel from earth—hell—to heaven, for a short visit, by means of an omnibus, a special-route bus. He is able to glimpse a portion of the reality of heaven and then to return, using that same omnibus. Miss Ruth's omnibus went the opposite direction. Bringing a taste, whether it was always wanted or not, of the genuine, the real thing, to those singings that sprang up outside of the tradition, and all too quickly the bus returned home. For many of us in the North, her bus riders—and their example [*turning to Southern singers on the alto bench*]—were our first real contact with the traditional—versus whatever it was we'd been doing—[*laughter*] of the Sacred Harp experience. . . . The influence of those trips is incalculable. And we are all profoundly grateful, for they brought to us [*choking up*] a true glimpse of heaven.[29]

Minnesota convention: September 25 & 26

Figure 27: Detail from a flyer for the 1999 Minnesota Convention, advertising a visit from the Southern bus. (Drawing by Jenny Willard.)

Stereotype Redux: Negotiated Compromise

Local-color narratives of Sacred Harp singing have changed much less than the singing community itself over the past century. Both journalists and singers still relish relating their end-of-the-line arrivals, their sense of stepping outside of time or back in history, the visceral power of the singing, and all the details of a strange land and a peculiar people. Like Frost in 1899, newcomers observe rural Southern culture "from the car window, with curious eyes, as we are whirled toward our Southern hotel," and some are struck by the guilty knowledge that "even yet" the traditional singers they have come to see "are scarcely distinguished in our thought from the 'poor white trash'" whose territory might still be fraught with peril for an outsider (Frost 1899: 311).

But while these basic themes have been consistent, they have been put to different uses across their history. In the early twentieth century, xenophobic writers deployed the end-of-the-line arrival scene to link isolation with racial purity. Today end-of-the-line isolation is more often celebrated as evidence of an endlessly diverse America where particularity still thrives in hidden places. The back-in-time quality attributed to Sacred Harp singing is now as often about resisting mass-mediated entertainments and reclaiming authentically felt experience as it is about giving America living ancestors to testify to its antiquity of national character. The old meanings of these tropes have not evaporated, and the new ones are not unprecedented; suspended in the liquid ambivalence of stereotype, any of them can rise to the surface to meet shifting needs. But the Sacred Harp diaspora, with its long-distance travel routes and its multimedia communications network, has given some "traditional singers" the impetus and the tools to perform stereotype in new ways and on a new stage.[30] Marginalized status becomes a point of pride through an emphasis on historical continuity and community values, the positive side of being a "living ancestor."

The old melting-pot model, which accommodated so many immigrant "white ethnics," dictated that those who could be fully assimilated should count it as a privilege: effaceable difference should be effaced if one really wants to participate on an equal footing in the mainstream. It's easy to imagine that white rural Southerners could choose to pass as just plain white people, with all the privileges that status conveys—and if they possess the necessary economic and cultural capital, many Southerners do exactly that. But as Barbara Ching writes in her work on country music, self-consciously choosing a rural persona can be empowering, especially for those who bear "the stigma of supposed unsophistication" (Ching 1997: 241). While Southerners often alter their own accents and mannerisms in order to "pass," they may also experience an obligation to perpetuate beliefs or practices bound up with essentialized Southernness. In certain contexts they choose to perform their difference rather than obscuring it.

The task of sorting out one's affiliations and perpetuating them through the medium of a given tradition has acquired new dimensions with new technologies. Classic transmission practices like singing around the table after a family supper can leave a reproducible trace, a floating commodity with consequences beyond the full control of the singers, the distributor of recordings, or the listeners. For singers who borrow the terms of pilgrimage to account for their travels, such a recording can seem like a sacred relic, bottled holy water, or perhaps Tollie Lee's soothing "oilll of gladness." But one still must "come to the source" and "drink from the fountain" in person to experience its efficacy (see Chapter 3). The inadequacy of recordings to represent the experience of Sacred Harp singing—the inadequacy that leads people to use "prettified" renditions to entice newcomers to come to a real singing—is a reminder that authentic Sacred Harp both requires and celebrates face-to-face interaction in the hollow square. Nothing else will do.

In keeping with this metaphor of healing waters, consider the second verse of "The Gospel Pool" (34t):

But whither can I go?
There is no other pool
Where streams of sovereign virtue flow
To make a sinner whole.[31]

The belief that "no other pool"—no other social forum or medium—can accomplish the same effect as the hollow square informs singers' choices as they circulate, interpret, and recontextualize this mediated music. Media representations circulate in unpredictable ways, but the hollow square meets their challenge with a different form of portability. Like a mirage oasis, it can spring up anywhere, but once it is there it holds still and gathers experience to itself. The square is "a gospel pool," a stable immersion point for experience and interpretation, saturated with local color. Recordings made in such a place are only meaningful inasmuch as they channel a "relational aesthetic," as Erlmann calls it, grounded in the conviction that "the essence of art no longer lies beyond the work of art, in a meaning, but in the interaction to which it gives rise" (Erlmann 1996: 481).

The Sacred Harp singers I have discussed in this chapter use all available media to negotiate personally acceptable and productive relationships with the stereotypes that cling to rural Southern culture and "old-time" American music. Some have traded on their Southernness through ironic performances like spelling out their accents, confirming their own authenticity as traditional singers while undermining assumptions about the people of their region. By some standards their efforts sound like a solid success story: Sacred Harp practice gets passed on, new liberal singers get the twin pleasures of ethical community and retrospective guilt, the Southern singers get respect, everyone becomes more tolerant, and the good American values—the ones about community and individual freedoms—live on.[32] But bear in mind that some lifelong singers have been criticized by family or fellow singers and rejected by church brethren for singing with the known liberals, gays, and unbelievers who revere them as tradition-bearers. At worst, it can seem that their options amount to little more than deciding which stereotype to mobilize and which heritage to betray.

However, singers who have considered these issues rarely sound this frustrated. They acknowledge that they have made a compromise, but their commitment to Sacred Harp has made it a satisfying one. Sacred Harp singers are far from unique in capitalizing on their own cultural marginality, but this process has special qualities in the Sacred Harp diaspora because so many different kinds of singers identify as marginalized—not only lifelong Southern singers but also gay and lesbian singers, radical leftists, folk music enthusiasts, singers who have left or been expelled from Christian congregations, and many who belong to several of these groups at once. These seemingly incompatible groups form bonds based on their shared rejection by or rejection of the "mainstream," now essentialized in its turn as corrupt and culturally bankrupt. New singers gradually identify with lifelong singers, remaking their own sense of alienation into membership in this musical community of the marginalized. The Sacred Harp diaspora has thus produced a vision of an ideal America out of the tensions between singers' performances of North and South, Christian and non-Christian, liberal and conservative, socially sanctioned intellectual and down-home traditional singer.

6

"At Home in Transience"

TRAVELING CULTURE AND
THE POLITICS OF NOSTALGIA

On the last day of February 2004, about forty Sacred Harp singers filed onstage and in front of millions of television viewers to perform at the Academy Awards. They were billed as the "Sacred Harp Singers of Liberty Church," which is in Henagar, Alabama, although in fact they came from Georgia, Alabama, Texas, New York, Rhode Island, Massachusetts, New Mexico, Illinois, Michigan, and Minnesota.[1] Most of these singers were among those who had sung at a recording session for the soundtrack to *Cold Mountain,* the 2003 Miramax film based on Charles Frazier's Civil War romance. Tim Eriksen—frontman for the band Cordelia's Dad, ballad singer with a master's degree in ethnomusicology, key figure in establishing the Western Massachusetts Convention—served as a musical consultant for the film and lobbied for the inclusion of Sacred Harp singing on the soundtrack. In 2002 he invited about fifty singers from around the country to a recording session at Liberty Baptist Church, along with "as many movie people as I could . . . hoping that they'd get to know the singers a bit and get to feel obliged to them."[2]

Two Sacred Harp songs were used in the film. "Idumea" (47b), a minor plain tune with a text about death and Judgment Day, was included as nondiegetic music—mixed with explosions and the cries of dying soldiers—during the devastating battle scene near the opening. Later, the film's stars and a crowd of Romanian extras were shown sitting in a hollow square and singing "I'm Going Home" (282) in the scene where the outbreak of war is announced. In an austere Southern-uplands parallel to the lavish plantation party scene in *Gone With the Wind,* the male singers gradually leave the plain church, built to resemble Liberty Baptist; the Sacred Harp singers mimicked this effect at the recording session by having male voices gradually drop out. Both songs appeared in what Eriksen called "straight ahead (and spirited)" versions on the soundtrack CD, which was marketed as a follow-up to the extremely successful *O Brother, Where Art Thou?* soundtrack released in 2000.[3]

But the "Sacred Harp Singers of Liberty Church" who traveled to California for the Oscars were not there to sing a Sacred Harp song. Eriksen had assembled them at the request of the studio to sing "a shape-note arrangement of the chorus"[4] of Elvis Costello's song "The Scarlet Tide," performed by Alison Krauss, which had been nominated for an Academy Award. As Rhode Island singer Kelly House noted in a singings posting that updated the singing community on the proceedings, "'Shape note style' is applied loosely here. The tune is very low and there are a few unshape-note-like harmonies involved."[5] Nor would there be any fasola syllables.

Eriksen and others involved with organizing the performance had tried to arrange for a Sacred Harp song to be included in the program, and until the last moment singers believed they would get a chance to perform on their own immediately after their back-up performance. Kelly House explained the rationale for this programming decision: "It is very unusual for the Academy to schedule music that wasn't nominated for an award, but it so happened that all five of the nominated songs this year are very low key, if not downright depressing. The Academy was concerned that they didn't have any showstoppers. Somehow, [the film's music producer] T Bone Burnett managed to convince them that the Sacred Harp singers could produce the showstopper they wanted. They decided they preferred a patriotic song, so Tim Eriksen chose Liberty."

"Liberty" (137) (Figure 28, Sound Example 15), a major-key fuging tune, has one of the least religion-oriented texts in *The Sacred Harp*:

> No more beneath th' oppressive hand
> Of tyranny we groan.
> Behold the smiling, happy land
> That freedom calls her own.[6]

A song like "I'm Going Home" (282), the equally upbeat major tune that actually appeared in *Cold Mountain,* might have seemed a better option for this performance. It is usually sung at a fast clip, it contains "showstopper" high notes, and its homophonic setting would project words more clearly in a non–hollow-square performance format. (See Figure 29, Sound

Figure 28: "Liberty" (137), the patriotic song that was almost performed at the 2004 Academy Awards.

Example 16.) But in an election year (2004), with the war in Iraq going badly, it is not surprising that decision-makers preferred to put the focus on America rather than using a song with lines like "Right up yonder, Christians, away up yonder" and "I'm glad that I am born to die."[7] Given a request for a patriotic song, "Liberty" was the obvious choice. It would also resonate nicely as a kind of theme song for the "Sacred Harp Singers of Liberty Church."

In the end, though, the singers did not perform "Liberty." It was cut from the program after the dress rehearsal, apparently due to time constraints. The disappointed singers carried their tunebooks onstage anyway, holding their closed books in front of their bodies in the hope that panning cameras would catch the title and pique the curiosity of viewers. As lifelong Texas singer Beverly Coates explained, "[W]e decided to carry our books to give some exposure to Sacred Harp. Since they did call us by the name

Figure 29: "I'm Going Home" (282), which appeared as diegetic music in *Cold Mountain*.

'Sacred Harp Singers,' perhaps it will cause some to investigate just what this 'Sacred Harp' is."[8]

In order to grasp the extraordinary nature of this whole chain of events, one must bear in mind the force with which diaspora singers have long expressed the ideas that Sacred Harp is not performance, that participation is always egalitarian, and that the most basic characteristics of Sacred Harp musical practice are singing the fasola syllables and sitting in a hollow square. While singing at folk festivals and the like may employ a performance format, singers retain control of representation; they virtually always include an explanatory element that describes shape-note notation or creates an opportunity for audience participation. These performances often draw on singing-school methods and are billed as "demonstrations" or "workshops," which distinguishes them from "real" Sacred Harp singing; moreover, any experienced singers in the area are usually welcome—or implored—to participate. At the Oscars, by contrast, some of the most prominent singers in the national community allowed that prominence to be publicly acknowledged in a commercial forum where they had to make numerous compromises. They went to California to sing something other than Sacred Harp while being billed as "from" a place that few of them actually called home. They were offered (but ultimately denied) the opportunity to represent Sacred Harp more accurately only in the context of a patriotic "showstopper" that would lend the Oscars nationalistic energy and gravitas in difficult political circumstances.

On the face of it, the Oscars performance was antithetical to the explicitly stated ideals of its singers in virtually every way. Yet Eriksen garnered the support of many devoted singers from around the country, creating a powerful portrait of the Sacred Harp diaspora: a group of committed travelers willing to compromise mightily to present a far-flung, varied practice under the banner of a single Alabama church with a politically fortuitous name. While some singers were not happy with aspects of the *Cold Mountain* affair—for example, the singling-out of particular singers and the commercial nature of the Oscars performance—their dissent remained in the sphere of private discourse and in individual choices not to accept Eriksen's invitation to come sing along at local venues during the "Great High Mountain" concert tour that followed the film.[9]

Because of the film, soundtrack, Academy Awards performance, and concert tour, Sacred Harp singing gained significant national media recognition. But that recognition was rooted in the film's depiction of the tradition as isolated, rural, Civil War–era music—anachronistically, as Eriksen ruefully observed:

> Historically, of course, a church in the North Carolina mountains ca. 1860 would have been more likely to house a singing from the Southern Harmony than the Sacred Harp, there probably wouldn't have been a hollow square, and in the case of 282 there wouldn't have been an alto part. My feeling, however, was that it would be good to give the audience as many clues as possible about Sacred Harp singing, increasing the likelihood that they'd check it out and see if it's something they wanted to pursue. And for the movie I think it's more effective to show the audience something that's more 'real' than speculatively and, I think, pointlessly 'accurate.' That was my reasoning, in any case.[10]

The film placed the voices of Sacred Harp singers from 2002 in the bodies of Romanian extras in 1860s period dress. The prop tunebooks pushed the tradition even further back in time. Eriksen reported, "The props department made up 60 replicas of the 1859 edition for everyone to sing from, and they looked pretty good (although I wasn't able to convince them they should look brand new rather than old, since the film is set soon after this edition came out)."[11]

Why did Sacred Harp singers—including Eriksen himself—agree to participate in this process? The answers, with their shadings of public willingness and private misgivings, recapitulate many of the themes of this book. In what might be termed a massively-mediated spin on Bealle's "public worship, private faith" paradigm, singers gave public support to this Hollywood-style veneration (in the senses of both sacralization and making-old) with the private faith that it would serve to promote Sacred Harp traditional practice and strengthen the diaspora community in the long run. Eriksen led the way in entering into cautious complicity with the hierarchical, invitation-only demands of the movie industry—which he has described to journalists as "the biggest enemies of life as it should be," noting he came "out of the hardcore punk tradition"—in the belief that it could not harm traditional singing (Walsh 2002). As he wrote to the singings list before the release of the film and long before the Oscars were on the horizon,

> I believe the proven resilience of the singing, the integrity and dedication of singers and, not least, the sheer intensity of community, sound and spirit will keep the singing safe, in the long run, from the charlatanism and triviality often associated with popular culture. It could also be that the whole thing will have little impact at all. I suspect, though, that what will happen is a flurry of activity as millions of people are exposed to the tradition, reduced to hundreds of thousands who care, several thousand who bother to try it out, and several hundred who love it enough to still be showing up at singings ten years from now.[12]

Eriksen's cautious predictions stand in counterpoint to the claims presented in newspaper articles about Sacred Harp and *Cold Mountain*, many of which suggested that the publicity afforded by the film was going to save a dying tradition in the nick of time. An Alabama reporter concluded that Sacred Harp's survival was "assured for the immediate future, thanks to 'Cold Mountain'" (Huebner 2004). A Minnesota reporter wrote that Eriksen "could have a hand in shepherding [shape-note singing] to the masses" (Walsh 2002). Like so many previous discoveries of a Sacred Harp tradition on the brink of vanishing, these accounts manufactured a crisis situation and its solution from the same cloth.

Complicity and Compromise

The hand-picked singers "of Liberty Church"—notably not "Liberty Baptist Church," its full name—show how the demands of media promotion lead Sacred Harp singers to articulate and crystallize what is ordinarily unspoken and flexible in the national singing community. The *Cold Mountain* phenomenon built on the compromises singers make whenever they try to gain recognition for the tradition, entice acquaintances to attend a convention, or encourage new Northern singers to travel South. Like the Southern singers who turn up or spell out their accents, singers everywhere play on stereotyped versions of Sacred Harp in order to attract newcomers and the media to the tradition. They are adept at marketing Sacred Harp, and they know the weaknesses of their regional targets. An agnostic singer at a newly established convention in an Alabama church might find himself talking up Sacred Harp's "spiritual fellowship" to local church members who dropped in to check out the singing. The same person might be overheard in Minneapolis telling a college student that "it's really powerful folk music" and you don't have to be a Christian to sing it.

A one-hour singing school held just before the official start of the 2004 Western Massachusetts Convention demonstrated the locally negotiated, contextual character of the habit of representation that I call "complicity and compromise." The schoolmaster was New York singer Bradford West—an occasional member of Eriksen's band, Cordelia's Dad—and he spent a portion of his lesson discussing the nature of the Sacred Harp tradition rather than explaining how to "sing the notes" or lead a song. West startled some experienced singers by saying that Sacred Harp is not worship, an unusual thing to announce to the class at a convention with close ties to Southern singing. Worship was a "fringe benefit" of Sacred Harp for some singers, West said, but it was not the main purpose at hand. He also drew attention to his own punk-rock, countercultural appearance as an implicit proof that the convention was not an exclusive or conservative event. But having established this platform—risking some of the good will of the lifelong singers who had traveled to this convention—West refused to compromise in another realm of Sacred Harp representation. He spent some time refuting the idea that Sacred Harp practice should be considered historical reenactment, stressing its historical continuity and imploring his audience not to "quaint-ify" it. He asserted that Sacred Harp "*has* history" but "*is not* history," and that the convention should not be compared to the activities of groups like the Society for Creative Anachronism. West knew his liberal, folk-music-loving Northampton audience: he did not want them to dismiss Sacred Harp for its religiosity, nor did he permit them to buffer themselves from the tradition's contemporary context and Southern history by projecting Sacred Harp into a charming, folksy, generically American past.

Afterward, I spoke to some Southern singers who were perplexed by this singing school. They wished that West had not sold religion short and didn't understand why he seemed to be minimizing Sacred Harp's historic status. But some diaspora singers from other states, accustomed to recruiting newcomers from a similar demographic pool, were impressed that West had taken a stand against historical reenactment. "Now they can't just claim the tradition for New England and ignore the South," one person told me, "no matter how much they want to channel William Billings."[13] These singers felt that West was providing more evidence that Western Massachusetts singing was different from New England Sacred Harp more generally. Yet there were also those present who viewed the singing school as disrespectfully complicit with the secularizing agenda of folk-revival singers. One longtime singer—neither Southern nor a Christian—told me, "Well, you just don't get up and say you don't believe in the words or it's not a religious thing. Especially not with those Southern singers two feet away from you." He suggested that West had been "pandering" to "hippies who're scared to sing about Jesus."[14]

The controversies raised within and in reaction to West's lesson drew on singers' ideas of sincerity, authentic experience, and hypocrisy. Clearly West did not believe "historical reenactment" to be an authentic form of Sacred Harp practice—but some of his critics would argue that there is no genuine Sacred Harp without religious feeling, either. To explore these issues I will return once more to the question of what constitutes "real Sacred Harp," this time not through singers' grapplings with the term "traditional" but through their use of humor and irony, their arguments over "performance" and "reenactment," and their convictions about diversity and dissent.

Earnestness and Irony

Chapter 5 touched on the way Southern singers like Tollie Lee can perform stereotypes in a way that challenges their audiences to decide whether it is okay to laugh. While such performances clearly parody typical representations of rural Southerners or Baptist preachers, they also preserve a sincerity of feeling and a seriousness of expression—of love and gratitude, for instance—that invite empathy and respect. This mixture of earnestness and irony is a hallmark of one kind of Sacred Harp humor. The proportions of the mixture can vary widely—for example, as widely as the difference between singing "the coffin, earth, and winding sheet will soon your active limbs enclose" to tease someone on her birthday and choosing to lead the same song when your friends know you are dying of cancer.[15] Both versions acknowledge mortality, both draw attention to a jarring combination of bleak words and a sprightly major tune, but one rendition is deadly serious in its deadpan humor.

It is this challenging, transgressive version that many singers find both funny and deeply moving, even those who usually complain that broad gallows humor and puns are annoying, trivializing, or disrespectful. It's one thing for a singer to enjoin the class to defy death with humor, they say, and another to lead a song for comic value when it might be meaningful to some people. The classic example is the temperance song "O Come Away" (334), which admonishes listeners to "hail the day that celebrates / the ransom of the inebriates / from all that does intoxicate"; this song is led quite earnestly by a few people and with evident hilarity by others.[16] (See Figure 30 for a visual example of a light-hearted treatment of dark lyrics.)

Playing around with earnestness and irony is one way to deal with conflicting demands for complicity in representing the tradition. For example, the flyer for the 2004 Midwest Convention combines direct references to *Cold Mountain* with antiquated poster design and language, exploiting the film's popularity by ironically endorsing its version of Sacred Harp. (See

Figure 30: Detail from the cover of *A Midwest Supplement, Or, A Choice Collection of Tunes, with Footnotes, Selected for and Compiled by Those of the Meanest Capacities* (cover art by Melanie Hauff). The intertwined worms that appear throughout the border are a reference to the lines "Why should we start and fear to die? / What tim'rous worms we mortals are!" (Isaac Watts, 1707).

Figure 31: Detail from a promotional flyer for the 2004 Midwest Convention, designed by Chicago singer Lisa Grayson.

Figure 31.) The flyer's designer, Chicago singer Lisa Grayson, used a quotation from the *New York Times* to make a competitive reference to the *O Brother, Where Art Thou?* soundtrack: "*Haunting, ancient harmonies and lyrics* that make Ralph Stanley's 'I'm a Man of Constant Sorrow' sound like a jingle by comparison." Grayson applied modern marketing techniques—the blurb, the piggy-back comparison to a popular predecessor, the prestige of the quoted source—to affirm Sacred Harp's antimodern depth of feeling. As she wrote to me, "I always loved the irony of creating high-tech materials for the lowest-tech entertainment."[17] And yet Grayson and the promoters of the Midwest Convention are also sincere in their claims: they *do* believe in a transformative, authentically felt Sacred Harp experience, and they are willing to borrow commercial marketing strategies and stereotypes of antiquated authenticity in order to lure newcomers to discover the real thing, something far too complicated to explain on a flyer.

Textual contrafacta present another realm of linked earnestness and irony. Altered texts circulate by word of mouth throughout the national community, ranging from plays on rhythm (see Figure 32):

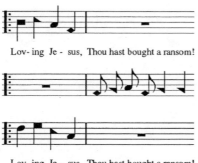

Lov- ing Je - sus, Thou hast bought a ransom!

Lov- ing Je - sus, Thou hast bought a ransom!

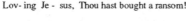

Figure 32: Excerpt from "Loving Jesus" (361).

> "Loving Jesus, Thou hast bought a ransom!" ". . . Jesse shot a possum" (or other variants)[18]

to simple twists on the sounds of words:

> "While shepherds watch'd their flocks by night" ". . . washed their socks . . ."[19]

> "Lo, Salem's daughters weep around" ". . . sleep around"[20]

Tiny changes can render an entire song near-pornographic. Consider the results of substituting "thong" for "song" in the second line of "Africa":

> Now shall my inward joys arise
> And burst into a song,
> Almighty grace inspires my heart
> And pleasure tunes my tongue.[21]

Some people sing contrafacta out loud at conventions. In the mass of sound no one will notice the difference, except perhaps a friend who sits nearby or notices one's raised eyebrows from across the room.

Such small-scale acts of sacrilege might appear childish, pettily offensive, or eye-rollingly trivial, but the context of their creation and use suggests otherwise. Virtually all of the contrafacta I know have been invented or reported to me by longtime singers who are committed to an intensely emotional and/or spiritual Sacred Harp experience. Contrafacta are the fruits of long familiarity with certain songs, familiarity that can breed boredom and dissatisfaction. Singers modify the texts of "chestnuts," songs that are sung over and over. Some singers consider these songs to be so "oversung" that they have lost their affective power; they inspire fatigue, annoyance with the leader who chose them, and other sentiments that can jar a singer out of her transcendent state. I know singers who will not even lead a song on the facing page of an overused song for fear that it will remind another leader of the existence of the despised "chestnut."

Making up new words to such songs trivializes their accumulated triviality, restoring an element of pleasure and in-group understanding to singing them while also cordoning them off from the rest of the repertoire. Simple sex jokes instantly dispel sentimentality. Deflating someone else's over-earnestness—rather than simply feeling alienated—preserves one's own capacity for earnestness in other contexts, and private humor expands one's capacity for public tolerance. The same instability of reference that allows singers to negotiate a meaningful relationship with a given text also leaves room for contained acts of sedition, from singing contrafacta with a straight face to winking at a friend across the square when someone is leading "Fly swift around, ye wheels of time" at an agonizingly slow tempo.[22] Creating contrafacta serves to quarantine oversung tunes; it opens up a gap in which they might become fresh and personally meaningful again under the right circumstances. It is deeply satisfying for singers to know that a song can survive a period of inverted value to emerge restored, a vessel for authentic experience after all.

"Firing Blanks": Reenactment and Performance

The deferred sincerity of contrafacta and the lessons of Bradford West's singing school must be understood in the context of diaspora debates over the basic nature of authentic Sacred Harp. These debates have been profoundly influenced by the overlap between new Sacred Harp groups and the historically-informed-performance movement of the "early music" community over the last thirty years.[23] Whether they live in Atlanta, Boston, or Ann Arbor, many of the singers who have been attracted to Sacred Harp in recent decades are early music devotees. They might have first sung Sacred Harp songs in choirs that focused on madrigals and motets or first heard them performed by Anonymous 4, the Boston Camerata, or Chanticleer. Many of these singers share an approach to Sacred Harp that emphasizes its role as a historical object and its connection to Revolutionary New England. It is important to them that some Sacred Harp songs were part of early American history—although of course the repertoire was neither called "Sacred Harp" nor printed in shapes at that point—and to some it is equally important to sing these songs "accurately" in accordance with their earliest performances. Historically oriented singers have also worked to integrate Sacred Harp into Civil War reenactments or to arrange singings at historical tourism sites staffed by costumed reenactors. In another example of "complicity and compromise," even singers who do not care for historical reenactment sometimes trade on Sacred Harp's historicity in order to gain access to the excellent singing spaces and potential new recruits that such venues can afford.

The linked questions of whether Sacred Harp should be performed for audiences and whether it constitutes historical reenactment come up often on the fasola.org lists and in Sacred Harp newsletters. These questions touch a nerve in the national community because answering them forces singers to draw on their differing convictions about authenticity and authority. The raised-sixth debate discussed in Chapter 3 is a common gateway to these issues: what happens when eighteenth-century evidence suggests a composer did not intend for sixths to be raised but an elderly lifelong Southern singer habitually raises them in that very song? The suggestion that it is more authentic to do what the composer or his contemporary singers would have done sticks in the craw of singers with strong commitments to Southern singing. It can give the impression that historically oriented singers are "claiming Sacred Harp for New England," or for America in general, and therefore denying the value of its embedded history in Southern culture and religious practice.

Even if the historical source and the present-day traditional singer concur on the raised sixth, questions of relative prestige remain: is an "accurate" sound valuable because the composer wanted it to sound that way, or because it is imagined to bring history into the present, or because it represents an impressive continuity of oral tradition? Reproducing such a historicized sound is evidently part of "a process of claiming pastness" (Radano 2003: 9), but is the claim's legitimacy rooted in a *reenactment* that skips back to a point of origin or in a claim of continuous *retention* from a distant past? Such questions create an implicit competition between the prestige of scholarly research and that of oral transmission. Meanwhile, the pressure to take a position on this historicist controversy can subsume a different ethos of vocal production, one that recognizes the value of reproducing a sound as a gesture of homage to one's teachers—whether they are "traditional" or not—as part of crafting a sonic representation of one's affiliations. A singer who had been strongly influenced by Tim Eriksen's distinctive timbre and ornamentation—derived partly from ballad traditions rather than any one regional Southern Sacred Harp style—told me how other diaspora singers had encouraged her to listen to historical recordings of Southern singing to recalibrate her own vocal style. But why shouldn't her singing reflect and acknowledge the attractive power of Eriksen's voice, the reach of his influence, and his own musical affiliations?

Orthopraxic obsessions in matters of musical performance practice also sideline the issue of authentic feeling in a way that frustrates many singers. Some suggest that no matter how perfectly one reproduces the musical characteristics of an eighteenth-century or Civil War–era performance, singing religious music without religious faith is not historically accurate: orthodoxy should trump orthopraxy (see Bell 1997: 191–97). In an online debate about Sacred Harp as historical reenactment, one singer pointedly summarized the issue as she saw it: "An easy way for me to tell the difference between re-enactments and my participation in Sacred Harp: When I sing Sacred Harp and praise God or pray through my singing, I don't believe I'm 'firing blanks.'"[24]

While Sacred Harp's interdenominational history and open-door policy have supported the idea that it is *possible* for a non-Christian to sing without "firing blanks," a sincerity akin to faith still seems to be a prerequisite for authentic Sacred Harp experience. Remember Richard DeLong's promise that "You'll be a traditional singer when you sing it from the heart." Karen House's family decided to bury her at Liberty Baptist Church in Alabama rather than closer to their New England homes; Karen's mother Sally remarked to an Alabama reporter that in the South, "There's more passion. It's a way of life in the South. In the North, it's an intellectual activity" (Huebner 2004). Lifelong Alabama singer Amanda Denson has often told me that Southern singing is different from Northern singing because in the South everyone believes the words, even though the doctrinal diversity of Southern Christian singers makes it plain that this is not literally true. As I discussed in Chapter 4, some singers implicitly support this view when they feel guilty for "smuggling" troubles into a cathartic atmosphere produced by a faith they don't share.

Many people believe that conceiving of Sacred Harp as "performance" undermines the value of sincerity, faith, and "singing from the heart." Historically informed performance, which one might expect to get a warmer reception than ahistorical renditions, actually opens a Pandora's Box of questions about different forms of authority. The "intellectual activity" of working through these questions is very satisfying to some singers, but it strikes others as irrelevant to the point of offensiveness—it seems to devalue "the real thing," to make a lot of noise but only fire blanks.

Singers who assert that true Sacred Harp is not performance are giving pride of place to sincerity rather than musical technique. Usually they also attribute higher status to Southern tradition than to early-music- or New England–oriented representations. As they defend faith-based singing and Southern authority, however, they may inadvertently reproduce the stereotype of traditional singers as "natural musicians," erasing the practiced, skillful nature of singing, reading music, and leading in the Southern singing school tradition. A noncompetitive, non-"performative" Sacred Harp ideology is very important to newer singers—both to bolster their own musical confidence and as a point of contrast with professional choral performances of shape-note singing—but in fact the singing schools and conventions of the nineteenth and early twentieth centuries encouraged individual excellence and competitive performance. Nineteenth-century minutes show that only the best leaders were even permitted to "give a lesson," which could last a half-hour or more. Newspapers reported on leaders' virtuosity, and lifelong singers still proudly report that their parents or grandparents could lead for long periods "without a book" (not an endorsement of oral tradition but rather akin to praising orchestral conductors who don't need a score).[25] Children won cash prizes for their performances in leading competitions; lifelong singer Violet Thomason, the daughter of a singing-school teacher, is always happy to tell the story of the five-dollar gold piece she won at a children's leading contest at the United Convention in 1928. George Pullen Jackson described a 1930 children's leading contest with two top prizes of thirty dollars—a substantial sum, equivalent to roughly $330 today (1933: 119).[26]

Today, too, being a skilled leader is a very public performance. Singers' assessments of these performances give a subtler cast to attributions of authenticity or of "firing blanks." Many singers consider being too emotionally self-involved—displaying an excess of sincerity—to be as bad as obsessing about the technical details of musical production. A leader who is too intent on his own emotional state to make appropriate choices of tune, tempo, and number of verses has a far more direct impact on others' experience than a leader who is devoted to historically informed performance on her own time. Local aesthetics and individual experience guide singers in drawing the line between admirable emotional involvement and self-involved "performance." The behaviors that some singers view as markers of sincerity—rhythmic rocking in one's seat, stamping one's feet, crying—

can strike others as tastelessly showy or potentially offensive, as fake as an adopted Southern accent. Some diaspora singers emphasize their embodied experience to distinguish themselves from the "intellectual" musicologists or reenactors, but their performances of uncontrollable emotion in the tightly controlled environment of the hollow square meet with criticism from life-long singers. If you lose your voice, you are singing too loud. If you move your body too much in your seat, you will tire yourself out and distract the class. Singing schools taught by such singers indicate that leading should be contained, controlled, masterful, subtle, and graceful—not at all like speaking in tongues. Shelbie Sheppard, a lifelong Alabama singer, longtime editor of the annual minutebook, and renowned singing school teacher, has been widely cited for saying that when a leader in the heat of emotion throws down his book to lead without it, "It just tears me out of my frame!"[27]

Christian singers have a wide range of responses to such "out-of-control" behavior, a range that points to their own doctrinal diversity. Some recognize and endorse the affinity of these intensely embodied displays with charismatic revival practices. Others dislike them for this very reason, since they believe Sacred Harp to have stronger links to their own more austere church traditions. Still others respect the authenticity of this kind of behavior in a church or revival context—whether they belong to such a church or not—but view it as a fake "performance" when they know the singers in question aren't Christian at all. They fear the trance-like states of some leaders are more indebted to New Age nonsense than to true religion, or they take offense at what seems to be a parody of being "in the spirit." Their concerns accidentally found a scholarly voice in an assessment by the ethnomusicologist Marin Marian-Bâlaşa, who visited three singings in the Midwest and concluded that "contemporary shapenote practitioners worship not a God and a song book, but rather their own enthusiasm. . . . [T]hese singers selfishly worship their own psychosomatic experience" (Marian-Bâlaşa 2003: 144). The musical characteristics that Marian-Bâlaşa identified as aesthetic priorities in a shape-note "psychodrama" (142) actually represent the worst fears of many diaspora singers, who found his description both embarrassing to the singings he attended and an unfair humiliation of the tradition as a whole.[28]

Singers who perform embodied emotion are subject to as many kinds of assessment as singers whose performances are "historically informed." First, if their behavior is akin to trancing, is it genuine or fake? Judith Becker has suggested that "believability" is always an important aspect of trance assessments; she also emphasizes the fact that "faking" trance characteristics often facilitates entrance into genuine trancing (Becker 2004: 42). But even if these singers are judged to be sincerely transported, the next question will be whether their behavior is appropriate to the hollow square. They may not be firing blanks, but some will still consider them to be "performing"—making a show of piety, a display of their own ability to be swept up in it all—rather than leading the class. Contrafacta, winks across the square, and the occasional physical parodies of particular leaders that are acted out in private are all ways of dressing down such performances, just as emotional displays implicitly dress down "intellectual" performances of historical knowledge. The proliferation of criteria used in making these judgments is daunting, but it also "allows for a flexibility of judgment in which every known person's merit is relative, and nobody's failure ever complete" (Baumann 1987: 188).

I come from a scholarly tradition that leads me to treat all Sacred Harp practice as "performative," in a broader sense than the concert tradition of performance that singers separate from their Sacred Harp experience. The question is, what is being performed? Is it religious faith? Patriotism? Fascination with the past? An idea of the rural South? Some singers indulge in ironic performances of stereotypes; others are intent on dressing appropriately, making authentic recipes, learning by ear, raising the right sixths, and somehow absorbing and reproducing the seemingly effortless social decorum of Southern hospitality.[29] Singers judge these performances all the time, assessing them as displays of skill, respect, knowledge, commitment, affiliation, and perhaps sincerity above all. If there is a single basic value of the community that I have termed "the Sacred Harp diaspora," it is an aversion to firing blanks.

Songs People Won't Sing

It may seem that such a statement excludes historically oriented singers from full community membership by definition. But there are many singers with period costumes in their closets who use history to take principled stands on challenges they encounter in Sacred Harp texts or the belief systems of other singers. In Chapter 4 I discussed singers' negotiations with Christian texts, but there are also songs in the book whose racist, sexist, or colonialist overtones pose a more pointed problem to the present-day community. These songs are very few in number, but they lead singers to address Sacred Harp's historicity and their own "performances" from a different angle than the musical performance practice and oral transmission debates.

Diaspora singers consistently identify three songs as the most problematic in lyric content: "Stafford" (78), "Edmonds" (115), and "War Department" (160t). "Stafford" is a straightforward major fuging tune with an Isaac Watts text; the words seem unremarkable until the last line:

> See what a living stone
> The builders did refuse,
> Yet God hath built His church thereon,
> In spite of env'ous Jews.[30]

"Edmonds" is a six-verse song on proper marital relations, the most controversial lines being

> This woman was not taken
> From Adam's head, we know;
> And she must not rule o'er him,
> It's evidently so.[31]

"War Department" previously appeared in the *Southern Harmony* (1835) and presents a one-sided account of the state of a contemporary conflict:

> No more shall the sound of the war-whoop be heard,
> The ambush and slaughter no longer be feared.
> The tomahawk, buried, shall rest in the ground,
> And peace and good-will to the nations abound.[32]

Singers also tend to bring one non-Sacred Harp tune into this company— "Indian Convert," a well-known tune in the *Christian Harmony* and *Southern Harmony* traditions in which some Sacred Harp singers also participate. Its faux-pidgin text makes it unusual among the many nineteenth-century songs featuring first-person conversion narratives:

> In de dark woods, no Indian nigh,
> Den me look Heb'n, and send up cry,
> Upon my knee so low;
> But God on high, in shiny place,
> See me at night, wid teary face—
> De preacher tell me so.[33]

"War Department" is very difficult to sing on musical grounds alone; its rarity at conventions is seldom mourned. But "Stafford" and "Edmonds" are widely regarded as lovely tunes, and singers express regret that their texts have made them pariahs. Online archives of annual minutebooks show that "Edmonds" was led only once in 2003; "Stafford" was led more often, but usually with an alternative text.[34]

Longtime singer Tim Cook brought up these issues on the discussions list in March of 2002. After summarizing the case of "Stafford," he described his first encounter with "Indian Convert," a popular tune in *Christian Harmony* circles:

> At my first Christian Harmony singing, I was ecstatic about these beautiful songs at once so new and somehow so familiar to me. Then we got to "Indian Convert" with its pidgin English and I could hardly mouth the words, so stunned was I at what is very hard not to take as racist, or at least paternalistic. After moving to Alabama in 1998, both my wife and I go to as many of Christian Harmony singings as we can, the singers having become our second family. But "Indian Convert" happens to be one of their favorite songs, which they sing with utmost sincerity and teary eyes, just like in the song ("But God on high, in shiny place, See me at night, wid teary face—De preacher tell me so"). I understand the words are supposedly dictated from an Indian back when Indians were struggling with the invaders' new language, but Native Americans nowadays go to great lengths to dispel the stereotypes that that song seems to promote.

Cook's description of the singers' sincerity—corroborated by their "teary eyes"—emphasizes his respect for their motives. These singers are moved by the conversion story, which parallels their own experience as Christians and uses the same prevailing metaphor as "Amazing Grace." As another singer observed later in this thread, "I would venture a guess that the people who find meaning in this song are also remembering a time when they were lost, and when God found them."[35]

Cook offered no such justification for the "envious Jews" reference in "Stafford." "Stafford" does not have the emotional resonance of a first-person conversion account from relatively recent American history; rather, it recounts an event in Biblical history. As Cook noted, "If this reflects any 18th-century prejudice on the part of Isaac Watts, he got it from no less a source than St. Paul, in Acts (e.g., ch. 17)."[36] But while Cook recognized the different contexts of these two songs' historical provenance and present-day reception, he placed them in the same category in terms of the challenge they pose to singers like himself: "One could say that this is all just historical music, that we don't really mean this 18th-century stuff anyway. But for the most part, when we're singing these songs, I think many of us really do mean it, even the scary parts. At least I do. But when we get to words that seem disrespectful, then it's hard to sing them without meaning them, which I don't want to do. Has anyone else been bothered by any of this?"[37]

Many others had been bothered. Singers who had made their peace with singing other Sacred Harp texts "without meaning them" in literal terms had trouble making the same flexible interpretations of these texts. The thread Cook started was one of the longest and most intensely argued that I encountered in six years of tracking the listservs, even though the discussion revolved around a few rarely sung songs in *The Sacred Harp* plus "Indian Convert."[38] Several singers observed that the offending Sacred Harp songs would likely be dropped from a future revision due to non-use, while "Indian Convert" appears in tunebooks whose nineteenth-century worldview is "frozen in time forever."[39] Still, the existence of these texts raised questions about tolerance, historical value, sincerity of intent, and ownership of the tradition that list participants took very seriously.

The postings in response to Cook's query suggested that singers have three basic responses to these problematic songs: a total refusal to sing them, a historicist approach that values these texts as object lessons about the past, and a middle path of cautious tolerance depending on the intent of the singers. As in the historically-informed-performance debate, singers often returned to the fundamental question of sincerity: is it ever authentic Sacred Harp to sing words "without meaning them"? Is it more of a betrayal to change texts to suit modern sensibilities or to mouth words that cannot be squeezed into any productive alignment with one's own beliefs? Might songs like "Stafford" be considered "living stones" refused by politically correct "builders" who are revising Sacred Harp history? What about singers who positively identify with the "Indian Convert"? How can faith-based integrity be accused of malice?

Singers who felt unable to sing one or more of these songs described a visceral reaction to them. Like Cook, who could "hardly mouth the words," they framed their discomfort as immediate physical resistance or pain. One singer felt "sand-bagged" when he first encountered "Indian Convert." Another wrote of "Stafford" that "it can keep a wound open that should have been allowed to close long ago." A singer who brought the song "Whitestown" into the debate said that singing it "just feels like pouring oil on an open wound." The text of this song describes a land ripe for colonization—"Where nothing dwelt but beasts of prey / Or men as fierce and wild as they"—and the singer observed that she lived "close to the Whitestown of the tune name. . . . The land ownership problems created about the time the song was written are still unresolved."[40]

This singer's explanation of her inability to sing "Whitestown" empha-sizes the painful modern resonances of this text, in which Watts para-phrased Psalm 107 under the heading "A Psalm for New England."[41] In general, despite their vivid descriptions of visceral reactions, most of these singers focused not on some essential, inherent offensiveness in these texts but on their potential for harm in the present-day singing community. Rather than condemning the authors outright, they acknowledged that these words were products of a different era. But they demanded in turn that others acknowledge the relevance of these texts to current cultural conflicts. Not being historical reenactors in the rest of their Sacred Harp practice, they could not cordon off these texts in a strictly historical space.

Even singers who could not sing "Stafford," "Indian Convert," or "Whitestown" without feeling as though they were endorsing derogatory content were inclined to assert that those who *did* sing them were *not* endors-ing prejudice. Rather, their individual life experience positioned them to sing one aspect of the text sincerely without recognizing another aspect as mali-cious. One Georgia singer wrote, "I have not heard 'Stafford' in several years. If the dear little lady I last heard lead it had ever met a Jew, she didn't know it and would never have intentionally offended them or anyone else. I decided not long after I first heard it to treat it as a historical document, bite the pc bul-let and sing it. Then I heard 'Indian Convert.' My Cherokee blood boiled!"

This singer implied that she had decided she could tolerate "Stafford" for reasons not so far removed from those of the "dear little lady": not being Jewish herself, she did not have a visceral response to the text and could approach it as a piece of history. Her stronger reaction to "Indian Convert" seemed to foreshadow a rejection of "Stafford," in light of a new under-standing of how it felt to be on the receiving end of these texts. However, she continued by explaining how she got over this feeling: "But sense pre-vailed; it is not meant to be derogatory, but as a dialect piece, like an Uncle Remus story." She went on to describe the layers of meaning and personal associations that accrue to songs, explaining how in the context of the sing-ing tradition even these texts could represent one's fond memories of a favorite relative rather than a "political statement."

These nuanced defenses of particular approaches to these songs showed how one might avoid condemning fellow singers as bigots for leading them, but did not preclude further debate about whether it would be a good idea to change the lyrics. Some considered "Stafford" to be an excellent candi-date for this kind of emendation, since only the words "in spite of envious Jews" would need to be changed: singers suggested substituting "lest we salvation lose" or "in spite of envious few." Others reported more tongue-in-cheek options in the tradition of irreverent contrafacta, taking the original text down a peg or two with lines like "in spite of empty pews," "in spite of drugs and booze," or (from a California singer) "in spite of envious dudes." The hymnody scholar Warren Steel suggested substituting a different Watts verse, preempting objections with an argument grounded in history and tradition: "To insist on this verse as 'traditional,' and to object to 'political correctness,' would be to ignore the tradition of interchanging music and words in congregational psalmody."[42]

Steel made it hard to argue that changing the words was an offense to tradition, especially if one substituted another Watts text in its entirety rather than patching over the offensive bits. It was the idea of patches that elicited the strongest concerns about diluting the "strong stuff" of Sacred Harp texts into the "bland" material found in contemporary church hymnals. But even as the strength of Steel's argument and his scholarly authority weakened counterarguments that claimed a basis in "the tradition," it also shifted the debate to questions of historical value. In this context, Texas singer Terre Schill made a strong argument for the importance of these songs. After citing the text of "Whitestown," she wrote:

> Now there's a relic of some outmoded thinking! But it probably taught me something more significant about my own history as an American than all my undergraduate studies of official policy toward native Americans in the 18th and 19th centuries. . . . I want to weigh in to point out that there is nothing whatsoever consistent at any level about these song lyrics as a group. They reflect social attitudes and values in flux over time. They reflect many contradictory theological beliefs. They represent our varied cultural inheritance, and the issues which have prevailed at different places and eras. That is a part of their richness. . . . This discussion reminds me of the movement to remove offensive racial terminology from the works of Mark Twain and other classics of literature for school use. If such a move were to truly succeed in banishing everything offensive, how would students ever learn to understand the social history of that period?[43]

Schill acknowledged that singers' approaches to these lyrics were flexible, writing "I believe that most of us are either singing lyrics that we don't agree with, altering the words that WE individually sing to suit our beliefs, or just remaining silent during passages that we can't with good conscience sing. I know I do all three." But despite this attention to individual standards of "good conscience," she promoted the value of these texts as historical documents of cultural heritage. Another singer spun this point a different way, implying that current singers' discomfort with these texts could be transmuted into a satisfying confirmation of a more liberal worldview: "The converts, . . . for instance, are clearly offered as pious examples for our edification. That we find them offensive now suggests that we've developed different ideas about strangers, about a sectarian God, about being 'right' and 'wrong.'"[44]

But how would a new singer know that others at a convention were singing these words with misgivings, with guilty reflections on social history, with satisfaction at the distance American culture has come, or with a sense of positive identification that precluded malicious intent? Teachers who work with charged material like Mark Twain texts are expected to contextualize them historically and engage students in discussion, whereas it would break many implicit social rules for a Sacred Harp singer to announce that she was leading "Whitestown" as a reminder of the evils of imperialist colonialism. As one singer asked, "how many Jewish folks would come to the next singing if 'Stafford' were their first exposure to SH? If we don't lose the verse, then we lose the song or the singers, or both."[45]

The Tolerance Paradox

This line of argument transformed a debate over rarely sung songs to a more contentious discussion of cultural ownership, diversity, and tolerance in the national Sacred Harp community. Several singers argued that a newcomer had an obligation to respect any beliefs made manifest at a traditional Sacred Harp convention, since the tradition was not hers to reform. Such people need not *embrace* an opposing or offensive ideology, but ought to withhold judgment as a sign of respect. Presumably that respect would be rewarded, over time, by the kind of nuanced understanding of historical context, tradition, and the diversity of singers' motives that had informed the listserv discussion. This argument was couched in terms that asserted the particularity of traditional Sacred Harp culture and criticized those who would claim it as their own without acknowledging that distinctiveness. Terre Schill summarized the issue this way: "Now other groups doubtless have their own fascinating and beautiful traditions, and I might also like very much to be welcomed into some of them. But as a white, rural, southern, King James-believin' somebody I wouldn't enter into their tradition, take umbrage at the fact that their culture does not legitimize and perhaps occasionally even opposes my beliefs or identity, and then set about to reform their literature."[46]

Schill's posting was not the first to point out the slippery-slope risks of changing Sacred Harp texts to avoid offending particular groups, but she recentered those risks around identity politics rather than the vague fear that Sacred Harp could become "bland." Schill situated Sacred Harp texts as "ethnic literature" (Sollors 1986: 237), in this case a tradition perpetuated by a community marked by race, region, rural lifeways, and religion. In so doing she sharpened the contours of Stephen Marini's sketch of Sacred Harp as "the public expression of what we might call the generic religion of the rural South, its consensus doctrines cast in compelling hymnic form" (Marini 2003: 88).

Other writers who defended the problematic texts on grounds of cultural ownership drew the circle-of-the-we around Christian singers generally rather than white, rural, "King James-believin'" Southerners. They asked why some singers were worrying over giving offense to Jewish people or Native Americans while appearing to malign or mock Christians. When a California singer described a group where "some of the singers were somewhat hostile to Christianity, or all organized religions" and "made the occasional irreverent, facetious comments," a Christian singer responded, "I do expect respect from others in singing SACRED music. I do not demand they believe, nor convert, but I do expect [them] to at least fake an attitude of respect when singing." The California singer's rejoinder dismissed that projected obligation outright: "Do you understand that it was 'our group'? We started it. A pious Christian who wanted to sing with us would be 'our guest' at first." This posting suggests that if traditional singers want to claim that Sacred Harp can be meaningful to anyone and is open to all, then they have to acknowledge the diversity of new singers and respect the development of new local traditions. Must all new Sacred Harp groups treat visiting lifelong singers with both the graciousness due to guests and the deference accorded to authoritative hosts?

Exchanges like this one demonstrate how the Sacred Harp ideology of inclusive, democratic participation in a fundamentally American tradition—the ideology that has earned Sacred Harp cultural capital and support from liberal folk revivalists—can come into conflict with the overlapping ownership claims of Christians, Southerners, and lifelong singers. While I have described some of the strategies that help non-Christian singers come to meaningful terms with the Christian aspects of Sacred Harp practice and repertoire, this does not really explain why Christian singers do not confront nonbelievers or discourage them from singing. In the past few decades an ideology of tolerance and inclusivity derived from a time when virtually all singers were practicing Protestants of different sects has been stretched to encompass a much broader range of participants. Many active travelers have strong Christian convictions, and their approaches to singing with non-Christians (or with Christians of substantially different beliefs) are as complicated as non-Christian approaches to Christian texts.

Some Christian singers are most comfortable assuming that other singers are faithful in their own way—as one woman put it, "I don't see how you can sing it and not believe in God and have faith of some kind, in some supreme Being."[47] Others apply the particular tenets of their own denominations to deal with the problem: evangelicals hope the texts and prayerful atmosphere will serve to proselytize, while predestinarians believe the matter is not in their hands. As Terre Schill put it, "There never has been nor will be any 'religious test' because of the long-standing belief that God will use these songs to melt the hearts of whom he pleases."[48]

Stephen Marini has described a similar controversy in a church-reform debate in 1720s New England. The question of whether noncommunicants should be allowed to sing psalms in church hinged on whether such singing constituted praise from the faithful or should be open to all due to its potential to arouse converting feeling. As Marini writes, the reformers "claimed that making restricted liturgical acts available to all would kindle piety and bring revival. But it could be asserted with equal cogency that to open the sacred ordinances to the reprobate would quench the Spirit" (Marini 1983: 77). Today, many Sacred Harp singers feel that there is something fundamentally different about singings where a majority of participants are practicing Christians, a sense of "Spirit" that could be diluted or quenched if too many nonbelievers are present. But there is still no "religious test," partly because openly discussing such matters would draw attention to the ideological schisms among the different Christian sects to which lifelong singers belong.

Justifications and celebrations of the diversity of present-day Sacred Harp singing rely on mutual good will, bringing the issue of sincerity and intent back to center stage. While unspoken intentions may not have an immediate impact on newcomers—e.g., the hypothetical Jewish newcomer who wouldn't understand why her friends sing "Stafford"—projections of sincere intentions are absolutely crucial in maintaining an atmosphere of tolerance. Singers use these projections to mount a defense of others who do not share their beliefs or background; they make deliberate efforts to account for others' behavior, whether that behavior involves leading

"Indian Convert," professing atheism, voting Republican, or being in a same-sex relationship.

These rationalizations often rely on assumptions about others' life experience that might seem dismissive or reductive: an atheist just wasn't raised with Christian values; if someone who led "Stafford" "had ever met a Jew she didn't know it"; it would never occur to certain people to find "Indian Convert" prejudicial. But as tactfully worded efforts to read others' behavior as well-intentioned, explanations like these shed light on the nature of tolerance in the Sacred Harp diaspora. Projections of sincerity can grant a reprieve in conflict situations; withholding judgment can make space for pluralist tolerance. Like claims of belonging, these statements of tolerance resemble Reddy's "emotives," the emotional utterances that can "alter the states of the speakers from whom they derive" (Reddy 1997: 327). They communicate good intentions in the form of "a pledge that alters"; if the pledge truly does shape and channel the speaker's feelings as promised, "the emotive, in a Western context, might be said to be 'sincere'" (332). Self-reinforcing expressions and projections of sincerity allow diaspora singers to confirm both their own authenticity of practice and the ethical nature of the Sacred Harp community.

One anecdote recounted by a liberal New England singer epitomizes what I have come to think of as the "tolerance paradox." She described how a Southern singer had revealed his political views to her in a way that assumed her agreement: "A gentleman of an age that he could have been my father—and I should mention I'd known this gentleman for several years so he felt comfortable talking to me—and he put his arm around my shoulders and said, 'Our man'—meaning Jesse Helms—'just made it back into the Senate this year.' I just took it as a sign that he thought I was a *very good person.*"[49] The paradox lies in the liberal singer's positive response to the conservative singer's violation of a social norm: the don't-ask/don't-tell standard of Sacred Harp political and religious discourse. If this standard is thoroughly established—"I'd known this gentleman for several years"—then violating it actually becomes a compliment, an expression of intimacy and a projection of common values. I have overheard subtle bargains being struck in conversations over dinner-on-the-grounds: a conservative singer bemoans the decline of family values when spouses must take jobs in different cities, a liberal singer sighs sympathetically and offers the corroborating example of a gay couple she knows whose long-distance relationship is under constant strain. Neither directly challenges the other, and their exchange falls within the bounds of "fellowship." Such tales have parallels in the stories lifelong singers have told me about their first trips to diaspora conventions—their embarrassment and confusion when faced with a table of food where "I really couldn't tell what anything *was!*" or the lesson learned when "I saw her with her boots and tattoos and my jaw dropped, and daddy said 'You just shut your mouth.'" When it comes to diasporic travels, the road runs in both directions, as theorists of diaspora have observed and as Sacred Harp singers often announce when they visit a distant convention. These stories show how the obligations of tolerance also run both ways.

The pointed challenges posed on the listservs reveal how much isn't said at singings—how a singing structures time *to prevent* these things from being said, how in a room full of singers people can subsume or conceal their dissent within an overwhelming group sound. Some are falling silent for a few words, singing contrafacta, "slipping out for water" (one singer's regular response to "Indian Convert"), or trying to think up ways to make a challenging text personally meaningful. Just as there are singers who feel they can't sing the words "envious Jews," there are those who feel doctrinally constrained not to sing texts that presume families will be reunited in heaven after death. As Reddy has observed, in a given social context "certain kinds of repression become collaborative efforts" (Reddy 1997: 338); singers tacitly agree to avoid particular subjects and to channel their feelings in certain directions. But these controversial topics are not simply covered over by silence. Instead, the gap they leave is filled in with singing, a very loud, very physical form of sounding resistance that need not be heard as an incitement to conflict.

Sacred Harp singers tend to be politically engaged, and they report that their Sacred Harp participation expresses their resistance to all sorts of things—among them the disintegration of community feeling, the pervasiveness of commercial broadcast media, the professionalization of music-making, the destruction of distinctive local traditions, the failure to respect one's elders, the decline of family values, the strip-mall homogenization of the American landscape, the secularist (or fundamentalist) drift of American culture, and the polarized atmosphere of national politics. Sometimes variants of these concerns are common to virtually all the singers at a given convention, and singers invoke them in prayers or memorial lessons without acknowledging that those present would disagree as to their causes and cures. Instead of debating these conflicts, they sit in the same room and sing until they can't speak. Maurice Bloch once asserted that "[i]n a song . . . no argument or reasoning can be communicated, no adaptation to the reality of the situation is possible. *You cannot argue with a song*" (Bloch 1974: 71, emphasis original). But in fact Sacred Harp singers frequently communicate arguments through song. Their powers of communication are enriched by this circumstance—not "impoverished," as Bloch would suggest—because they are at liberty to choose *when to recognize* songs as arguments.

Both the tunebook and the singers are more diverse than they appear, even than they appear to experienced singers. I have tried to emphasize that diversity to move beyond assumptions of commonality based on the visibly huge majority of white, middle-class American singers at Sacred Harp conventions. Regional and religious divisions have been the most obvious wedge issues in my analysis, but many other important sites of difference exist in this community—class, political ideology, rural versus urban background, musical experience, formal education, and more. Yet even as participants are aware of this diversity, their racial nondiversity and the fact that socioeconomic divisions are largely occluded make it possible for them to temporarily ignore their differences in a manner unavailable to more visibly diverse groups. Sacred Harp singers constantly posit differ-ence—between traditional and new singers, Southern and Yankee, Chris-tian and non-Christian, family and visitors, locals and strangers—without recourse to racial difference. This might be one reason why these other dif-ferences, which are real but not visible, can be rhetorically erased as often as they are established, the "circle of the we" repeatedly reinscribed to include different representations of authentic Sacred Harp singing.

While Sacred Harp is no longer directly implicated in white supremacist ideology—indeed, many singers throughout the country actively recruit non-white participants—the overwhelming whiteness of the current sing-ing population undoubtedly shapes the nature of performed dissent and tolerance in the national community. It also contributes to the ability of new singers to claim ownership of the tradition, to start a new singing that is "our group" and suggest that lifelong Christian singers would be "guests" there—a deeply controversial point, but one whose fundamental logic has vastly increased the number of Sacred Harp singings around the country. Sacred Harp offers white Americans of whatever spiritual orientation the rhetorical means to address marginality, alienation, exile, and community through eighteenth-century Christian poetry, when other folkish rep-ertoires might feel less authentic in their mouths (for example, the slave songs, black vernacular spirituals, and multicultural freedom songs that have become folk-revival staples). This musical practice lends their own

trials, tribulations, and anxieties a measure of legitimacy, the stamp of tradition, and a sense of kinship in hard times. But when new singers become
involved in the diaspora and its travel networks their sense of ownership
becomes less direct and more contingent: having come to Sacred Harp for
its promise of unfettered individual expression, a place where everyone can
lead and no one will say you are singing too loudly or out-of-tune, they
come to realize they have entered a culture of mutual obligation where
their own authenticity is predicated upon respect for a tradition that is no
more naturally "theirs" than any "ethnic music." This process is hastened
by some singers' guilty feelings about Sacred Harp's whiteness, feelings that
encourage them to look for signs of authentic diversity in the singing population. They find it in the lifelong Southern singers who have accepted the
mantle of culturally distinctive "tradition-bearers."

In this way new singers who espouse a liberal multiculturalist worldview
find themselves required to take a second look—a look influenced by cultural relativism—at fellow Americans they previously viewed as ideological
opponents or dismissed with negative stereotypes. In another spin on the
"tolerance paradox," these liberal singers often express surprise at the level
of tolerance exhibited by Southern conservative Christians. Indeed, when
asked what impact Sacred Harp has had on their lives, many diaspora singers reply that it has made them more tolerant of difference. In recognizing
Southern singers as culturally distinctive—in the tradition of local-color
journalists discovering "a strange land and a peculiar people"—new singers
predicate the authenticity of their own practice on respect for the authority
and values of rural Southerners. With the aid of some temporal distancing
to divide Southern singers from contemporary politics, even the most liberal, urban, and Northern-identified newcomers can "envision the old rural
South as a spiritual Mecca where respect for religion, family, hard work,
and strict morality form the foundation of social life" (Allen 1992: 117).[50]

But if some new singers get a grip on Sacred Harp's value by turning from
negative essentialisms to positive ones—celebrations of depoliticized folk
wisdom, "pilgrimages" to meet singers who are conceived as isolated relics of an idealized past—they often find themselves unable to maintain the
boundaries of fundamental difference. The travel practices of the national
diaspora, with its network of conventions and personal affiliations, do not
permit singers to maintain the sense that they are individual free agents
moving between bounded cultures. They cease to be cultural tourists who
can make firm distinctions between "home" and "away."

At Home in Transience

Sacred Harp conventions and the travels they entail create a sense of recurring homecoming that punctuates the everyday lives of singers. These annual reunions of particular "classes" in particular hollow squares are the traces of a transcendent community that exists no-time and no-place. William Safran has noted the parallels between the "myth of return" that characterizes diasporas—the repeatedly imagined and wished-for return to the homeland—and the eschatological promise of a home in heaven (Safran 1991: 94). Sacred Harp discourse makes this connection explicit. For some singers the repeated returns "home" to annual conventions themselves trace the contours of a utopia, signaling the presence of an idealized Sacred Harp community that is never quite in the same place at the same time. For others, these periodic returns are a foretaste of the afterlife, the "home in heaven" or "over Jordan" to which songs and memorial lessons refer. This sense of homecoming does not rely on a religious test, and it constitutes a powerful aspect of the "diaspora consciousness" that binds singers together.

Sacred Harp holds special appeal for people whose lives involve frequent uprootings—the long-distance moves connected with schooling, jobs, marriage, or retirement. In a memorial lesson in Western Massachusetts, where the core singing community includes many college students who may not live in the area for long, a young man summed up this appeal with the suggestion that Sacred Harp provides "a way to feel at home in transience."[51] It was a powerful promise, and it kept resurfacing in my memory as I contemplated the singing community's affinity with pilgrims and ethnic diasporas. Sacred Harp travels are closely associated with anxieties of transience, based not only on individual life experience but also on broader, more abstract fears about globalization and modernity that singers express through their concerns about pollution, dilution, and homogenization of the tradition. Amid these anxieties the convention network offers a form of repeatedly enacted transience that situates "home" in the hollow square. The visits "home" are fleeting; like Turnerian pilgrimage, these travels consist in "movement from a mundane center to a sacred periphery which suddenly, transiently, becomes central for the individual" (Turner and Turner 1978: 34). Each homecoming to the periphery has the potential to recenter experience.

Like pilgrims—and unlike many members of ethnic diaspora communities—singers *choose* to travel. This self-induced transience is a way of announcing one's vulnerability, submitting oneself to traditional relationships and the established transmission process, stating an intention and desire to be part of the national community. Travel constructs the hollow square as a destination that can afford transcendent experiences, in part because the places through which singers must travel—the inevitable airports, interstates, and strip malls of the American landscape—raise expectations that the hollow square will be different: a marked and distinctive place at the end of the line. Holding a convention becomes an act of "reterritorialization," in Morley's terms, a counter-process to globalization in which "borders and boundaries of various sorts are becoming more, rather than less, strongly marked" (Morley 2001: 427). The travel networks of the Sacred Harp diaspora and the spatial structures of the hollow square create a powerful sense of boundaries and borders but simultaneously make the promise that no one will be turned away. Morley proposes the gated community as the correlative of postmodern hypermobility (432), and in some ways these housing developments are not a bad stand-in for the hollow square: they can spring up anywhere, they have clear boundaries and behavioral norms, their spatial arrangements structure particular relationships among their residents. But the key difference is that Sacred Harp's inclusive, pluralist ideology stipulates that the gate is always open.

Sacred Harp singers make seemingly contradictory claims in assessing the tradition. They attach value to Sacred Harp's particularity—that it's local, kinship-oriented, tied to particular places, musically distinctive. In the same breath they describe it as universally accessible and relevant—portable, open to anyone, potentially meaningful for anyone, with no musical prerequisites. The portable and generic qualities of the tradition offer an invitation to join in creating authentic experience: the hollow square will reconfigure space into place, the convention protocols will reconfigure strangers into family. This is the paradoxical promise of being "at home in transience."

These promised attributes of Sacred Harp—universal relevance, a community open to outsiders, freedom of individual expression, miraculous conversion of empty space into meaningful place—are also the attributes of American exceptionalism. Sacred Harp's much-discussed fundamental "Americanness" is rooted not only in its historical connections to early New England composers, its democratic institutional style, and its folk music credentials, but also in its more subtle ideological resonances with long-standing American narratives. It evokes what Sollors terms "the classic American idea of the newcomers' rebirth into a forward-looking culture of consent" (Sollors 1986: 4), framing that rebirth in the terms of "the classic trope of American national character as polarized between individualism and egalitarianism" (Tick 2003: 723). The idea of Sacred Harp as a haven for wandering outsiders and strangers transplants an American exceptionalist theme to the more circumscribed terrain of the hollow square, drawing on the "typological imagination" through which America has been conceived as the New Jerusalem or New Canaan, a fulfillment of millenarian prophecies (Sollors 1986: 43).[52]

Sacred Harp singing is commonly understood to have developed and been perpetuated at the margins, by and for outsiders, although these outsiders differ as to what constitutes the mainstream. In her 1999 survey response, a Chicago singer neatly expressed the seeming paradox of locating Sacred Harp's Americanness in its marginality: "Sacred Harp is the most American thing I've ever done (authentically American i.e. home-grown, as opposed to Americanized imports) and makes me feel finally as though I'm really a member of this society, which is weird since Sacred Harp is really a pretty marginal activity as compared to, say, watching the World Series." This account supports Sollors's suggestion that "In America, casting oneself as an outsider may in fact be considered a dominant cultural trait" (Sollors 1986: 31; cf. Bailyn 2003). Sacred Harp historical and textual narratives certainly encourage participants to identify with strangers, outsiders, pilgrims, and transients of all kinds. But recognizing oneself as a stranger, a marginal person—"Oh is there anyone like me?" as one song asks[53]—not only draws on established notions of the American character but also provides a haven from guilt about the privileges of Americanness, or those of whiteness, wealth, and cultural capital. A weak wanderer, a penitent, a "poor wayfaring man of grief"—these are not exploiters, cultural imperialists, people who would appropriate the traditions of others. They are seekers of a welcoming community of consent.

One can hardly blame new singers for adopting Sacred Harp as their own on the grounds of its Americanness, since that is exactly how the tradition is advertised to them. Besides, Sacred Harp *is* American. Its Americanness consists not only in geography, history, and the democratic ideology of egalitarian participation that singers and scholars constantly invoke, but in the delicate bargains the tradition strikes among competing forms of dissent and marginalization, its rapid incorporation of new technologies, the staging ground it provides for regional rivalries, and its embedded racial and religious history. Nor can one blame newcomers for relating to Sacred Harp on nostalgic grounds, since experienced singers constantly encourage those feelings in order to cement commitments to the tradition. The Sacred Harp memorial lesson is nothing if not a deliberate incitement to nostalgia, an "emotive" genre of formal speech that brings both the speaker and the audience to nostalgic tears and makes a song into a synecdoche, an artifact of absence (cf. DeLyser 2001).

But not all nostalgia is the same. Nostalgic subjectivity depends on how the claimant positions herself—for example, as a modern, mainstream person wistful for an authentic past or as a marginal, resistant person being threatened by modernity. At a minimum, a catalogue of forms of nostalgia includes the one that makes a pastiche of accessories from different pasts (Jameson 1991), the "wilful nostalgia" promoted by a nation-state as it seeks to create a loyal citizenry (Robertson 1990, following Nairn 1988), imperialist nostalgia (Rosaldo 1989), and nostalgia from the margins, which Stewart describes as "a pained, watchful desire to frame the cultural present in relation to an 'other' world" (Stewart 1988: 288).[54] Discourses of antiquity and vanishing tradition provide grist for all kinds of nostalgia, but nostalgia situated at the margins also entails a sense of obligation—"a responsibility to remember what happens" and to value certain people and experiences in the expectation that they will disappear (Stewart 1988: 235). This is the politics of nostalgia that characterizes Sacred Harp memorial lessons, where painfully dwelling on the loss of the dead leads to an exhortation to be true to their ideals and to make contact with the elderly and sick before they're gone. It is the same preemptive sentiment that led a singer to write, "Whenever I attend a convention, I have the feeling of time running out" and to describe her constant anticipation of "going out into a world where, if you try to tell someone about your experience, they won't understand."[55]

Understanding Sacred Harp's politics of nostalgia clarifies Ted Mercer's position in his *Chicago Sacred Harp Newsletter* article entitled "Should Northerners Learn to Sing Sacred Harp?" (see Chapter 1). Mercer seemed to reproduce a classic discourse of the vanishing, writing that "each year death and disability shrink the traditional core of singers, each loss a sliver of that shared experience and that distinctive sound that is Sacred Harp Singing." But Mercer co-opted this nostalgic discourse in order to protect Sacred Harp from those who were using the same ideas to support folk-revival or "early music" approaches without acknowledging the primacy of Southern tradition. Mercer warned of the threat of "dilution" from such sources, urging Northern singers to go South and absorb the "actually-made sounds" that "set Sacred Harp Singing apart from all other music." He wrote of the transmission process,

> Sacred Harp Singing can be *taught* but it's more easily, and more naturally, *caught*. Sing with traditional singers as much as you can. Think of it as a bit of an apprenticeship. Go to Georgia, go to Alabama. Yes, *you* can do it. Put off mowing your lawn (or shoveling your snow) until *next* weekend, get a cheap ticket now and *go*. Sit by these folks and sing with them. *Listen and absorb*. Breathe with them, pulse (accent) with them, phrase with them.[56]

The article implies that face-to-face experience will make Sacred Harp more distinctive to new singers, lifting it out of its initial position in a vague space triangulated from concepts of world music (exotic, primitive, incomprehensible), medieval music (ancient, austere, sacred), and American music (egalitarian, folkish, common property). Mercer asks folk-revival singers who pay lip service to "oral tradition" to put their money where their mouth is and buy a plane ticket. Traveling South will alert singers to their obligations and restrict their indulgence in "coating the sounds of the fully commodified present with the patina of use value in some other time and place" (Erlmann 1996: 483).

One lifelong singer's response to this article corroborated Mercer's description of traditional singers—that they "are fiercely proud of the old sound, of which they have long and faithfully been the custodians"—and reinforced his exhortations to new singers. When Mercer's article was posted to the singings list in 2003, some years after its appearance in the *Chicago Sacred Harp Newsletter,* Alabama singer Darlene Dalton offered a gracious invitation to new singers on the terms defined by Mercer, but emphasizing that not all newcomers are Northern: "I do welcome 'foreigners' (Northerners and others, even Southerners who are new to the tradition) to our way of singing, and I hope I portray that welcome. I know that many of you have come to love it as I do, and I am made glad by that knowledge. I especially appreciate those who want to avoid 'diluting' it or changing it to something less 'raw' and more refined."

Rather than suggesting that outside participation will inevitably destroy local Southern traditions—which might imply that would-be revival singers should learn from recordings and leave Southern singers in peaceful isolation—Mercer and Dalton seem confident that exposure to traditional singing can create relationships and obligations that will engender authentic continuation of a living tradition, not merely reenactment or preservation. From such a perspective Sacred Harp could be said to constitute what Bernhard Giesen calls a traditional code—a means of "constructing collective identity by assuming and defending a particular continuity between past, present and future" (Giesen 1998: 30). That code is contagious; it can be "caught" by new singers if they expose themselves to Southern singing. Trading on the appeal of nostalgia and the fear of vanishing tradition, Mercer and Dalton gave the old celebration of isolated Southern culture a twist: they suggested that newcomers would inevitably dilute those raw, pure, and powerful sounds if they isolated *themselves* from Southern singing.

This chapter dwells on controversies, conflicts, and competing claims, the political discourses that singers are enjoined to leave at the margins of the hollow square. But no community is without conflict, and one as diverse and mobile as the Sacred Harp diaspora would seem particularly prone to schism. The fact that participants repeatedly characterize it as unusually cohesive, a rare find in a fragmented world, only reinforces the importance of considering "the means through which such contradictions are mediated or masked, so that members of communities come to experience their 'system' as forming a coherent whole" (Sugarman 1997: 198). Nostalgia—as it is performed, incited, and projected onto others—is a crucial aspect of the coherent community feeling that I have referred to as "diaspora consciousness" or being "at home in transience."

Even if one argues that nostalgia can rely heavily on essentialism, it would be a mistake to underestimate its power and flexibility as a kind of politicized emotion. Like stereotype, that other multivalent and unstable form of expression, nostalgia has objectifying tendencies: it "reifies the 'everyday' experience of the folk" (Sorensen 1997: 46–47) and performs an "aesthetic intervention" on recollections of experience or ideas of history (Steinwand 1997: 10). In Sacred Harp diaspora consciousness, the "myth of return" to an imagined homeland is oriented more around temporal than geographical distance; the defining values of the homeland have been lost to historical time and the destructive powers of modernity but can be partially, temporarily revisited through traditional singing.

Staking a claim to nostalgia is a self-reinforcing processual act. Singers affirm their ownership of the tradition by professing the pain of loss, whether that loss is anticipated (the "vanishing tradition" in crisis) or already complete (the deaths of previous generations and the end of their way of life). In this sense nostalgia can be a form of activism rather than a passive, wistful sentiment (cf. Allon 2000: 284). Out of such acts, unlikely alliances have emerged from Sacred Harp's diasporic relationships. New singing communities affiliate themselves with Southern traditional singing partly on the basis of shared nostalgia, and from this foundation these groups support one another in making claims to cultural authenticity and value. At the same time, committed diaspora singers and lifelong Southern singers continually find ways to remind newer participants that their nostalgia has to be earned to count as authentic.

Mercer, Dalton, and other singers who emphasize the importance of travel are challenging newcomers to prove the sincerity of their intent to participate in an authentic Sacred Harp community. I have discussed how that community can be read through theories of descent, consent, affinity, and dissent, each of which frames ethnicity and affiliation a little differently (Sollors 1986, Shelemay 2003). The American exceptionalist qualities of Sacred Harp discourse draw attention to the community's consent-oriented characteristics: it promises membership to anyone who will agree to a particular social contract. But the Sacred Harp emphasis on individual agency—in travel, song choice, performance practice, and interpretation—suggests that *intent* presents an important complement to consent. The Sacred Harp diaspora is characterized by so many competing local discourses, such a deep concern with distinguishing the authentic from the inauthentic, and such transient community gatherings that singers must convincingly and continually perform their forward-directed intentions rather than merely offering consent. Sincere intentions affirm the existence of shared values that cross-cut the diaspora, whether these intentions are performed through vocal ornaments, expressions of nostalgia, commitments to travel, or efforts to avoid conflict in the hollow square. Consider one survey respondent's answer to the question "Do you consider yourself a traditional singer?"—"I would say that my motives are traditional."

With its egalitarian ideology and its focus on participatory music making, Sacred Harp has clear affinities with folk-revival jam sessions, drum circles, and singalongs of all kinds. But it is worth remembering that Sacred Harp singers do not sit in a circle. They structure space and individual positions in a way that is both more hierarchical and less exclusive, affording a wider variety of potential communications and relationships. The hollow square has corners, aisles, many different sightlines, seats suited to displaying or concealing one's feelings and one's voice. It encourages sectional alliances and private communication in the midst of a crowd, across the square or behind the leader's back. Its hierarchical arrangement is repeatedly destabilized by the succession of individuals who briefly occupy the center of the square, and its discourses are marked by sectional counterpoint, imitation, repetition, and dissonance.

In the hollow square singers acknowledge that words fail them. At times they can only hope to communicate by offering up their voices as proof of their sincere intent, their belief that "these actually-made sounds count for something," as Mercer wrote. Singing together communicates intent in uniquely powerful and multivalent ways: as a shared visceral experience and a form of physical and emotional intimacy, it continually points to the failures of speech. The undeniably forceful feelings engendered by singing encourage singers to discount apparent conflicts and marks of difference. A group of people with sharply different political ideologies can occupy the same space because singing keeps them from talking and talking reminds them of how different they feel when they're singing. Even as singers communicate their affiliations and convictions through their decisions in the hollow square, the flexibility of the medium makes definitive interpretations impossible. Unable to make hard judgments about other people's choices, one can only fall back on assuming that the leader's intentions are good and the class's efforts are sincere. In so doing, each singer lives out the contradictions, obligations, and intense pleasures of being "a stranger here below" who also belongs to a far-flung community, creating a common authentic experience out of difference and a sense of home out of transience.

Notes

Introduction

1. George Atkin (1819)—William Moore (1825). Parenthetical citations for song texts refer to page numbers in *The Sacred Harp*, 1991 revision (McGraw 1991). All song citations in the notes give the source of the text followed by the composer or arranger, with the respective dates; they duplicate attributions printed in *The Sacred Harp*. When two songs appear on the same page, it is conventional to append "t" or "b" to the page number to indicate "top" or "bottom."

2. Well-known films that provide variants on such "discovery" scenes include *Deliverance* (1972; banjo and clogging in a decrepit end-of-the-line locale), *The Apostle* (1997; a white child discovers black Southern preaching styles), *Songcatcher* (2001; a professor on vacation discovers Appalachian ballads), and *Cold Mountain* (2003; a Civil War–era urban sophisticate discovers rural traditions that include Sacred Harp singing; see Chapter 6). *O Brother, Where Art Thou?* (2000) is a feature-length love letter to this genre.

3. George Pullen Jackson provides examples of many different shape-, number-, and letter-based notation systems (1933: 337, 343).

4. Thanks to singer Dick Hulan, who posted this information to the listserv discussions@fasola.org on February 12, 2004: "Some copies of William Smith, The Easy Instructor . . . Part II (1803) contain this affidavit on the verso of the title page: 'This is to certify, that I have granted to Mr. Willm. Little and to Mr. William Smith, the sole and exclusive right to publish the following characters to designate Sol [picture of a round note], La [square], Mi [diamond], Fa [triangle]. Upon condition that the books by them made should be sold upon the most easy terms for the benefit of the public. Given under my hand at Philadelphia this tenth day of March, A.D. 1798. John Connelly. Attest, N. Jones. Copy right secured.'"

5. Thomas Morley published this system in his *Plain and Easie Introduction to Practicall Musicke* (1597); it was adopted in the 1698 edition of the *Bay Psalm Book* in the form of letters placed under the pitches on the staff (Marini 2003: 79).

6. E.g., Epstein 1983 and Garst 1986 on the contested relationship of shape-note singing to African American spirituals; Eskew 1966 on nineteenth-century singing in the Shenandoah valley; Marini 1983 and 2003 on the role of sacred song in the Great Awakening; Campbell 1997 on turn-of-the-twentieth-century tunebook revision controversies; Patterson 1970–71 for a review of scholarship and discography; Taddie 1996 on issues of solmization and mode; and Tallmadge 1984 on "folk organum." See especially Bealle 1997 and his continually updated *Shape Note Bibliography* at http://fasola.org/bibliography/.

7. For historical and ideological connections between contemporary Sacred Harp practice and the Second Great Awakening, see Vinson 1999. Marini suggests that some present-day Southern Sacred Harp conventions "faithfully preserve the historic practices of the early American singing school," which permits him to assert that the tradition has been "practiced continuously since the 1720s" (Marini 2003: 68). While the current geographic spread of Sacred Harp conventions and some aspects of their terminology owe a great deal to singing schools, these two types of Sacred Harp gathering have had clearly differentiated structures since the mid-nineteenth century.

8. Cincinnati *Musician and Intelligencer* 2, no. 1: 21ff, cited in Jackson 1933: 20.

9. Some of these sects also consider the use of musical *notation* to be inappropriate during worship; congregations sing from books that contain only the words to songs, such as Benjamin Lloyd's *The Primitive Hymns, Spiritual Songs, and Sacred Poems* (1841). Members of such congregations typically engage in singing notated sacred music outside of church services.

10. The 1832 date refers to Joseph Funk's four-shape tunebook *A Compilation of Genuine Church Music,* which was retitled as the *Harmonia Sacra* and reset in seven-shape notation in its fifth edition (1851).

11. Bealle presents a detailed analysis of the relative influence of Jackson's book and Carl Carmer's *Stars Fell on Alabama*—now the motto on the state's license plates—which also came out in 1933 and contained a widely read description of a Sacred Harp singing. Carmer's book sold much better than Jackson's, providing "an emotional roadmap by which Americans for decades afterward, if only in their imaginations, navigated native Alabama culture and Sacred Harp tradition" (1997: 97–98). But it was Jackson's work that had scholarly authority and dealt directly with matters of race.

12. Work's letter is undated but was evidently sent in 1931; Brown's is dated April 8, 1931. These scrapbooks are currently in the possession of Jackson's granddaughter, Pam Helms, in Atlanta. I am extremely grateful for her generosity with these materials.

13. The reproduction also appears in Jackson 1943: 140, attributed to "Paul Petrovich Svenin some time between 1811 and 1813," with reproduction credit to the Metropolitan Museum of Art in New York.

14. Review by the Agrarian Donald Davidson, *New York Herald Tribune Books,* May 14, 1933; vol. 2 of Jackson's scrapbooks.

15. Contemporary reviewers echoed this argument. One referred to black spirituals as "a natural and integral part of American life. . . . The spirituals, white and black, are as native to this country as the camp-meeting, and the real origin of each is bedded deep in English Protestantism" (Parks 1933: 169)

16. Boyd 2002 provides detailed biographical and ethnographic work on Judge Jackson, his family, and their participation in folk revival events. This volume also includes an excellent CD compilation of African American shape-note singing. See also my review (Miller 2004b) and Dyen 1977.

17. See Stewart 1996, Wray and Newitz 1997, and Wiegman 2002 [1999].

18. George Pullen Jackson popularized two of these expressions in his book *White Spirituals in the Southern Uplands: The Story of the Fasola Folk, Their Songs, Singings, and "Buckwheat Notes"* (Jackson 1933). He previously referred to "The Fa-Sol-La Folk" in a 1926 article bearing that title (Jackson 1926).

19. Parts of this section are adapted from Miller 2003b. I am grateful for Leo Treitler's guidance and feedback as I drew an American parallel to his work on medieval song.

20. A substantial scholarly literature explores and critiques similar tropes of antiquity. A sampling of critical approaches might include Shelemay's work on the Beta Israel in Ethiopia (1989); Ginsburg et al. on how First Peoples reflexively engage with these discourses (2002); Hatfield on Taiwanese pilgrimage (1997); and di Leonardo on the trope's exploitation in American anthropological literature, journalism, and popular culture (1998).

21. Cf. Gene Wise (1999) on American "paradigm dramas" and Judith Tick on American exceptionalism as "the compass charting a course for American music scholarship for the last fifty years" (2003: 722).

22. Cf. Finnegan 1989, on pathways of musical practice, as well as Sacred Harp singers' frequent references to "seeking the old paths" (see Chapter 2).

23. Along these lines, Bryan Turner provides a useful "nostalgic paradigm" with four dimensions: the attribution of historical decline; "loss of personal wholeness and moral certainty"; "loss of individual freedom and autonomy"; and "loss of simplicity, personal authenticity and emotional spontaneity" (1987: 150–51).

Chapter 1: A Venture to the Field

1. *Collection of Hymns and Spiritual Songs* (1814).

2. This question presents a rhetorical and ideological parallel to many conference sessions sponsored by the Society for Ethnomusicology; one such presentation was entitled "Should I Feel Distressed About Teaching Gamelan Music in the Cornfields of Iowa?" (Roger Vetter, November 19, 1999 in Austin, Texas) in an edited collection stemming from these sessions.

3. Mercer's article was posted to the singings@fasola.org list by another singer on August 3, 2003. Since both Sacred Harp listservs are open to anyone with an email address and all past postings can be searched and retrieved using automated archiving commands, I have not obtained explicit permission for every quotation from listserv postings. However, in most cases I have attempted to contact the writer to explain how I plan to use the quoted material and to ask whether he or she would like to be identified by name.

4. I distributed the survey at singings around the country, publicized it on the listserv singings@fasola.org, and made it available in electronic form as a webpage, eventually receiving 109 responses. Survey respondents were self-selecting but nevertheless represented a broad range of Sacred Harp singers in terms of age, origin, and experience. The vast majority of the respondents had not met me before. See the appendices to Miller 2005 for my survey questions and basic demographic statistics on the respondents.

5. Posted to discussions@fasola.org on November 1, 1999.

6. I make these points with care because singers' interactions with scholars have not always been positive. Most recently, the ethnomusicologist Marin Marian-Bălașa visited three Midwestern singings and published an article which he described as "intellectual polyphony," in which he integrated singers' written comments on a draft into his footnotes, without addressing their factual corrections to the main text or fully explaining to the singers how their comments would be used. In the article he characterized the singers' corrections as the defensive gestures of an intrinsically conservative, hegemonic shape-note culture: "Criticism, rectilinear logic, improvement or innovation—all are irrelevant in this tradition. . . . Overall, their self[-]representations should be anyone's perception, their projections are the unique truth, their narrative is hegemonic" (2003: 153, 167).

7. One dispersed community that *does* have some close resemblances to my "Sacred Harp diaspora" is the one oriented around the Native American pow-wow circuit, as described by Tara Browner (2002).

8. Cf. Zheng 1994 on diasporic "cultural brokers," and Sheffer 1986 on the triangular relationships between the diaspora community, the host country, and the homeland.

9. Recorded interview, December 2000.

10. The Lee family, who live in southern Georgia, sang Sacred Harp in their local community for several generations without participating in the national convention network. In the 1990s, when members of the family began attending singings outside their home region, their very slow, densely ornamented performance style became influential in the diaspora. See Chapter 3.

11. Recorded interview, June 2003.

12. See for example Sugarman 1997, Rasmussen 1998, Zheng 1994, Gopinath 1995, Rouse 1991, and Ragland 2003.

13. Herman 1997 is a detailed study of the relationships among these California singing groups.

14. Handwritten field notes, Pacific Northwest Convention, Seattle, Washington, February 14, 2004.

15. The Sunday conflict arises from the historical practice of holding Sacred Harp singings in churches that did not have services every week; the weekend convention was a faith-oriented social activity that could fill an unused church. Church leaders can be sensitive to the idea that singings are competing with preaching or church attendance, but they also want to maintain the good will of singing families in their congregations (and they welcome the donations a convention can bring). Some singers have created or renewed a relationship with a particular church in order to use it as a venue for singings.

16. My discussion of affiliation is indebted to Hollinger 1993.

17. Anonymous (1774)—Arr. T. W. Carter (1844).

18. Turner and Turner characterize Christian pilgrimage as a liminoid rather than a strictly liminal experience because of its elective, leisure-based nature, in contrast to obligatory rites of passage (1978: 35, 231).

19. Here I follow Shelemay's reframing of the Sollors consent/descent model (Sollors 1986) to emphasize processes of "descent, dissent, and affinity" (Shelemay 2003: 11).

20. See, for example, di Leonardo 1998, Foster 1988, Stewart 1996, Ware and Back 2002, Wiegman 2002 [1999], and the essays collected in Wray and Newitz 1997.

21. See Herzfeld 1997: 164, for a discussion of stereotyping as a fundamental privilege.

22. "West Savannah," from the 1998 Outkast album *Aquemini* (La Face). Lyrics by Big Boi. Produced by Organized Noize.

23. Cf. Peter Manuel's discussion of "audible *difference*" (1995: 232) as an aspect of world music samples, sounds that might not have specific referential meaning to the listener but instead index generalized difference.

24. The rural Southerner is by no means the only white subaltern in America. The Irish American population has occupied a similar position at various times and places, as have other "white ethnics." We should also remember the class-based (rather than regional) category of "white trash," which overlaps with but is no longer limited to the rural South.

25. Recorded interview, June 2003.

26. I am not suggesting that *all* lifelong Southern singers are delighted with the diversity of the contemporary national singing community; those who find it objectionable do not become regular visitors at diaspora conventions. However, singers of all political stripes have reported that Sacred Harp encourages them to suspend judgment and to continue attending particular conventions despite concerns about the ideological convictions of the host community (see Chapter 6).

27. I will return to the concept of "orthopraxy," typically used in contrast to "orthodoxy" to distinguish societies that emphasize "proper performance of ritual obligations" (Gk. *orthos* + *praxis*: "correct action") from those that emphasize "proper doctrinal beliefs" (*orthos* + *doxa*) (Bell 1997: 171, 191–97). Cf. Hannerz's discussion of cosmopolitan travelers' "concern with achieving competence in cultures which are initially alien," an orthopraxic approach to cultural tourism that can eventually yield "a sense of mastery" and free choice with respect to one's culture of origin; "surrender abroad [is] a form of mastery at home" (Hannerz 1990: 240).

28. Recorded interview, June 2003.

Chapter 2: Travels to the Center of the Square

1. Recorded interview conducted by singer John Plunkett on October 12, 2001, printed in Miller 2002: 275.

2. Recorded interview, January 9, 2002, printed in Miller 2002: 312.

3. These phrases come from "Wayfaring Stranger" (457; Bever's *Christian Songster* [1858]—Arr. John M. Dye [1935]), "Irwinton" (229; Anonymous [1774]—Arr. T. W. Carter [1844]), "White" (288; *Dobell's New Selection* [1810]—Edmund Dumas [1856]), "The Better Land" (454; O. A. Parris [1935]), "Bound for Canaan" (82t; John Leland [1793]—Arr. E. J. King [1844]), and "Journey Home" (111t; *Mead's Collection* [1807]—R. F. Mann [1868]). The "Sacred Harp Online Index" (http://www.fasola.org/index/oIndex.html) shows the word "home" appearing in eighty-nine songs, virtually always as a reference to heaven and used in conjunction with implied travels or exile. A search sampling some of the many words used for directed motion in *The Sacred Harp* reveals variants of the word "travel" (e.g., trav'ling, traveler) in twenty-two songs, "journey" in fourteen, and "walk" in fifteen.

4. In this section I am indebted to Richard Wolf's work on how music and dance provide "conventionalized categories" that function as "signposts" for emotional experience and aid in the navigation of ceremony (Wolf 2001: 380, 413).

5. Turner and Turner have eloquently described the enveloping quality of such spaces (Turner and Turner 1978: 10–11).

6. Judith Becker has written on the role of sensory over-stimulation in triggering ecstatic or transcendent "trancing" experiences connected with music (Becker 2004).

7. Recorded on March 11, 2001, in Northampton, Mass.

8. "The Better Land" (454), O. A. Parris (1935): "I'm going to a better land, / Where troubles are unknown, / All sorrow will be gone, / We'll sing around the throne in sweet accord, /Adoring Jesus, our dear Lord."

9. E.g., "Living Hope" (500), Isaac Watts (1707)—Hugh W. McGraw (1959): "He gave our souls a living hope / That they should never die."

10. See Hatfield 1997: 3, on the crowd as "a spectacle with the power to cajole, convince, or convert."

11. This terminology is uncommon outside the South. Some singers use the noun "sing" instead of "singing"; the two terms convey different information about a singer's influences, affiliations, and geographical origin.

12. Posted February 18, 1999.

13. Posted February 18, 1999.

14. Cf. Bohlman 1988: 71 on the reduction of individual tradition-bearers to "an innocuous sameness" in folk music research.

15. Recorded interview, December 2000.

16. Marian-Bâlaşa is mistaken in his assumption that "since every individual takes in turn the role and place of the leader any criticism is automatically taken away" (2003: 164). Singers are adamant that anyone has the right to lead, but they vigorously compare, praise, and critique individual leaders.

17. My thanks to Steve Warner for this observation.

18. Recorded on January 14, 2001.

19. Recorded on June 3, 2001, near Bremen, Ga.

20. Recorded interview, January 9, 2002, printed in Miller 2002: 309–10.

21. I follow Richard Wolf's lead in discussing nonlinguistic forms of expression as emotives; Reddy makes space for this possibility but mostly discusses verbal examples (Wolf 2001).

22. Recorded interview conducted by John Plunkett on October 12, 2001, and printed in Miller 2002: 273.

23. Recorded June 4, 2000.

24. Recorded interview, January 13, 2002, printed in Miller 2002: 325–26.

25. Cf. Glassberg 2001: 123 and Casey 2001: 408.

26. I'm grateful to Aaron Girard for suggesting this insight about mistakes. A lifelong Alabama singer told me that on occasion she deliberately gives an inappropriate starting pitch when she is leading so as to demonstrate to young people and new singers that it's all right to make mistakes.

27. Alto distinctiveness is also connected with the variability of sung alto parts, discussed in Chapter 3. See Girard 2002.

28. This self-imposed vulnerability calls into question Marian-Bâlaşa's assertion that Sacred Harp singers lead in order to achieve "prestige, power, and dominance" (2003: 161).

Chapter 3: "Well, You'll Learn"

1. An earlier version of this chapter appeared as Miller 2004a.

2. Recorded January 12, 2003. This story emerged in a virtually identical form in an interview John Bealle conducted with Ted Johnson (Marcia's husband) thirteen years earlier (Bealle 1997: 201).

3. For the sake of brevity, this survey is oriented around the pragmatic function of genre categories for singers rather than an analysis of the many harmonic styles

and compositional processes represented in the three centuries of music contained in *The Sacred Harp*. Such analysis can be found in Jackson 1933, Horn 1970, Seeger 1940, Tallmadge 1984, Taddie 1996, and many more general surveys of American hymnody.

4. English country parish composers include William Tans'ur, Aaron Williamson, and William Knapp. See Marini 2003: 77.

5. See Jackson 1943, Epstein 1983, Garst 1986, and Radano 2003.

6. Chicago singer Lisa Grayson's "Anatomy of a Sacred Harp Tune," which appears in her *Beginner's Guide to Shape-Note Singing* (Grayson 1997), dissects this layout to show how a single song can stand in for the entire repertoire.

7. Recently some singers have begun to sing out of both the Denson and Cooper books, but even then almost never during a single convention.

8. Some of these compositions originally had four parts; B. F. White excised many alto parts in compiling *The Sacred Harp* because "he felt that it was unnatural for women to sing in the low part of the voice" (Bruce 2000: 140). These parts were restored or recomposed in twentieth-century editions.

9. Handwritten field notes during informal discussion, September 8, 2001.

10. As I will discuss in Chapter 6, some singers feel that newcomers become obsessed with orthoprax performance to shield themselves from Sacred Harp's religious nature. Stephen Marini writes that Northern singers "simply do not share" the evangelical worldview of Southern singers; while this is an over-broad generalization, Marini makes a good point in suggesting that "in order to participate authentically in Sacred Harp, therefore, they valorize the procedures of the singing school and its lore through which they, too, can become true Sacred Harp singers" (Marini 2003: 93).

11. Cf. Ruth Katz on "mannerism" in Aleppo Jewish singing (Katz 1968: 77).

12. Personal email correspondence, January 9, 2004.

13. Posted January 6, 2004.

14. http://users3.ev1.net/~amity/ (accessed January 7, 2004). The very existence of a website that will "orally transmit" tunes to singers who don't read music raises a host of issues, especially given the pedagogical history of shape-notes. Such technologies are filling the transmission gap created by the decline of long-term singing schools and the fact that new adult singers often did not learn to read music as children.

15. An interesting parallel can be found in Turino 1990, which recounts how Andean flute players refused to acknowledge the dissonance of an ensemble performance that was forced to combine differently tuned instruments. This sounding dissonance arose from issues of localism and ascribed authority similar to those I have discussed here, but for Turino they indexed a vanishing tradition rather than an expanding one.

16. Cf. the "highly constrained, notated, literate, yet orally transmitted repertoire" discussed in Shelemay, Jeffery, and Monson 1993: 117.

17. George Pullen Jackson made a similar observation about a 1930 Texas convention (1933: 116).

18. Recorded interview, December 2000.

19. Marini refers to the tenor part as "the lead" and the alto as "the counter," a terminology still used in some Southern singing areas. "Lead" is far more common than "counter" in current usage; I have never heard a singer refer to the altos as "counters."

20. Summarized from Bealle 1997: 265–66.

21. Personal correspondence, March 15, 2004.

22. In fact, this proved a complicated issue for members of the Lee family in their local community, as I discuss in Chapter 5.

23. Posted to discussions@fasola.org on December 6, 2003.

24. See Marini 2003: 95.

25. Posted to discussions@fasola.org on April 10, 2000.

26. Personal correspondence, March 15, 2004.

27. Diligently adding prestigious and remote singings to one's list might indeed be viewed as an aspect of the "fetishism of commodities" that Batteau has associated with twentieth-century folk culture (Batteau 1990: 11).

28. Cf. Treitler 2003 for a medieval case.

29. Personal correspondence, March 15, 2004.

30. Recorded March 4, 2001.

31. Jackson lists many of the Southern counties, rivers, towns, and people who lend their names to songs in early-twentieth-century tunebooks (1933: 151–52).

Chapter 4: "Speaking May Relieve Thee"

1. "Jackson," 317b, *Mercer's Cluster* (1810)—M. F. McWhorter (1908).

2. "I'm Going Home," 282, Leonard P. Breedlove (1850).

3. "Prospect," 30b, Isaac Watts (1707)—Graham (1835).

4. "Distress," 32b, Anne Steele (1760)—*Southern Harmony* (1835).

5. "Africa," 178, Isaac Watts (1709)—William Billings (1770).

6. "Ragan," 176t, Arr. W. F. Moore (1869).

7. See Fernandez 1966 and Fernandez 1986: 45 on the "time-binding" effect of metaphor.

8. *Revival Melodies* (1842)—Arr. J. T. White (1844).

9. *New England Sunday School Hymn Book* (1830)—S. M. Denson (1911).

10. Posted August 1, 1999.

11. The reader may note the shift to first names here. In general, I refer to singers by full name or surname when citing written words or formal speech and by first name when describing informal personal interactions.

12. Personal email correspondence, January 2005.

13. The origins of this local practice are murky, but New England singers often compare this system to the egalitarian procedures governing spontaneous speech at Quaker meetings.

14. Bealle has summed up this separation with the phrase "public worship, private faith" (1997); his distinction remains relevant outside the realm of religious affiliation and expression.

15. See Goody 2000: 83, on storytelling and domination.

16. Personal correspondence, March 15, 2004.

17. Stephen Jenks (1800).

18. Joseph Hart (1759)—M. A. Hendon (1859).

19. Eriksen has since become famous in Sacred Harp circles for his consulting and performance work on the *Cold Mountain* soundtrack and ensuing "Great High Mountain" tour, discussed in Chapter 6.

20. Posted March 20, 2002.

21. Recorded March 4, 2001, in Amherst, Mass. Names of singers are provided when I could definitively identify them on my recording.

22. Posted August 26, 1999.

23. Recorded interview, June 2003.

24. This 1707 Isaac Watts text is set in "Arlington," 73b, by Thomas Arne (1762); in "The Enquirer," 74t, by B. F. White (1844); and in "Eternal Light," 483, by H. N. McGraw (1960).

25. "Corinth," 32t, Joseph Grigg (1765)—Arr. John Massengale (1844).

26. This 1707 Isaac Watts text is set in "Webster," 31b, which is reprinted from the *Southern Harmony* (1835); in "Albion," 52t, by Robert Boyd (1816); and in "Novakoski," 481, by P. Dan Brittain (1989).

27. Isaac Watts (1709)—H. S. Reese (1859).

28. Isaac Watts (1719)—*A Sett Of Tunes* (1720).

29. Joseph Hart (1759)—B. F. White (1844).

30. Cf. Fernandez on metaphor as a device "for leaping beyond the essential privacy of the experiential process" and on its self-fulfilling potential (Fernandez 1986: 6, 20).

31. Posted August 26, 1999.

32. Arr. W. F. Moore (1869).

33. Reddy makes a distinction between emotives and Austin's "performatives" (Austin 1975 [1962]). I posit that "I belong" has an instrumental, reflexive, self-exploratory character that places it in the "emotive" category.

34. My discussion of hoarseness as an index of authentic affect is indebted to Feld 1982, Briggs 1993, Tolbert 1990, and Urban 1988.

35. Recorded March 11, 2001, in Northampton, Mass.

36. Posted August 30, 1999.

Chapter 5: A Strange Land and a Peculiar People

1. I encountered this article and several others cited in this chapter in the media scrapbooks at the Sacred Harp Museum in Carrollton, Georgia. Partial citations

appear in endnotes when full citations were not available from the scrapbooks. This article was written by Judi Johnston and appeared in a Sumter County, Georgia, newspaper on April 23, 1980.

2. These articles appeared in the *Atlanta Journal* or *Atlanta Constitution* newspapers; they are collected in Plunkett 2003 without full citations.

3. Sacred Harp Museum scrapbook; first page and byline missing. "Sacred Harp singers refuse to let unique musical tradition fade away," *Houston Chronicle* (August 22, 1987), section 6, page 2.

4. Recorded telephone interview, August 21, 2001, printed in Miller 2002: 258.

5. This list should make it clear that I cannot make a comprehensive survey of Sacred Harp–related media in a single chapter. John Bealle has already provided insightful analysis of newsletters and minutebooks, two major genres of Sacred Harp representation that I will not discuss (Bealle 1997). Here I focus on recordings and web-based media; see Miller 2005: 357–67 for a discussion of documentary video representation.

6. Personal correspondence, March 15, 2004.

7. See Shapiro 1978, Batteau 1990, and Stewart 1996.

8. This tendency has been analyzed in exhaustive detail from within the discipline; see especially Fabian 1983 on temporal distancing and di Leonardo 1998 for a discussion of this issue in the context of American identity politics.

9. Rural African American Southern communities and musical traditions have played a somewhat different role. Folk revival discourse in the second half of the twentieth century often attributes equivalent authenticity and atemporality to black and white rural Southern traditions without addressing race relations or the racist implications of the earlier folk-celebrating literature I discuss here. Meanwhile, rural Southern black musicians have played a "living ancestors," nostalgia-inspiring role for urban black populations (see Allen 1992).

10. Fabian 1983 provides a broader discussion of "coevalness denied."

11. The literature on this subject is vast; see, for example, Newcombe 1979–80, Whisnant 1983, Foster 1988, Batteau 1990, and Stewart 1996.

12. Article by Mimi Altree, quoted here from the version posted to singings@fasola.org on August 8, 2002.

13. Article by Cathy Taylor for *The Old Times,* a Minneapolis monthly focused on antiques and preservation, quoted here from the version posted to singings@fasola.org on November 8, 2001.

14. Article by Max McCoy for the *Joplin Globe,* quoted here from the version posted to singings@fasola.org on March 20, 2001.

15. Sacred Harp singers will recognize this phrase from the text of "Warrenton" (145t).

16. Personal correspondence, March 15, 2004.

17. Ibid.

18. Ibid. Lee is referring to Cobb 1989.

19. Typographical errors corrected.

20. Personal email correspondence, July 28, 2004.

21. Posted to singings@fasola.org on April 26, 2000.

22. Posted to singings@fasola.org on October 19, 1999.

23. Bealle locates a similar quality in the "postmodern pastiche texture" in the *Chicago Sacred Harp Newsletter* (Bealle 1997: 203).

24. Personal correspondence, March 15, 2004.

25. Cf. Lausevic's analysis of Balkan music's appeal to a similar demographic: that repertoire is "distant enough—neither inherited nor 'lily white' American—and at the same time close enough, being still European" (1998: 451).

26. Bealle's discussion of these album notes places Gordon's "vast boundaries" in a wider discursive context: he writes, "I mean not to suggest that these 'vast boundaries' did not exist but that a discourse of irreconcilable difference had long prevailed, largely in culture writing, over a discourse of possible sameness" (1997: 193).

27. Article by Sarah Bryan Miller, *Post-Dispatch* Classical Music Critic, quoted here from the version posted to singings@fasola.org on March 28, 2001.

28. E.g., Anonymous 4 2003, Boston Camerata 1990, and Boston Camerata 1992.

29. Recorded February 15, 2004, at the Pacific Northwest Convention (held at the Sunset Hill Community Club in Seattle, Wash.).

30. Cf. Foster 1988: 182–83.

31. John Newton (1779)—Edmund Dumas (1869).

32. Cf. Stephen Marini's summary of North-South Sacred Harp relations: "Northern singers now use evangelical language more freely, southern singers are more comfortable with postmodern quirkiness, and everyone loves the new tunes" (Marini 2003: 97).

Chapter 6: At Home in Transience

1. Kelly House provided this state breakdown in a posting to singings@fasola.org on February 24, 2004.

2. From a letter Laura Clawson posted to singings@fasola.org on Eriksen's behalf on October 10, 2003.

3. Ibid.

4. Posted to singings@fasola.org by Tim Eriksen on February 14, 2004.

5. Posted February 24, 2004.

6. Stephen Jenks (1800).

7. Leonard P. Breedlove (1850).

8. Posted to singings@fasola.org on March 2, 2004.

9. Eriksen expressed regret that he had to choose an exclusive group of singers, writing to singings@fasola.org that "it's been a heartbreak to have to invite (and therefore not invite) people to sing on a few occasions" (posted February 14, 2004).

10. Letter from Eriksen posted to singings@fasola.org by Laura Clawson on October 10, 2003.

11. Ibid. The fact that Romania provided a more convenient, cheaper filming location than Appalachia, down to the replacement of nineteenth-century mountaineers with Romanian extras, might inspire discussion of the historical parallels between Eastern Europe and Appalachia as economically exploited sites of cheap labor and folk culture.

12. Ibid.

13. Handwritten fieldnotes, March 13, 2004.

14. Ibid.

15. "Morning Sun," 436, *New England Sunday School Hymn Book* (1830)—S. M. Denson (1911). See Chapter 4 on Jerilyn Schumacher.

16. Hauser's *Hesperian Harp* (1848)—William Hauser (1848).

17. Personal email correspondence, January 28, 2005.

18. "Loving Jesus," 361, Anonymous—Pietro Guglielmi (1772), Arr. White & Searcy (1850).

19. "Sherburne," 186, Nahum Tate (1700)—Daniel Read (1783).

20. "Morning," 163t, Isaac Watts (1709)—Amos Pilsbury (1799).

21. 178, Isaac Watts (1709)—William Billings (1770).

22. "Northfield," 155, Isaac Watts (1707)—Jeremiah Ingalls (1800).

23. See the preliminary ethnography presented in Shelemay 2001.

24. Posted to discussions@fasola.org on November 16, 1999. The singer is referring to the guns fired in Civil War battle reenactments.

25. See the primary sources reprinted in Miller 2002.

26. Currency conversion performed using the Consumer Price Index calculator at Economic History Services (http://eh.net).

27. Quoted in Minnesota singer Keith Willard's description of Sheppard's leading workshop at Camp Fasola in the summer of 2003. Posted to singings@fasola.org on July 2, 2003.

28. Thanks to Chicago singer Ted Johnson for providing me with an even-handed account of singers' sometimes vitriolic responses to Marian-Bâlaşa's fieldwork methods and to a rough draft of his article that was widely circulated without his permission. These events clarified my understanding of diaspora singers' anxieties about their own fitness to represent traditional Sacred Harp.

29. This approach, which I have previously glossed as "orthopraxic," has a strong affinity with ethnomusicological fieldwork (especially the "bimusicality" branch pioneered by Mantle Hood) and with apprenticeship practices in general (cf. Herzfeld 2004, Solis 2004).

30. Isaac Watts (1719)—Daniel Read (1782).

31. Edmund Dumas (1869).

32. Jackson uses the first line of this text as the epigraph for his intriguing (if dated) chapter on "Shape Notes and Dorayme Songs among the Indians" (Jackson 1933: 410–18).

33. "Indian Convert" appears on page 133 in the *Southern Harmony* (William Walker, 1835) and is attributed to "Johnson." The *Southern Harmony* is available for online study at http://www.ccel.org/s/southern_harmony/. See also "The Romish Lady" (82 in the *Southern Harmony*), a conversion narrative about a young Catholic woman who is burned to death by the clergy after secretly studying a Bible on her own.

34. Annual minutebooks from 1995 through 2004 can be searched by keyword at http://www.fasola.org/minutes/.

35. Posted March 25, 2002.

36. This kind of controversy is not limited to Sacred Harp circles, of course; for example, the depiction of Jews in Bach's *St. John Passion* has engendered much public debate, particularly when the piece is to be performed by students or community choruses.

37. Posted March 22, 2002.

38. Interested readers can peruse the whole discussions thread by sending an email to discussion-subscribe@fasola.org and using automated archive-retrieval commands. "Stafford" was the subject of renewed listserv debate in October 2005.

39. Posted March 29, 2002, by a Kentucky singer.

40. 211, Isaac Watts (1719)—Howd (1800). Message posted March 25, 2002.

41. A public-domain electronic edition of Watts's psalms is available at http://www.ccel.org/w/watts/psalmshymns/TOC.htm.

42. Posted March 23, 2002.

43. Posted March 25, 2002.

44. Posted March 26, 2002.

45. Posted March 24, 2002.

46. Posted April 8, 2002.

47. Posted to singings@fasola.org on August 10, 1999.

48. Posted to discussions@fasola.org on April 8, 2002.

49. Handwritten fieldnotes, September 8, 2001.

50. Allen is writing about urban African American performance and reception of rural Southern musical genres, but his observations about nostalgia and Southern identity hold true for the Sacred Harp diaspora.

51. Handwritten field notes, Pioneer Valley Singing, July 5, 2003.

52. Many of the composers represented in the Sacred Harp explicitly subscribed to this ideology as it applied to America—including William Billings, for whom "the Revolution could be squarely placed in a biblical typology" (Stowe 2004: 52). Sacred Harp song titles often reflect typological convictions (e.g., "New Jordan" [442], "New Jerusalem" [299], and many songs dealing with the "new Canaan").

53. "Jackson," 317b, *Mercer's Cluster* (1810)—M. F. McWhorter (1908).

54. See Robertson 1990: 55 for a proposed historical sequence of several forms of nostalgia.

55. Posted to singings@fasola.org on August 9, 1999.

56. First published in the 1990s, posted to singings@fasola.org by another singer on August 3, 2003.

Bibliography

Allen, Ray. 1992. "Back Home: Southern Identity and African-American Gospel Quartet Performance." In *Mapping American Culture,* ed. W. Franklin and M. Steiner. Iowa City: University of Iowa Press.

Allon, Fiona. 2000. "Nostalgia Unbound: Illegibility and the Synthetic Excess of Place." *Continuum: Journal of Media and Cultural Studies* 14, no. 3: 275–87.

Anonymous 4. 2003. *American Angels: Songs of Hope, Redemption, and Glory.* Compact disc. Harmonia Mundi USA 907326.

Austin, J. L. 1975 [1962]. *How to Do Things with Words,* 2nd ed. Cambridge, Mass.: Harvard University Press.

Bailyn, Bernard. 2003. *To Begin the World Anew: The Genius and Ambiguities of the American Founders.* New York: Alfred A. Knopf.

Batteau, Allen W. 1990. *The Invention of Appalachia.* Tucson: University of Arizona Press.

Baumann, Gerd. 1987. *National Integration and Local Integrity.* Oxford: Clarendon Press.

Bealle, John. 1997. *Public Worship, Private Faith.* Athens: University of Georgia Press.

Becker, Judith. 2004. *Deep Listeners: Music, Emotion, and Trancing.* Bloomington: Indiana University Press.

Bell, Catherine. 1997. *Ritual: Perspectives and Dimensions.* New York: Oxford University Press.

Bloch, Maurice. 1974. "Symbols, Song, Dance and Features of Articulation: Is Religion an Extreme Form of Traditional Authority?" *European Journal of Sociology* 15: 55–81.

Bohlman, Philip V. 1988. *The Study of Folk Music in the Modern World.* Bloomington: Indiana University Press.

———. 1996. "Pilgrimage, Politics, and the Musical Remapping of the New Europe." *Ethnomusicology* 40, no. 3: 375–412.

Boston Camerata. 1990. *New Britain.* Compact disc. Erato 2292-45474-2.

———. 1992. *The American Vocalist.* Compact disc. Erato 2292-45818-2.

Bourdieu, Pierre. 1990. *The Logic of Practice.* Stanford, Calif.: Stanford University Press.

Boyd, Joe Dan. 1971. "Negro Sacred Harp Songsters in Mississippi." *Mississippi Folklore Register* 5, no. 3: 60–83.

———. 2002. *Judge Jackson and The Colored Sacred Harp.* Montgomery: Alabama Folklife Association.

Briggs, Charles. 1993. "Personal Sentiments and Polyphonic Voices in Warao Women's Ritual Wailing: Music and Poetics in a Critical and Collective Discourse." *American Anthropologist* 95, no. 4: 929–57.

Browner, Tara. 2002. *Heartbeat of the People: Music and Dance of the Northern Pow-Wow.* Urbana: University of Illinois Press.

Bruce, Neely. 2000. "Sacred Choral Music in the United States: An Overview." In *The Cambridge Companion to Singing,* ed. J. Potter. Cambridge: Cambridge University Press.

Caldwell, Mary French. 1930. "Change Comes to the Appalachian Mountaineer." *Current History* 31: 961–67.

Campbell, Gavin James. 1997. "'Old Can Be Used Instead of New': Shape-Note Singing and the Crisis of Modernity in the New South, 1880–1920." *Journal of American Folklore* 110, no. 436: 169–88.

Carlton, David. 2003. "To the Land I Am Bound: A Journey into Sacred Harp." *Southern Cultures* 9, no. 2: 49–66.

Casey, Edward S. 2001. "Body, Self, and Landscape: A Geophilosophical Inquiry into the Place-World." In *Textures of Place: Exploring Humanist Geographies,* ed. P. C. Adams, S. Hoelscher, and K. E. Till. Minneapolis: University of Minnesota Press.

Ching, Barbara. 1997. "Acting Naturally: Cultural Distinction and Critiques of Pure Country." In *White Trash: Race and Class in America,* ed. M. Wray and A. Newitz. New York: Routledge.

Clifford, James. 1997. *Routes: Travel and Translation in the Late Twentieth Century.* Cambridge, Mass.: Harvard University Press.

Cobb, Buell E., Jr. 1979. *Rivers of Delight: American Folk Hymns from the Sacred Harp Tradition.* Liner notes. Nonesuch Records H-71360.

———. 1989. *The Sacred Harp: A Tradition and Its Music.* Athens: University of Georgia Press.

Crawford, Richard. 1990. "'Ancient Music' and the Europeanizing of American Psalmody, 1800–1810." In *A Celebration of American Music: Words and Music in Honor of H. Wiley Hitchcock,* ed. R. Crawford, A. Lott, and C. J. Oja. Ann Arbor: University of Michigan Research Press.

———. 2001. *America's Musical Life: A History.* New York: Norton.

Crowley, John G. 2004. "The Sacred Harp Controversy in the Original Alabama Primitive Baptist Association." *Baptist Studies Bulletin* 7. http://www.mercer.edu/baptiststudies/july04.htm (accessed November 2004).

DeLaughter, Jerry. 1964. "Sacred Harp Singers Preserve Fading Art They Might Revive." *The Clarion-Ledger,* October 4, 1964.

DeLyser, Lydia. 2001. "When Less Is More: Absence and Landscape in a California Ghost Town." In *Textures of Place: Exploring Humanist Geographies,* ed. P. C. Adams, S. Hoelscher, and K. E. Till. Minneapolis: University of Minnesota Press.

di Leonardo, Micaela. 1998. *Exotics at Home: Anthropologies, Others, American Modernity.* Chicago: University of Chicago Press.

Dyen, Doris J. 1977. *The Role of Shape-Note Singing in the Musical Culture of Black Communities in Southeast Alabama.* Ph.D. diss., University of Illinois.

Epstein, Dena. 1983. "A White Origin for the Black Spiritual? An Invalid Theory and How It Grew." *American Music* 1, no. 1: 53–59.

Erlmann, Veit. 1996. "The Aesthetics of the Global Imagination: Reflections on World Music in the 1990s." *Public Culture* 8: 467–87.

Eskew, Harry L. 1966. *Shape Note Hymnody in the Shenandoah Valley, 1816–1860.* Ph.D. diss., Tulane University.

Fabian, Johannes. 1983. *Time and the Other: How Anthropology Makes Its Object.* New York: Columbia University Press.

Feld, Steven. 1982. *Sound and Sentiment.* Philadelphia: University of Pennsylvania Press.

Fernandez, James W. 1966. "Unbelievably Subtle Words: Representation and Integration in the Sermons of an African Reformative Cult." *Journal of the History of Religions* 6: 43–69.

———. 1986. *Persuasions and Performances: The Play of Tropes in Culture.* Bloomington: Indiana University Press.

Finnegan, Ruth. 1989. *The Hidden Musicians: Music Making in an English Town.* Cambridge: Cambridge University Press.

Foster, Stephen William. 1988. *The Past Is Another Country: Representation, Historical Consciousness, and Resistance in the Blue Ridge.* Berkeley and Los Angeles: University of California Press.

Fox, John, Jr. 1901. "The Southern Mountaineer." *Scribner's Magazine* 29: 387–99, 556–70.

Friedson, Steven. 1996. *Dancing Prophets: Musical Experience in Tumbuka Healing.* Chicago: University of Chicago Press.

Frost, William Goodell. 1899. "Our Contemporary Ancestors in the Southern Mountains." *Atlantic Monthly* 83: 311–19.

Garst, John. 1986. "Mutual Reinforcement and the Origins of Spirituals." *American Music* 4, no. 4: 390–406.

———. 1991. "Rudiments of Music." In *The Sacred Harp, 1991 Revision,* ed. H. McGraw. Bremen, Ga.: Sacred Harp Publishing Company.

Giesen, Bernhard. 1998. *Intellectuals and the German Nation: Collective Identity in an Axial Age.* Cambridge: Cambridge University Press.

Ginsburg, Faye, Lila Abu-Lughod, and Brian Larkin. 2002. "Introduction." In *Media Worlds: Anthropology on New Terrain,* ed. F. Ginsburg, L. Abu-Lughod, and B. Larkin. Berkeley and Los Angeles: University of California Press.

Girard, Aaron. 2002. "Alto Parts and Alto Voices in Sacred Harp Singing." Paper presented at the annual meeting of the Society for Ethnomusicology, Estes Park, Colo.

Glassberg, David. 2001. *Sense of History: The Place of the Past in American History.* Amherst: University of Massachusetts Press.

Goody, Jack. 2000. *The Power of the Written Tradition.* Washington, D.C.: Smithsonian Institution Press.

Gopinath, Gayatri. 1995. "'Bombay, U.K., Yuba City': Bhangra Music and the Engendering of Diaspora." *Diaspora* 4, no. 3: 303–21.

Gordon, Larry. 1979. *Rivers of Delight: American Folk Hymns from the Sacred Harp Tradition.* Liner notes. Nonesuch Records H-71360.

Grayson, Lisa. 1997. *A Beginner's Guide to Shape-Note Singing,* 2nd ed. Chicago: Chicago Sacred Harp Singers.

Hannerz, Ulf. 1990. "Cosmopolitans and Locals in World Culture." *Theory, Culture & Society* 7: 237–51.

Harney, Will Wallace. 1873. "A Strange Land and a Peculiar People." *Lippincott's Magazine* 12: 429–38.

Hatfield, Donald John W. J. 1997. *Disappearing in the Crowd, or How Taiwanese Pilgrimages Became Culture.* Ph.D. diss., University of Chicago.

Hayde, Monica. 1995. "Sing Out Loud, Sing Out Strong." *Palo Alto Weekly,* January 13, 1995.

Herman, Janet Lyn. 1997. *Sacred Harp Singing in California: Genre, Performance, Feeling.* Ph.D. diss., University of California at Los Angeles.

Herzfeld, Michael. 1997. *Cultural Intimacy: Social Poetics in the Nation-State.* New York: Routledge.

———. 2004. *The Body Impolitic: Artisans and Artifice in the Global Hierarchy of Value.* Chicago: University of Chicago Press.

Hollinger, David A. 1993. "How Wide the Circle of the 'We'? American Intellectuals and the Problem of the Ethnos Since World War II." *American Historical Review* 98, no. 2: 317–37.

Horn, Dorothy D. 1970. *Sing to Me of Heaven: A Study of Folk and Early American Materials in Three Old Harp Books.* Gainesville: University of Florida Press.

Huebner, Michael. 2004. "Sacred Harp: The Power of the Spirit Is Given Voice." *The Birmingham News,* June 15, 2004. http://www.al.com (accessed June 17, 2004).

Ivy, Marilyn. 1995. *Discourses of the Vanishing: Modernity, Phantasm, Japan.* Chicago: University of Chicago Press.

Jackson, George Pullen. 1926. "The Fa-Sol-La Folk." *Musical Courier* 93, no. 11: 6–7, 10.

———. 1932. "The Genesis of the Negro Spiritual." *American Mercury* 26: 243–48.

———. 1933. *White Spirituals in the Southern Uplands: The Story of the Fasola Folk, Their Songs, Singings, and "Buckwheat Notes."* Chapel Hill: University of North Carolina Press.

———. 1943. *White and Negro Spirituals, Their Life Span and Kinship, Tracing 200 Years of Untrammeled Song Making and Singing among Our Country Folk, with 116 Songs as Sung by Both Races.* New York: Augustin.

Jameson, Fredric. 1991. *Postmodernism, or The Cultural Logic of Late Capitalism.* Durham, N.C.: Duke University Press.

Katz, Ruth. 1968. "The Singing of Baqqashot by Aleppo Jews: A Study in Musical Acculturation." *Acta Musicologica* 40: 65–85.

Kirshenblatt-Gimblett, Barbara. 1996. "The Electronic Vernacular." In *Connected: Engagements with Media,* ed. G. E. Marcus. Chicago: University of Chicago Press.

Kymlicka, Will. 1995. *Multicultural Citizenship.* Oxford: Oxford University Press.

Lausevic, Mirjana. 1998. *A Different Village: International Folk Dance and Balkan Music and Dance in the United States.* Ph.D. diss., Wesleyan University.

Lauter, Paul. 2001. *From Walden Pond to Jurassic Park: Activism, Culture, and American Studies.* Durham, N.C.: Duke University Press.

Lomax, Alan. 1960. *All Day Singing from "The Sacred Harp."* LP record album. Prestige/International Records 25007.

Lornell, Kip, and Anne K. Rasmussen. 1997. *Musics of Multicultural America: A Study of Twelve Musical Communities.* New York: Schirmer Books.

Manuel, Peter. 1995. "Music as Symbol, Music as Simulacrum: Postmodern, Premodern, and Modern Aesthetics in Subcultural Popular Musics." *Popular Music* 14, no. 2: 227–39.

Marian-Bâlaşa, Marin. 2003. "Performing Religiousness through Joyful Noise and Playful Order: Notes on Shapenote Singing." *European Meetings in Ethnomusicology* 10: 117–76.

Marini, Stephen A. 1983. "Rehearsal for Revival: Sacred Singing and the Great Awakening in America." *Journal of the American Academy of Religious Studies* 50, no. 1: 71–91.

———. 2003. *Sacred Song in America: Religion, Music, and Public Culture.* Urbana: University of Illinois Press.

Massey, Doreen. 1995. "The Conceptualization of Place." In *A Place in the World? Places, Cultures and Globalization,* ed. D. Massey and P. Jess. New York: Oxford University Press.

McGraw, Hugh, ed. 1991. *The Sacred Harp, 1991 Revision*. Bremen, Ga.: Sacred Harp Publishing Company.

McNeil, W. K., ed. 1995. *Appalachian Images in Folk and Popular Culture*. Knoxville: University of Tennessee Press.

Miller, Kiri, ed. 2002. *The Chattahoochee Musical Convention, 1852–2002: A Sacred Harp Historical Sourcebook*. Carrollton, Ga.: Sacred Harp Museum.

———. 2003a. "Americanism Musically: Nation, Evolution, and Public Education at the Columbian Exposition, 1893." *19th-Century Music* 27, no. 2: 137–55.

———. 2003b. "A Middle Ages for America: Song/Politics/Praxis in the Rural South." Paper presented at the annual meeting of the Society for Ethnomusicology, Miami, Fla.

———. 2004a. "'First Sing the Notes': Oral and Written Traditions in Sacred Harp Transmission." *American Music* 22, no. 4: 475–501.

———. 2004b. Review of J. D. Boyd, *Judge Jackson and The Colored Sacred Harp* (2002). *The Alabama Review: A Quarterly Journal of Alabama History* 57, no. 3: 206–7.

———. 2005. *A Long Time Traveling: Song, Memory, and the Politics of Nostalgia in the Sacred Harp Diaspora*. Ph.D. diss., Harvard University.

Morley, David. 2001. "Belongings: Place, Space and Identity in a Mediated World." *European Journal of Cultural Studies* 4, no. 4: 425–48.

Nairn, Tom. 1988. *The Enchanted Glass: Britain and Its Monarchy*. London: Hutchinson Radius.

Newcombe, Horace. 1979–80. "Appalachia on Television: Region as Symbol in American Popular Culture." *Appalachian Journal* 7, nos. 1–2: 155–64.

Nora, Pierre. 1989. "Between Memory and History: *Les Lieux de Mémoire*." *Representations* 26: 7–25.

Noren, Christopher, ed. 2002. *September Psalms: Being a Choice Collection of the Finest Hymn-tunes, Anthems and Fuging-tunes Newly-Composed by Eminent Authors from the United States and Abroad, Together with a Selection of Historical Patriotic and Revival Songs Presented in Memory of the Victims of September 11, 2001*. Beverly, Mass.: self-published.

Parks, Edd Winfield. 1933. Review of G. P. Jackson, *White Spirituals in the Southern Uplands* (University of North Carolina Press, 1933). *The Vanderbilt Alumnus*: 169.

Patterson, Beverly Bush. 1995. *The Sound of the Dove: Singing in Appalachian Primitive Baptist Churches*. Urbana: University of Illinois Press.

Patterson, Daniel W. 1970–71. "Hunting for the American White Spiritual: A Survey of Scholarship, with Discography." *ARSC [Association for Recorded Sound Collections] Journal* 3, no. 1: 7–18.

Pen, Ron. 1994. Review of H. McGraw, ed., *The Sacred Harp, 1991 Revision* (Sacred Harp Publishing Company, 1991), and B. E. Cobb, Jr., *The Sacred Harp: A Tradi-*

tion and Its Music (University of Georgia Press, 1989). *American Music* 12, no. 1: 93–98.

———. 1997. "Triangles, Squares, Circles, and Diamonds: The 'Fasola Folk' and Their Singing Tradition." In *Musics of Multicultural America: A Study of Twelve Musical Communities,* ed. K. Lornell and A. K. Rasmussen. New York: Schirmer Books.

Plunkett, John. 2003. *Newspaper Accounts from the* Atlanta Constitution *and* Atlanta Journal *of the United Sacred Harp Musical Association 1904-1956.* Self-published. Available at The Sacred Harp Museum in Carrollton, Ga.

Qureshi, Regula Burckhardt. 1994. "Exploring Time Cross-Culturally: Ideology and Performance of Time in the Sufi Qawwali." *Journal of Musicology* 12, no. 4: 491–528.

Radano, Ronald. 2003. *Lying up a Nation: Race and Black Music.* Chicago: University of Chicago Press.

Radway, Jan. 2002 [1999]. "What's in a Name?" In *The Futures of American Studies,* ed. D. E. Pease and R. Wiegman. Durham, N.C.: Duke University Press.

Ragland, Cathy. 2003. "Mexican Deejays and the Transnational Space of Youth Dances in New York and New Jersey." *Ethnomusicology* 47, no. 3: 338–54.

Rasmussen, Anne K. 1998. "The Music of Arab Americans: Aesthetics and Performance in a New Land." In *Images of Enchantment: Visual and Performing Arts of the Middle East,* ed. S. Zuhur. Cairo: American University in Cairo Press.

Reddy, William M. 1997. "Against Constructionism: The Historical Ethnography of Emotions." *Current Anthropology* 38, no. 3: 327–51.

———. 2001. *The Navigation of Feeling: A Framework for the History of Emotions.* New York: Cambridge University Press.

Robertson, Roland. 1990. "After Nostalgia? Wilful Nostalgia and the Phases of Globalization." In *Theories of Modernity and Postmodernity,* ed. B. S. Turner. London: Sage.

Rosaldo, Renato. 1989. *Culture and Truth: The Remaking of Social Analysis.* Boston: Beacon Press.

Rouse, Roger. 1991. "Mexican Migration and the Social Space of Postmodernism." *Diaspora* 1: 8–23.

Safran, William. 1991. "Diasporas in Modern Societies: Myths of Homeland and Return." *Diaspora* 1: 83–99.

Sant Cassia, Paul. 2000. "Exoticizing Discoveries and Extraordinary Experiences: 'Traditional' Music, Modernity, and Nostalgia in Malta and Other Mediterranean Societies." *Ethnomusicology* 44, no. 2: 281–301.

Seeger, Charles. 1940. "Contrapuntal Style in the Three-Voice Shape-Note Hymns." *Musical Quarterly* 26: 483–93.

Seiler, Jean. 1999. *Joe Beasley Memorial Sacred Harp Album: Northwestern Alabama 1954-1976-1977-1978.* Two compact discs. SH-159D-1/2.

Shapiro, Henry D. 1978. *Appalachia on Our Mind: The Southern Mountains and Mountaineers in the American Consciousness, 1870–1920.* Chapel Hill: University of North Carolina Press.

Sheffer, Gabriel, ed. 1986. *Modern Diasporas in International Politics.* New York: St. Martin's Press.

Shelemay, Kay Kaufman. 1989. *Music, Ritual, and Falasha History.* East Lansing: Michigan State University Press.

———. 2001. "Toward an Ethnomusicology of the Early Music Movement: Thoughts on Bridging Disciplines and Musical Worlds." *Ethnomusicology* 45, no. 1: 1–29.

———. 2003. "Ethnicity and Beyond: Reconsidering Notions of Community in the Study of American Musical Life." Paper presented at the annual meeting of the Society for American Music, Phoenix, Ariz.

Shelemay, Kay Kaufman, Peter Jeffery, and Ingrid Monson. 1993. "Oral and Written Transmission in Ethiopian Christian Chant." *Early Music History* 12: 55–117.

Sheppard, Shelbie, and David Ivey, eds. 2000. *Sacred Harp Singings: 1999 and 2000.* Gadsden, Ala.

Smith, Harry. 1997 [1952]. *Anthology of American Folk Music.* Six compact discs. Smithsonian Folkways Records 40090.

Solís, Ted. 2004. *Performing Ethnomusicology: Teaching and Representation in World Music Ensembles.* Berkeley and Los Angeles: University of California Press.

Sollors, Werner. 1986. *Beyond Ethnicity: Consent and Descent in American Culture.* New York: Oxford University Press.

Sommers, Laurie Kay. 2000. "Continuity and Change in the Hoboken, Georgia Sacred Harp Tradition." *Bulletin of the Society for American Music* 26, nos. 2–3: 33–36, 44.

Sorensen, Janet. 1997. "Writing Historically, Speaking Nostalgically: The Competing Languages of Nation in Scott's *The Bride of Lammermoor*." In *Narratives of Nostalgia, Gender, and Nationalism,* ed. J. Pickering and S. Kehde. New York: Macmillan.

Spivak, Gayatri. 1988. "Can the Subaltern Speak?" In *Marxism and the Interpretation of Culture,* ed. C. Nelson and L. Grossberg. Urbana: University of Illinois Press.

Steinwand, Jonathan. 1997. "The Future of Nostalgia in Friedrich Schlegel's Gender Theory: Casting German Aesthetics Beyond Ancient Greece and Modern Europe." In *Narratives of Nostalgia, Gender, and Nationalism,* ed. J. Pickering and S. Kehde. New York: Macmillan.

Stewart, Kathleen. 1988. "Nostalgia: A Polemic." *Cultural Anthropology* 3, no. 3: 227–41.

———. 1996. *A Space on the Side of the Road: Cultural Poetics in an "Other" America.* Princeton: Princeton University Press.

Stock, Brian. 1974. "The Middle Ages as Subject and Object: Romantic Attitudes and Academic Medievalism." *New Literary History* 5, no. 3: 527–47.

Stowe, David W. 2004. *How Sweet the Sound: Music in the Spiritual Lives of Americans*. Cambridge, Mass.: Harvard University Press.

Sugarman, Jane C. 1997. *Engendering Song: Singing & Subjectivity at Prespa Albanian Weddings*. Chicago: University of Chicago Press.

Taddie, Daniel. 1996. "Solmization, Scale, and Key in Nineteenth-Century Four-Shape Tunebooks: Theory and Practice." *American Music* 14, no. 1: 42–64.

Tallmadge, William H. 1984. "Folk Organum: A Study of Origins." *American Music* 2, no. 1: 47–65.

Tick, Judith. 2003. Review of D. Nicholls, ed., *The Cambridge History of American Music* (Cambridge: Cambridge University Press, 1998). *Journal of the American Musicological Society* 56, no. 3: 721–33.

Titon, Jeff Todd. 1988. *Powerhouse for God*. Austin: University of Texas Press.

Tolbert, Elizabeth. 1990. "Women Cry with Words: Symbolization of Affect in the Karelian Lament." *Yearbook for Traditional Music* 22: 80–105.

Treitler, Leo. 2003. *With Voice and Pen: Coming to Know Medieval Song and How It Was Made*. New York: Oxford University Press.

Turino, Thomas. 1990. "Structure, Context, and Strategy in Musical Ethnography." *Ethnomusicology* 34, no. 3: 399–412.

———. 1999. "Signs of Imagination, Identity, and Experience: A Peircian Semiotic Theory for Music." *Ethnomusicology* 43: 221–55.

Turner, Bryan S. 1987. "A Note on Nostalgia." *Theory, Culture & Society* 4: 147–56.

Turner, Victor, and Edith Turner. 1978. *Image and Pilgrimage in Christian Culture*. New York: Columbia University Press.

Tyson, Ruel W., Jr., James L. Peacock, and Daniel W. Patterson, eds. 1988. *Diversities of Gifts: Field Studies in Southern Religion*. Urbana: University of Illinois Press.

Urban, Greg. 1988. "Ritual Wailing in Amerindian Brazil." *American Anthropologist* 90, no. 2: 385–400.

Vinson, Laurence Duncan. 1999. *The Second Great Awakening Meets the New Spirituality: New and Lifelong Singers in Alabama and New England*. M.A. thesis, Brown University.

Walser, Robert. 2004. "Musical Translation." Paper presented at the annual meeting of the Society for Ethnomusicology, Tucson, Ariz.

Walsh, Jim. 2002. "Local Musician Helps Hollywood Get into Shape." *St. Paul Pioneer Press*, July 23, 2002. http://www.twincities.com/mld/pioneerpress/3712587.htm?1c (accessed November 15, 2004).

Ware, Vron, and Les Back. 2002. *Out of Whiteness*. Chicago: University of Chicago Press.

Warner, R. Stephen. 1993. "Work in Progress toward a New Paradigm for the Sociological Study of Religion in the United States." *American Journal of Sociology* 98, no. 5: 1044–93.

———. 2005. *A Church of Our Own: Disestablishment and Diversity in American Religion*. New Brunswick, N.J.: Rutgers University Press.

Waterman, Christopher A. 1990. "'Our Tradition Is a Very Modern Tradition': Popular Music and the Construction of Pan-Yoruba Identity." *Ethnomusicology* 34, no. 3: 367–79.

Whisnant, David E. 1983. *All That Is Native and Fine: The Politics of Culture in an American Region.* Chapel Hill: University of North Carolina Press.

Wiegman, Robyn. 2002 [1999]. "Whiteness Studies and the Paradox of Particularity." In *The Futures of American Studies,* ed. D. E. Pease and R. Wiegman. Durham, N.C.: Duke University Press.

Willard, Keith. n.d. "A Short Shaped-Note Singing History." http://fasola.org/introduction/short_history.html (accessed November 15, 2004).

Wilson, Charles Morrow. 1929. "Elizabethan America." *Atlantic Monthly* 144: 238–44.

Wise, Gene. 1999. "'Paradigm Dramas' in American Studies: A Cultural and Institutional History of the Movement." In *Locating American Studies,* ed. L. Maddox. Baltimore: Johns Hopkins University Press.

Wolf, Richard K. 2001. "Emotional Dimensions of Ritual Music Among the Kotas, a South Indian Tribe." *Ethnomusicology* 45, no. 3: 379–422.

Wray, Matt, and Annalee Newitz, eds. 1997. *White Trash: Race and Class in America.* New York: Routledge.

Zheng, Su. 1994. "Music Making in Cultural Displacement: The Chinese-American Odyssey." *Diaspora* 3, no. 3: 273–88.

INDEX

Place-names refer to singing locations/regions unless otherwise noted. Appended f denotes figure, n denotes endnote, t denotes table.

MUSIC IN AMERICAN LIFE

Aaron Copland: The Life and Work of an Uncommon Man   *Howard Pollack*
Louis Moreau Gottschalk   *S. Frederick Starr*
Race, Rock, and Elvis   *Michael T. Bertrand*
Theremin: Ether Music and Espionage   *Albert Glinsky*
Poetry and Violence: The Ballad Tradition of Mexico's Costa Chica
    John H. McDowell
The Bill Monroe Reader   *Edited by Tom Ewing*
Music in Lubavitcher Life   *Ellen Koskoff*
Zarzuela: Spanish Operetta, American Stage   *Janet L. Sturman*
Bluegrass Odyssey: A Documentary in Pictures and Words, 1966–86
    Carl Fleischhauer and Neil V. Rosenberg
That Old-Time Rock & Roll: A Chronicle of an Era, 1954–63   *Richard Aquila*
Labor's Troubadour   *Joe Glazer*
American Opera   *Elise K. Kirk*
Don't Get above Your Raisin': Country Music and the Southern Working Class
    Bill C. Malone
John Alden Carpenter: A Chicago Composer   *Howard Pollack*
Heartbeat of the People: Music and Dance of the Northern Pow-wow   *Tara Browner*
My Lord, What a Morning: An Autobiography   *Marian Anderson*
Marian Anderson: A Singer's Journey   *Allan Keiler*
Charles Ives Remembered: An Oral History   *Vivian Perlis*
Henry Cowell, Bohemian   *Michael Hicks*
Rap Music and Street Consciousness   *Cheryl L. Keyes*
Louis Prima   *Garry Boulard*
Marian McPartland's Jazz World: All in Good Time   *Marian McPartland*
Robert Johnson: Lost and Found   *Barry Lee Pearson and Bill McCulloch*
Bound for America: Three British Composers   *Nicholas Temperley*
Lost Sounds: Blacks and the Birth of the Recording Industry, 1890–1919   *Tim Brooks*
Burn, Baby! BURN! The Autobiography of Magnificent Montague
    Magnificent Montague with Bob Baker
Way Up North in Dixie: A Black Family's Claim to the Confederate Anthem
    Howard L. Sacks and Judith Rose Sacks
The Bluegrass Reader   *Edited by Thomas Goldsmith*
Colin McPhee: Composer in Two Worlds   *Carol J. Oja*
Robert Johnson, Mythmaking, and Contemporary American Culture
    Patricia R. Schroeder
Composing a World: Lou Harrison, Musical Wayfarer
    Leta E. Miller and Fredric Lieberman
Fritz Reiner, Maestro and Martinet   *Kenneth Morgan*
That Toddlin' Town: Chicago's White Dance Bands and Orchestras,
    1900–1950   *Charles A. Sengstock Jr.*
Dewey and Elvis: The Life and Times of a Rock 'n' Roll Deejay   *Louis Cantor*
Come Hither to Go Yonder: Playing Bluegrass with Bill Monroe   *Bob Black*
Chicago Blues: Portraits and Stories   *David Whiteis*

KIRI MILLER is Assistant Professor
of Music at Brown University.

The University of Illinois Press
is a founding member of the
Association of American University Presses.

Composed in 10.5/13 Adobe Minion
with Meta display
by BookComp, Inc.
for the University of Illinois Press
Manufactured by Thomson-Shore, Inc.

University of Illinois Press
1325 South Oak Street
Champaign, IL 61820-6903
www.press.uillinois.edu